'Whatever your role – manager, coach, parent or performer – making the most of the talent development process is always complex and challenging. Therefore it is good to get a clear and concise road map to work from, and this book offers that. Dave and Áine have a wealth of experience as managers, coaches and parents. In fact Dave might even remember his time as a performer! They bring knowledge as researchers *and* practitioners, offering a considered and well-informed but also clear and readable coverage of the development process, stage by stage. This is an informative and useful read that you can go back to time and again as a reference.'

Neil Bath, Head of Youth Development, Chelsea FC

TALENT DEVELOPMENT

The process of talent development (TD) is essential to success in any sport. Drawing on the latest evidence and a considerable experience base, this book dispels myths about talent development and offers practical advice on the TD pathway from pre-school to elite level. Aimed at practitioners and other stakeholders involved in the TD process – including coaches, scientists, administrators, educators, students, parents, policy makers and senior development athletes – this is the only up-to-date practical guide to TD in sport.

Written by experts with more than 20 years' experience in TD training, coaching and research, it covers key topics from deliberate practice and fundamental movement skills to designing and managing a TD pathway. It also includes contributions from professionals working in a wide range of sports, providing real-world insights into important topics including:

- the recruitment process
- academy and apprenticeship preparation
- the coach–athlete relationship
- what to do to stay ahead
- considerations for parents and coaches.

Talent Development: A Practitioner Guide is an indispensable resource for all those interested in talent identification, talent development and coaching practice in elite sport.

Dave Collins is Professor of Coaching and Performance at the University of Central Lancashire, UK and Director of Grey Matters Performance Ltd. Dave has published over 300 peer-reviewed articles and more than 60 books and book chapters. From an applied perspective, he has worked with over 60 World or Olympic medallists plus professional sports teams, dancers, musicians and executives in business and public service. As a performer, he was excessively average at high contact sports (at least the way he played them) such as rugby, American football, martial arts and outdoor pursuits. He has coached rugby to national level, is a senior coach in weightlifting, a 5th Dan in karate and a qualified and experienced PE teacher/teacher educator. Dave is a Director of the Rugby Coaches Association, Director of Coaching for iZone Driver Performance and current lead psychology consultant to, amongst others, Chelsea FC and the New Zealand ski and snowboard teams. He is also a Fellow of the Society of Martial Arts, the Zoological Society of London and the British Association of Sport and Exercise Sciences, an Associate Fellow of the British Psychological Society and an ex-Royal Marine. He is also the proud (and legal) father of five children, spanning 31 to 9, plus a plethora of grandchildren.

Áine MacNamara is a Reader in Elite Performance in the Institute of Coaching and Performance at the University of Central Lancashire, UK. Áine's background is in physical education and coaching and she has worked with young people in a range of sporting environments as an educator, coach and sports psychology consultant. Her main research interest is in Talent Development (TD) and she has published widely in peer-reviewed journals, book chapters and technical reports. She has consulted with a range of sporting organisations in the UK and Ireland to help them develop Talent Development pathways and policies as well as providing coach and parent education to support the implementation of these ideas. She is the mother to two long-term TD projects called Síofra and Iarlaith whom she endeavours to support with an evidence-based approach!

TALENT DEVELOPMENT

A Practitioner Guide

Dave Collins and Áine MacNamara

Routledge
Taylor & Francis Group

LONDON AND NEW YORK

First published 2018
by Routledge
2 Park Square, Milton Park, Abingdon, Oxon OX14 4RN

and by Routledge
711 Third Avenue, New York, NY 10017

Routledge is an imprint of the Taylor & Francis Group, an informa business

© 2018 Dave Collins and Áine MacNamara

British Library Cataloguing in Publication Data
A catalogue record for this book is available from the British Library

Library of Congress Cataloging in Publication Data
A catalog record for this book has been requested

ISBN: 978-1-138-67252-9 (hbk)
ISBN: 978-1-138-67253-6 (pbk)
ISBN: 978-1-315-56247-6 (ebk)

Typeset in Bembo
by Wearset Ltd, Boldon, Tyne and Wear
Printed and bound by CPI Group (UK) Ltd, Croydon, CR0 4YY

To Lily, Ruby and Helen
To Síofra, Iarlaith and Damian

CONTENTS

FIGURES

TABLES

CONTRIBUTING EXPERTS

David Court, Talent ID and Development Education Lead, Football Association (FA).

Nigel Edwards, Performance Director, England Golf.

Joni Harding, Education Manager, Swim Ireland.

Deirdre Lyons, Player Development Manager, Rugby Players Ireland.

Kevin Mannion, Academy Athletic Performance Manager, Gloucester Rugby Club.

Neil McCarthy, Academy Manager, Gloucester Rugby Club.

Toni Minichiello, Athletics Coach.

Anne Pankhurst, Coach Education Consultant, Professional Tennis Registry, Virgin Active, and the United States Tennis Association.

David Passmore, Lecturer in Coaching, Dublin City University, Ireland and Coach, Ireland Hockey.

Robert Reid, Director, FIA Institute Young Driver Excellence Academy.

Dave Rotheram, Head of Coach Development, Rugby League.

Erin Sanchez, Head of Student Welfare and Dance Science, London Studio Centre.

Iain Simpson, Director of Sport, Oakham School, UK.

Tynke Toering, Associate Professor, Norwegian School of Sport Sciences, Oslo, Norway.

Paul Waldron, Lead Foundation Phase Coach, Chelsea FC.

PREFACE

We have been working at developing talent for most of our professional lives. Early training and employment as PE teachers, then training and working as coach educators, through to later roles as sport psychologists with the added bonus of almost 20 years each researching it. One of the biggest kicks across this work has been seeing young performers 'make it'. However big or small our contribution, there is something really fulfilling in seeing a youngster able to achieve his or her potential and even, perhaps, his or her dream of attaining the elite level. There is a parallel warm glow from helping parents and coaches to facilitate this. In summary, we love helping people to achieve.

In parallel to this, however, we have been 'irritated' by the number of gurus, journalists and social media twitterati who have jumped on the bandwagon. No doubt most are well-meaning and some propose good ideas, but developing an understanding of 'why' and ensuring that advice is as good as you can make it depend on longer study, effort and experience. We are not silly enough to suggest that those with letters after their name have a unique claim on correctness … in fact, far from it, as anyone who reads the critical nature of our research would know. The point is that understanding the 'why and why nots', the 'it depends-ness' and how things which have been normal and accepted practice might be made better requires a level of criticality that is the mark of the best practitioners … and a few of those might be researchers as well!

So, building on the knowledge and experience gained from study, investigation, doing it ourselves and working with some very good practitioners, we present this book aimed at those most concerned with talent development, namely coaches and parents. We have hopefully kept it simple and practical, or at least as simple as it can be made! We have used some old methods such as s/he or alternating her and his as a way of stressing that this applies to both sexes. We have also used 'performer' to hopefully encompass all those physical performance domains which use talent development. As such, what is presented here holds implications for young team players, individual sports athletes and dancers. We hope you enjoy it but even more, we hope it is useful.

Dave and Áine

PART I
Underpinning talent development principles

1

MYTHS AND TRUTHS IN TALENT DEVELOPMENT

Introduction

Within the competitive landscape of sport there is always a pressure to try and identify, and then select, the best young performers. Indeed, Talent Identification and Development (TID) has become a key focus for National Governing Bodies (NGBs), professional clubs, and individuals across all sports. Unfortunately, the efficacy and scientific foundations of most Talent Identification (TI) programmes employed has been strongly questioned. These criticisms are mainly based on the low predictive value and lack of validity attributed to TI programmes; simply, TI programmes have not been very effective at detecting and identifying young people with the potential to develop into successful senior performers. Unfortunately, despite this lack of underpinning evidence *and* the considerable data that illustrates the inefficiencies of early TI (for example, over 90 per cent of those recruited to Premiership football academies will never play first team football), sports continue to invest considerable resources, time and funding into 'talent spotting' initiatives. Indeed, in recent times there has been exponential growth in this area that has even spawned a new genre of sport scientist – the 'talent scientist'! In this opening chapter we explore some 'myths and truths' in TID and suggest that it seems more sensible to consider the range of factors that underpin the capacity of a young performer to realise their potential, rather than focus on those 'snapshot' characteristics, or once-off performances at 'trials', which hint at unrealized capacity. Building on this, we present some health warnings for practitioners working in Talent Development (TD) and some clear criteria that should be used to enable coaches, parents and other stakeholders to act as critical consumers of knowledge.

Transforming ability into talent

To begin, let's consider what we mean by 'talent'. Talent is typically viewed as an individual's ability, with little consideration of the process of development required to achieve expertise. This misunderstanding presumably underpins TI processes (scouting in soccer, or more structured TI models such as Talent Search in Australia) that seek to 'talent spot' young athletes. However, these approaches to TI fail to distinguish between current performance (i.e. how well a young athlete is performing at the time of testing) and that individual's capacity for future development. Furthermore, since these TI models typically select young athletes based on a limited range of discrete variables (usually once-off performance and/or physical measurements), they fail to recognise the dynamic nature of talent development. In this book, we are mostly concerned with the *process* of TD, which refers to the 'path from rank-novice to the most outstanding and distinguished accomplishments' (Sternberg, 2003). It might be easiest to think of this in terms of 'inputs and outputs' (see Figure 1.1). Giftedness, the possession and use of high levels of natural abilities or aptitudes to a level that places a person in the top 10 per cent of their peers, is essentially the *input* to the TD pathway. This is the product that you will work with in your coaching environment. Talent is the superior mastery of systematically developed abilities or competencies to a level that places an individual in the top 10 per cent of individuals active in that field – essentially the *output* of the system.

Gagné's Differentiated Model of Giftedness and Talent (DMGT) (Gagné, 1999) is a useful way to understand this process. Essentially, the DMGT describes the coaching process that transforms gifts or natural ability (the input) into expert performance or talent (the output) via learning and practice. When a performer enters the TD pathway they have potential that can be transformed into talent. Think of talent as a developmental construct (Sternberg, 2003) that is influenced by a range of factors. Gagné's proposition is that the rate of development is influenced by three significant catalysts: chance factors (e.g. good or bad luck), intrapersonal factors (e.g. motivation, persistence) and environmental factors (e.g. coaching, access to resources). Viewing talent as a developmental construct is important as it places the emphasis on the process of development rather than the identification of potential. Simply, talent is something that develops over time and in response to a good coaching and development environment. This is where you will make the difference!

The DMGT considers natural abilities to be the raw materials of talent and, even though it is unlikely that an individual will become talented without these natural abilities, the opposite is not always true. In fact, underachievement and talent loss can be seen across performance domains where outstanding natural gifts remain as untapped potential because of the moderating role of different catalysts and variables. Even if a young performer has a natural ability, he or she must also have the motivation to engage in the requisite practice and training to fulfil this potential. Similarly, a young performer may possess outstanding natural ability but may have little interest in pursuing excellence unless forced by external agencies (parents, for

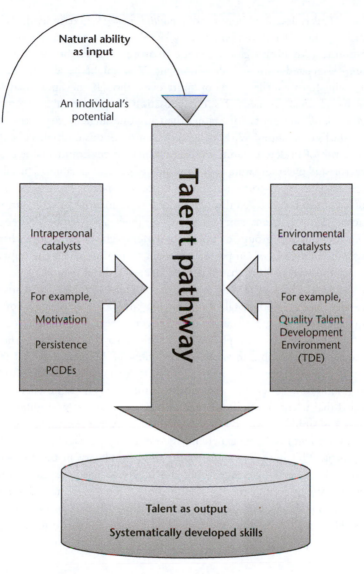

Natural ability
as input

An individual's
potential

Talent pathway

Intrapersonal
catalysts

For example,

Motivation

Persistence

PCDEs

Environmental
catalysts

For example,

Quality Talent
Development
Environment
(TDE)

Talent as output

Systematically developed skills

FIGURE 1.1   Inputs and outputs on the TD pathway

example). Conversely, there are examples of elite athletes who were able to compensate for physical disadvantages (e.g. height in rugby) with strengths in another
factor (e.g. commitment, determination, hard work; Abbott and Collins, 2002). As
such, deficiencies in one area of performance can be compensated for by strengths
in another. What does this mean for TID? It means that there isn't a single profile
that typifies 'success' and that different types of performers can get to the top by
exploiting their own strengths and compensating for their weaknesses.

   To illustrate this point, consider an analogy between abilities and potential
muscles; without exercise and training the genetic potential of muscles will not be

actualised. This is described in terms of a *multiplier effect* where individuals with less potential for muscular development may develop more muscle because of their motivation to take advantage of relevant environmental factors (such as access to coaching) associated with skill development. You might be able to name some athletes who have excelled in your sport even though they possessed less than remarkable physical profiles. This 'compensation phenomenon' suggests that it is the *interaction* of different factors, rather than any one single factor, that determines an individual's capabilities. Without an appreciation of this multiplicative approach there is a risk of underestimating the importance of environmental and intraper-sonal factors and overestimating the magnitude of genetic variables. The take-home message? Excellence in sport is not idiosyncratic to a specific set of skills or physical attributes but can be achieved through unique combinations of skills, attitudes and behaviours. Simply, talent emerges from 'complex and unique choreographies' between the different groups of causal influences. The suggestion is that greater emphasis should be placed on providing young performers with the opportunities to develop those capabilities that underpin successful development.

This understanding of TD also helps us appreciate that there are many ways to initiate talent and the optimal talent domain may not be stable. As new components develop, the developing performer may discover a greater inclination for a related but distinct domain. For example, a young athlete may begin their journey in one sport but end up excelling in another. This view of TID suggests that talent can develop in different ways for genetically distinct or even genetically similar individuals (Simonton, 2001). In other words, adults with the same talent may have developed that talent through different routes, while adults with different talents may have had similar childhood experiences. Moreover, even adults who have the same mature talent may have experienced contrasting spurt and lull periods during development. TID initiatives must reflect this complexity in their procedures if they are to be worthwhile endeavours and meet the needs of their participants. Unfortunately, prescriptive methods dominate TID; if a performer doesn't fit into the prescribed pathway, they are likely to miss out on lots of development opportunities. How well does your sport or performance domain cater for this non-linearity?

A summary

Much of what we have presented thus far contradicts some practices that typify applied initiatives in TID – most notably, early selection and specialisation. In fact, the lack of evidence concerning early signs of excellence suggests that the import-ance placed on these factors is overestimated – an example of the atheoretical approach to TID that currently prevails in sport. Given these arguments, Talent Development (and note the emphasis on *development*) initiatives must begin to adopt frameworks that conceptualise development as dynamic and non-linear. Thus, TD processes must be aware of the multiple pathways that individuals may take as they progress in their activity. When this non-linearity is coupled with the importance of key events and transitions in the development pathway, the case for support systems that offer flexibility, individual optimisation and return routes as characteristic factors is strengthened. As a consequence, it makes sense to consider both the pathway to excellence and the multiple components that contribute to the realisation of potential. We hope the remainder of the book addresses these questions and importantly provides you with an understanding as to how to optimise your pathway.

Myths, truths and health warnings in talent development

Before we move on, we will begin by presenting some of the 'myths, truths and health warnings' in TID. As in other domains, some practices have become so embedded in the sporting landscape that they are generally accepted even though they may not reflect best, or even good, practice. It is worth taking a look!

Pyramid thinking

Development in sport has typically been explained in terms of a pyramid-based model: a broad base of foundation skills participation, with increasingly higher levels of performance, engaged in by fewer and fewer people. Despite its popularity among policy makers, there have been numerous criticisms levelled at the pyramid approach. One line of attack has been the moral one: built into the pyramid's design is the systematic exclusion of players, no matter how good they are in absolute terms, as fewer and fewer players can play at each level. There are a number of other problems with pyramid thinking.

The problem of prediction

Pyramid models presume successful progression from one level to the next is indicative of later or emergent ability; in most cases, this is not accurate. Indeed, the low conversion rates of successful junior performers to successful seniors points to the dangers of predicting who is likely to 'make it'. Furthermore, identifying talent involves predicting both an athlete's potential and the type of player required for future success in that sport. Sports change and what might constitute the 'perfect' athlete in 2017 might look a lot different in 2037. Rugby players, for example, look a lot different now compared to the start of the professional era in the early 1990s. Indeed, when the timeframe between identification and performance is large, the accuracy of predictions will surely decrease. Simply, the performance, anthropometric or skill profiles currently used to identify talent when a child is 12 years of age might look appreciatively different when that child reaches their mid-twenties. Therefore, if TI is to be effective, we would have to be able to predict the future and that isn't possible!

The problem of participation

Pyramid models also presume that selection for progressively higher levels within the system is based on merit. In practice, participation is influenced by a host of psychosocial and environmental factors, such as the ability to take part in the first place. Consider, for example, the role of the family in high-level sports performance (see Chapter 7). We might also add factors like availability and quality of coaching and facilities, access to funding and choice of sport (see the discussion on the talent development environment in Chapter 9) as variables that influence selection. Since young players can hardly be held responsible for the quality of their families, schools, cities and so on, it seems fair to say that, to some extent, their sporting achievement, or even engagement in sport, is mediated by 'blind luck', irrespective of their ability. Another issue with pyramid thinking is that the logic of the model means that the quality of performers at the higher levels is dependent on the experiences and resources offered to those at the lowest levels: a poor foundation undermines the whole system (see Chapter 4 for a discussion on the importance of Deliberate Preparation).

Systematic bias in TID

TID models take it for granted that current performance represents a player's ability, while there are numerous reasons to doubt this is, in fact, the case. TI procedures are highly subjective, often based on the 'coach's eye' or measurements such as current performance, anthropometric profile and/or results on a skill test. A striking example of such arbitrariness is the effect of relative age on performance (see Chapter 8 for a thorough examination of the relative age effect). Numerous studies have shown that players born early within a selection year have a considerable advantage over those born later. This seems, in part, because of the relative physical size and strength and further matured coordination of players who can be up to one or two years older than their peers. Those with the benefit of extra months, or even years, of development are more likely to be identified as talented and progress to the next level of the pyramid, where they would be expected to receive better coaching, play with a higher standard of teammates and opposition, compete and train more frequently.

These problems might explain two perplexing findings, which seem to raise doubts about the efficacy of early TI: the majority of young people identified as talented do not go on to elite, or even sub-elite, careers; and, conversely, many adult elite performers did not come through the standard talent pathways, nor were they precociously gifted as young children. We further suggest that the apparent success of some traditional approaches to TID is ultimately an optical illusion, as there is no way of knowing who might have succeeded through different systems, and who were deselected from the system but might have (under different circumstances) gone on to achieve high performance. Indeed, since those cut from systems are rarely, if ever, the focus of study, it is unlikely that much evidence for TI models' lack of efficacy will be available.

Athletic progress is complex and non-linear

Traditional models (such as the pyramid approach or Jean Cote's Developmental Model of Sport Participation, DMSP) present talent development as a relatively linear progression along a continuum from childhood to retirement. Simply, athletes move from one stage of development to another as they progress along the pathway. However, even a cursory look at the biographies of successful performers will highlight the non-linear, dynamic and idiosyncratic nature of development. Reflecting this, it seems sensible to consider the range of factors that underpin the capacity of a young performer to realise their potential and cope with a dynamic pathway. Unfortunately, TID programs often ignore those very factors that may form the mechanisms for achieving success – the psychological and environmental factors that help transform potential into ability (see Figure 1.1). This dearth in understanding and employment of key psychological characteristics is in stark contrast to the large body of literature examining the physical and anthropometric factors that contribute to elite performance, a bias driven perhaps by inbuilt preference for 'harder', more (apparently) objective measures and the universal attraction of an objective measure-based predictive test – the 'Holy Grail' of TID. In this book we offer evidence and guidance about the mechanisms which underpin progression and transfer in and between sporting activities. For those at the coalface of coaching and development, this should increase the effectiveness of the pathway, since crucial factors that contribute towards the fulfilment of potential are not ignored and scarce resources are not (mis)invested in a select few who may not develop into mature, elite performers.

'Sticky ideas' in talent development

The longevity and widespread acceptance of some TID practices suggest that they are 'sticky'. Simply, sticky ideas are accepted and repeated because they share certain basic qualities, including simplicity, concreteness and credibility; other ideas, despite their efficacy, wither and die because they lack these same characteristics. As such, the stickiness of ideas has nothing to do with their truthfulness or validity; some practices, early specialisation and the 10,000-hour 'rule', for example, are sticky and prevalent and have been passed on both vertically (from one generation to the next) and horizontally (between sports or countries) despite a lack of evidence supporting their usefulness. What are the implications of 'stickiness' for you and others working in TID? Popularity and 'stickiness' cannot be taken as sufficient evidence in favour of theory or practice. Just because an idea is tenacious, or has been touted as 'successful', does not mean it is correct. Based on these contentions, coaches and other TID practitioners need to critically examine their practices making use of the emerging body of literature base available in talent development. As you read this book, we encourage the same criticality.

'Scienciness'

All performance domains are continually searching the global marketplace for practices that might add a competitive edge and give them an advantage over their competitors. We often presume that the initiatives adopted and employed are the result of rigorous scientific testing and underpinned by reasonable evidence. Unfortunately, this is not always the case in sport and in fact the glossy, PR-friendly TID programmes that form the basis of (some) sport's initiatives often lack this evidence and instead are sold (we contend) to practitioners and key stakeholders on the basis of 'scienciness'.

Scienciness refers to the illusion of scientific credibility and validity that provides a degree of authority to otherwise dubious ideas. Scienciness is conveyed through, for example, esoteric language and complex statistical representations, and supplemented by association with an apparently successful foreign system. Our use of this new term was inspired by the American political satirist Stephen Colbert (2005), who talked about 'truthiness', which is the conviction that something is true, despite there being absolutely no evidence in favour of it. Scienciness follows the same logic. It is essentially a rhetorical device to attribute the authority of science to methods and ideas which possess little or no underpinning evidence or theoretical base.

We suggest that scienciness in rife in TID! Indeed, some of these ideas are so pervasive and have been so strongly promoted that even a scientific, empirically based refutation has trouble in making an impact. First, consider the Long–Term Athlete Development (LTAD) model (e.g. Balyi and Hamilton, 2003), an approach explicitly grounded in the Eastern Bloc philosophy which has been, and largely remains, the fundamental driver for government, sporting organisations, quangos, trusts and coach education in the United Kingdom, as well as Ireland, Canada and elsewhere. In the current climate, which stresses the need for evidence-based practice, one would expect such a pervasive policy to be strongly supported by scientific rigour. We suggest that this is not the case. The approach incorporates much face-valid and simple advice, guidance that is so fundamental and sound that it is almost irrefutable (the progression of 'learn to train' through to 'learn to compete' stages, etc.). However, LTAD includes a veneer of scienciness that covers several more questionable statements. Consider as an example the concept of critical periods, which are described as developmental phases that, if not fully exploited at that time, will prevent an individual ever achieving his/her genetic potential (Balyi and Hamilton, 2003). Empirical evidence for this principle is somewhat lacking, and few of the source papers cited in support of LTAD seem to be peer reviewed.

This offers some interesting speculations on how 'sciencey' constructs get a hold and why they seem so pervasive and persuasive. Perhaps, once an agency, sport, or even individual coach has invested a lot of money and other resources for a construct, it is difficult to evaluate it impartially; after a certain level of investment, one becomes committed to being committed! Whatever the reasons, such reluctance to consider alternatives represents another characteristic of 'scienciness' constructs. As

John F. Kennedy stated: 'The great enemy of the truth is very often not the lie, deliberate, contrived and dishonest, but the myth, persistent, persuasive and unrealistic.' What can you do? There is surely a need to establish policy against a strong evidence base and evaluate initiatives against the total contribution they can make. We encourage readers to adopt a critical stance, ask questions and seek answers before they adopt any practice.

It depends! Hume's Law and avoiding obvious answers

In TID, there has been a tendency to adopt ideas as fact without careful consideration of the mechanisms underpinning these approaches. For example, a considerable amount of research has explored the developmental histories of elite and non-elite performers – what they experienced, when they specialised, who supported them, etc. Much of this work is completed in the hope that results will offer clues to best practice, generating clearly 'evidence-based' practices which can be adopted and applied by nations, sports, organisations and even parents in the pursuit of excellence. Unfortunately, this apparently laudable pursuit is complicated by a major problem, the underlying basis of which is well described by Hume's 'is–ought' problem. This originally philosophical, but actually very pragmatic point, states that caution must be exercised in explanations of how directive, 'we ought to' statements often follow uncritically and automatically from observational, 'we found that the champion does this' descriptions. In short, just because champion X did Y does not necessarily mean that doing Y will inevitably generate championship performances in Z! As we will repeat throughout the book, the answer to most questions in TD is 'it depends!' This approaches requires the practitioner to weigh up the evidence and make informed decisions relevant to their context; there isn't a blueprint of what to do because every context, and every performer, is different.

There are many reasons which underlie this philosophically based but accurate advice. One significant but often neglected factor is the context in which champion X succeeds and behaviour Y takes place. We know that TID is a biopsychosocial issue; that is, optimum solutions will be contextualised, indeed best designed, on the basis of the interaction between physical and mechanical attributes (the 'bio'), psycho-behavioural characteristics (the 'psycho') and the sociocultural environment/milieu in which the individual exists (the 'social'). Unfortunately, the lack of application of, and consideration for, this approach leads to the uncritical adoption of systems from one culture to another, the continuation of methods in the absence of missing-though-critical features or the support of approaches which may exist due to tradition or other pressures. Caveat emptor: buyer beware!

TD from a biopsychosocial perspective

We hope to demonstrate throughout this book that the use of a biopsychosocial approach can offer a useful checklist for practitioners, enabling a structure which encourages a more critical evaluation for the validity and worth of a particular model, system or idea. We will first examine the underpinnings of the biopsycho-social approach, providing examples of its beneficial use in human settings.

The biopsychosocial approach has become an increasingly popular way of char-acterising human development. This model suggests a dynamic interaction between biological, psychological and social factors, all of which can play a significant role in human functioning. When these dynamic interactions are considered as part of the development process you are likely to arrive at more parsimonious if complex explanations and, even more crucially, better solutions. In contrast, approaches to TD that focus too narrowly on physiological or psychological processes are in danger of missing the complex, dynamic and non-linear nature of development (Abbott *et al.*, 2005) and are, therefore, inherently inadequate. Of course, reducing development to any one factor cannot capture the complexities of the phenom-enon, which is clearly influenced by a range of additional factors such as the educa-tional and sporting system, access to resources and facilities, and psycho-behavioural skills.

The main message here is that, whilst the different factors impacting on TD can be analysed as discrete elements that offer value, they should not be used solely and in isolation as the basis of policy and recommendations. This warning is especially noteworthy in light of the fact that the two most influential models of development (LTAD and DMSP) are explicitly based on relatively narrow disciplinary perspec-tives (physiology and developmental psychology, respectively). In contrast, a biopsychosocial perspective recognises that any feature of human development is far too complex and individualised to be reduced in this mono-disciplinary fashion.

Expert perspective on Chapter 1

David Court has worked as a practitioner within Talent ID and Development for 18 years in varying roles, including coaching Under 10 players through to a profes-sional squad before moving to the England and Wales Cricket Board developing talent pathways in cricket. David now works for the Football Association as Talent ID and Development Education Lead.

As I read this opening chapter I was able to relate a lot of its content to both good and not so good practice I have encountered in cricket and football. It is widely agreed by practitioners that effective Talent ID is vital to the success of both individuals and teams. So strong is this belief that many coaches and organisations believe they live and die by their recruitment, both at senior and junior level and, as such, vast amounts of time and money is spent trying to identify the next great player. However, the time and money that is spent identifying younger and younger athletes hasn't added to the quality of the output. There are still many issues within the current practice of Talent ID, which this book will help you to understand in greater detail. As Talent ID has become big business people look for and are often sold the magic bullet or 'answer to all the problems', but in reality this doesn't exist; to quote Áine and Dave, it depends! Predicting the future is impossible to do. As such it is important that those working within a talent system have a critical mind and are able to challenge the popular rhetoric.

It is vital that our Talent Systems are organised in the most effective way to provide maximal opportunity to a large number of athletes. Now, I understand that a 'more for longer' approach has practical challenges. You likely only have a limited amount of resources, in terms of time and money. However, I strongly believe it's not always about resources but *resourcefulness*. It's important to think long and hard about where resources should be allocated within the pathway, how much return on that resource do you get identifying very young athletes? Research consistently tells us that the most promising young players are often surpassed and fall away when they reach adulthood, and that other players either from within the group or often from outside of the group go on to be the stars. As such, how do we ensure that our systems, programmes and squads account for this with the non-linear and multi-dimensional nature of talent development and ensure we create a fluid pathway ensuring players have the chance to come in at any age and still achieve their full potential, whether that be a long-term participant in grassroots sport or Lionel Messi and, if they are removed from the pathway, they retain a love of the sport to continue playing? All of us working in sport must work harder to look at the whole person and their long-term development versus the snapshot, trial-based talent ID model, which many still use – and particularly the early (de)selection model.

We don't stop assessing talent when athletes are selected onto a pro-gramme. We should be continually challenging and supporting athletes to assist their development and continue to learn more about who they are, what they can do, what they are learning, are they improving, how they overcome setbacks and what motivates them and, importantly, how these change as athletes develop and mature. After all these look to be the key components of someone achieving their potential.

I would urge all practitioners to grasp the research nettle and to critically review what you do and why you do it. Some key concepts will be raised throughout this book, which can assist in guiding practitioners through the maze that is Talent ID and Development. I would urge you to reflect on your own practice and context based on what you learn in this book and engage in discussion and debate with those around you.

In conclusion

As you read this book, we suggest that you act as a critical consumer, weighing up the evidence against the realities of your landscape. Despite some of the glossy initi-atives that you might have come across in your domain, we suggest that solutions are typically complex, context-specific, and influenced by a range of factors. We are not sitting on the fence by failing to offer a template or blueprint for TID, after all 'it depends!' What we do provide in this book are evidence-based guidelines and principles that should inform your practice.

References

Abbott, A. and Collins, D. (2002). A theoretical and empirical analysis of a 'state of the art' talent identification model. *High Ability Studies*, 13(2), 157–178.

Abbott, A., Button, C., Pepping, G. and Collins, D. (2005). Unnatural selection: talent identification and development in sport. *Nonlinear Dynamics, Psychology and Life Science*, 9(1), 61–88.

Balyi, I. and Hamilton, A. (2003). Long-term athlete development update: trainability in childhood and adolescence. *Faster, Higher, Stronger*, 20, 6–8.

Colbert, S. (2005). *The Colbert Report*. Los Angeles, USA: Comedy Central.

Gagné, F. (1999). Nature or nurture? A re-examination of Sloboda and Howe's (1991) interview study on talent development in music. *Psychology of Music*, 27(1), 38–51.

Simonton, D. K. (2001). Talent development as a multidimensional, multiplicative, and dynamic process. *Current Directions in Psychological Science*, 10, 39–43.

Sternberg, R. J. (2003). WICS as a model of giftedness. *High Ability Studies*, 14, 109–137.

PART II

Developing the base
Pre-school and early preparation

For a variety of reasons, many societies worldwide reflect an increasing focus on physical factors at younger and younger ages. Parents, teachers and government agencies all express concerns about the 'obesity epidemic' – a genuine and important concern which is increasingly but, as we will suggest, only partly correctly addressed by providing activity classes for kids. In parallel, as high-level sport reaches down and down into the 'talent pool' and sports offer ever younger specialist pathways for kids, both parents and coaches get involved in early preparation training in an attempt to give their son or daughter the best possible start and chance of eventual success.

Unfortunately, these two 'agendas', often characterised as participation (taking part for health) or performance (preparing to perform at a high level), are often seen as distinct. We will address this mistaken dichotomy later. For the moment, let us reassure you that the two aims are well catered for by a large and common core of principles and practices, with the overlap making it sensible to keep a broad focus. Of course, things do get specialised later; you won't usually see Olympic champions in your local jogging club. For the early stages, however, and totally for the age groups covered in Part II, the same principles and practices will apply. Put simply, the same early foundation can equip youngsters for a career in professional sport, or a lifetime of enjoyable participation or recreational physical activity. Even more importantly, the same foundation can enable individuals to move seamlessly between these categories, as their aims, time available, resources and needs evolve.

So, all concerned with sport and physical activity – parents, coaches, teachers and sports administrators – are increasingly involved in early preparation. From parenting your superstar books and websites, through to toddler training classes, there is a lot available, only some of which is useful, well thought through or even, in some cases, well intentioned! So, 'let's start at the very beginning – a very good place to start', as the song goes. The next three chapters offer some underpinning principles, evidence-based ideas and practical examples of what a good base preparation might look like. For most children, this will cover the pre-school and early primary years; usually up to the age of 7–9 years old. In some cases, however, talent selection systems will get children involved from age 6, even earlier in activities such as gymnastics or dance. As this, and subsequent parts of the book, will suggest, this only *might* be a good idea. Read through our ideas and see what you think.

Finally, starting with this part and subsequently throughout the book, we will highlight implications for practitioners and what are now termed stakeholders. In English, parents, coaches and teachers for the early sections, with sports administrators receiving increasing coverage as we progress through the age bands, and the chapters.

2

THE ESSENTIALS OF MOVEMENT, CONFIDENCE AND ATTITUDE

The importance of fundamentals

It is well accepted that movement competence, an effective foundation of fundamental motor skills, is an essential feature of development. These skills underpin participation in physical activity from elite performance, through taking part in sport, to habitual patterns of daily movement. Without these skills, children can be limited in their ability to do *anything* physical. They are limited in play interactions with their peers, stand out in social physical challenges such as dancing and often become increasingly self-conscious, resulting eventually in a decision to quit, or at least avoid, situations where their 'weaknesses' may be exposed. In this respect, learning to move is as important as learning to read. Fortunately, literacy issues seem far less common, at least in the UK. However, you can just imagine how limiting a lack of reading and writing skills could be, even in this digital age. Well, we would suggest that lack of movement competence can also be a major challenge; socially, for your self-confidence and, in the long term perhaps for your health.

Before we consider what sort of 'diet' might work to address this problem, just a little more on why it is so important. Figure 2.1 shows what would be for us the ideal potential development from early age through to adulthood.

Developed from work we completed with several other colleagues (MacNamara *et al.*, 2011), the figure shows how basic movement competence is the essential first step to a lifetime of physical activity achievement and participation. Our suggestion was that, in an ideal world, people are equipped to move up and down a continuum of activity, running from Elite Reference Excellence (ERE) on the right through Personally Referenced Excellence (PRE) to Participation for Physical self-Worth (PPW) on the left. Most people will live in the PPW (e.g. 'I love working in my garden' or 'Walking on the hills is great') or PRE ('I am aiming for my first under the hour 10 km' or 'I love playing rugby with my mates in the fourth team

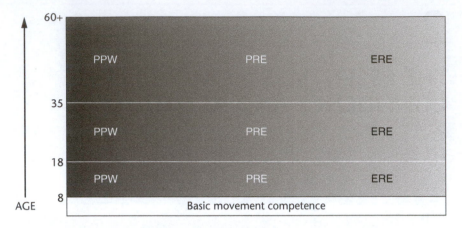

FIGURE 2.1 The ideal lifetime development model

Note
PPW – Participation for Physical self-Worth; PRE – Personally Referenced Excellence; ERE – Elite Reference Excellence.

… but I'm aiming to get in the seconds this season'). For some, however, taking a trip into the ERE section ('I won the medal at the local 10 km' or even 'This is my third premiership title') is their driving aspiration. Wherever you want to be on the continuum, however, it is important to be able to move across as things change. Both of us played on the right side when younger but, now of more 'mature' years, we still try to stay active, living in the PPW box with occasional forays into PRE, just to show that the old magic is still there!

Our point here is that, whatever your eventual aim (and that might change as you discover new activities, make new friends, etc.) an effective base of movement competence is needed so that you can go (or try to go) where you please. For parents, coaches and teachers the message should be clear. Equipping a child with the right tools for effective movement enables them to take part at whatever level they want to try for, for as long as they want. Movement competence is the basis for both high achievement and lifelong physical activity participation, with all the benefits they both can bring.

So what is needed?

On the basis of the ideas above, there are now many providers of 'fundamental movement skills' training. As we will examine later in the book, many of these may involve too much *fun* and not enough *de mentals*! For the moment, however, let's think what the absolute essential would be. Strangely, there is a need for a good deal more than some basic movements.

As Figure 2.2 shows, there are three interacting components, three legs of a stool if you like, that are needed for a programme to be really effective. Different authors

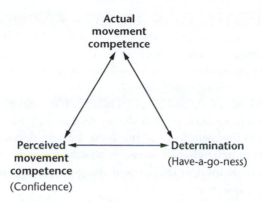

FIGURE 2.2 The physical literacy triangle

have used slightly different terms, but those in the figure work for us. Taken together, these terms form an important construct called *physical literacy*.

The point is that actual movement competence is only one element of what is needed. For a start, having confidence in that ability is also crucial. We have done several studies where children were equal in movement ability at a certain age, but differences in *perceived* ability at that age resulted in differences in *actual* ability a few years later. Whether the children became what they thought they were, or got worse because they avoided the activities which, they thought, made them look foolish, is an interesting question – we come back to this in Chapter 4. For the moment, however, the point is that all of us, children or adults, will tend to avoid doing things at which we lack confidence. Physical activity is no different.

More positively, perhaps, a child with 'have a go-ness' (our technical term!) may well overcome lack of confidence. Even more importantly, they will give new things a go, persist in the face of failure (especially if the thing is important to them) and can often galvanise their friends into involvement. We will talk about 'have a go-ness' in a slightly more technical and applicable way in Chapter 6. For the moment, notice how useful this capacity is: for the child him/herself, his/her friends and siblings, and for the class or group that you teach or coach. In other words, such individuals are worth developing and worth using!

Focusing on the right combination – the obesity trap

So, we now know what is needed for young children: not just physical activity, which affects them now but only might work to keep them involved in the future. Only by working on physical literacy can parents, teachers and coaches give children the lifelong physical activity habit which they need, and which we all need to have.

Of course, that isn't to challenge the importance of obesity as an issue for all of us. Recent data from the Millennium study (Centre for Longitudinal Studies, 2012), which tracks children across the UK as they get older, shows that over one-third of children in England are obese or overweight. The picture elsewhere in the UK is even worse. Our point is that just making children more active is a temporary solution, unless they pick up on a lifelong physical activity habit.

That's why we emphasise physical literacy, as the nearest thing to a magic bullet that we have. If children are equipped with the skills to do activity, the confidence in those skills, and the 'get up and go' to try them out in a variety of circumstances, then we are much more likely to get a slightly thinner and much happier population! Returning to the main focus of this book, namely developing the talented towards ERE, developing physical literacy is equally important. So, unusually but fortunately, we can do more or less the same things with everyone, whatever their eventual goals – truly a sporting utopia!

As one of many consequences, children should be focused on physical *education* as opposed to just physical activity! Of course, PE should be active, but the aim is to teach skills and build confidence, rather than just run them around a bit. Just imagine if children did reading as an activity – two hours reading a week instead of lessons on how to read and write. They would never be pushed to read anything above their level, and achievement would be very dependent on what they had done beforehand, either at home or with another teacher. We suggest that, for too many children, especially those outside the sports system, this is indeed the case. Getting out of breath is a novel experience for many kids. We have taken trips to the mountains where several children have complained that they were having a heart attack as they walked upwards. Fortunately, this was just breathlessness and we were able to encourage them through it (N.B. *not* what to do if you are having a heart attack!). So, good quality PE will both stretch and teach youngsters, keeping them active but equipping and enthusing them for a lifelong habit – once again, we repeat, whether they are an aspiring professional/Olympic medallist or not.

General movement ability – the essentials

So, before addressing the slightly more subtle issues of confidence and determination, let's look at what movement skills should actually be addressed in young aspiring superstars as well as 'normals' like us. In this book, we will refer a lot to a construct called General Movement Ability or GMA. For us, GMA is built on the movement competences that should form part of every child's development. We offer some examples of activities later in this section but, first, let's consider what GMA is, and isn't.

Many years ago, when one of the authors was young and the other wasn't yet born, GMA was thought of as agility. Developing this general skill was done through a variety of games and activities, together with whole-body activities such as circuit training. The 'general' bit here is the important one. Most people think of someone as agile if they can twist and turn when chased; also, when they can pick up new skills quickly and, finally, if their movements look smooth and well coordinated. Today, agility is often defined as abilities related to Change of Direction, or CoD. This has led a number of coaches, and not a few scientists, to put some rather annoying limits on agility. As a result, 'agility' training is often developed around shuttle runs, fast footwork ladders or responding to visual signals. Of course, all these elements are a *part* of agility, but they don't represent the *whole* thing.

So, what are the essentials for agility, or GMA as we will now return to calling it? Well another way to think of it is as a 'movement vocabulary'. Imagine being in an argument or writing a learned article. You will do better if:

1   you have a large vocabulary, and;
2   you are well practiced and confident in using it.

So, any youngster, whether destined for world domination or simple participation, will do better if s/he:

a   has experienced a wide variety of movement challenges, and;
b   had lots of experience in solving novel movement problems with *some* success.

Hopefully, the link from one set of requirements/principles to another set of prac-tices is clear. We return to these ideas later when we look at the ideal pre-academy and academy experience in Part III and Chapter 9. For the moment, and before we go into the what, when and how of a pre-school and primary movement diet, just consider the italicised 'some' in point (b) above. We suggest that learning is often effectively paired with challenge, and that avoiding any challenge will produce a rather doughy and dependent child. However, this challenge must be proportion-ate, with the child getting success some of the time, thereby increasing confidence and determination. Special Forces style selection procedures, what our friends in the military call 'beasting', is *never* appropriate for young children. This may seem obvious, but there are still some examples of this 'treat them mean' philosophy out there. It's not only cruel but it doesn't work! Scaring children into doing things will always lose its power, albeit eventually.

So, sermon over: now back to the positive stuff. What then are you to do with the developing youngster to optimise development?

The GMA 'curriculum'

First of all, a disclaimer! It would be wrong of us to prescribe any one method or set of activities as the best. There are lots of other factors to be considered. So Dave might suggest judo for his youngsters whilst Áine looks for a Gaelic equivalent. What is available in your society and, therefore, what your children watch and aspire towards, is one key criteria. You may also find that teachers or coaches will decide to work through a particular medium. This coach might use netball, that one rugby. What matters is that the principles and practices shown above are followed.

When done effectively then, children are well equipped to glean all the other benefits of other approaches. So the approach known as 'Deliberate Play' will enable them to develop good social skills and challenge themselves in different ways. In contrast, the more training-like 'Deliberate Practice' will help children to groove essential skills, gaining confidence in their ability to use them, and also in their ability to progress – more of this in Chapter 4. For the present, we will focus on an idea called Deliberate Preparation (Giblin *et al.*, 2014) and how it can be applied to a pre-school audience.

As a general guideline, pre-school children should be looking to get some experiences in the following broad areas. We offer some detail for each one, together with a rationale for its inclusion, what to look for in a good provision, and how the messages can be enhanced by parents at home. No surprises with the first and second, however, which are as near to essential as you can get.

Swimming

Hopefully, we will face no argument over the safety advantages of learning to swim. People often fail to recognise the additional benefits, however. Here is an activity which you can start with very young babies, which is challenging them in a novel environment and one which offers a number of different movement elements, such as weightlessness. In short, swimming is an essential part of any pre-schooler's agenda.

So, look for instructors who offer more than just 'water fun'. They should be teaching safety skills, such as turning and gripping the rail/edge in case you fall in, using the steps and manoeuvring yourself around the pool. Instructors should ensure that the baby/child is fine with getting their face wet and, eventually, get them swimming underwater. Finally, training should work on stroke technique, not just achieving a distance. As stated above, this is all about the learner satisfactorily meeting challenge. Parents can offer significant help here. Indeed, good programmes will offer advice and training drills, so that parents can practice alone with their children.

Gymnastics

Gymnastics is another key skill, but not because your son or daughter will ever compete at high level. Only gymnastics (or a more modern derivative such as parkour or free running) can offer sufficiently varied movement challenges to really develop the movement vocabulary. So, make sure that your chosen training gym provides a full range of movement; rolling, tumbling and balances, ideally with movement from one to the next. Children should find the activities challenging, and this challenge should extend to more than just an insistence on correctness of movement. For both swimming and gym, there are a lot of providers out there, of varying quality. Take your time; watch a few sessions and note the levels of supervision and challenge. Good instructors will be a lot more than just friendly child minders; make sure you stay and watch, asking questions if you are not sure about what you see. Once again, good gyms will encourage practice at home, but with some moderation. After all, not every home is carpeted with crash mats!

Striking skills and hand-eye coordination

We now go onto a few skills where specialist instruction is not necessary, at least at these ages. The first is perfect for home development. Beach versions of most striking games, particularly cricket, tennis and badminton, will offer the patient parent or teacher more than enough scope for developing hand-eye coordination. Start with a static target; a traffic cone (out of the traffic!) offers a perfect tee on which the ball can start. This is commonly used in the US as T-Ball. As coordination develops, you can move to an easy predictable toss as serve. Note that, if the ball is to bounce off the ground first, overarm, dart-like throws are better than an underarm lob.

If you do seek out instruction, make sure that there is lots of activity and much less talk. Some coaches and adults evaluate their worth on the volume (amount not loudness) of verbal instruction. Remember that we learn by doing more than listening!

If you are focused on an early start towards high-level performance, avoid the 'drill it into them' schools which, unfortunately, are still about and happy to take your money. Particularly common in tennis and golf, but certainly apparent in other sports, these (sometimes well-meaning) coaches are often convinced by the 'groove the basics' arguments which dominated coaching in the 1950s and 1960s (one of your authors was on the receiving end of it – and a lot of good it did him … not!). Room for individuality within a certain structure is now acknowledged as the best way, certainly at this age.

Gross motor movements

Perhaps because they are difficult to measure, these are the skills that get missed out from many movement programmes. A pity because they really are the basis of most sports and game, plus dance (at least the disco/club kind which can actually play an important part in the youngster's life). Once again, however, a lot can be achieved without specialist input. A simple game of tag, with several chasers (or one very agile one) can work well to develop the whole (gross) body movement patterns which will be essential building blocks for games later. Running slalom patterns around cones is another good one (timing kids to see who is fastest will help with motivation) whilst classic party games such as musical chairs will also work well. Help kids to acquire a sense of rhythm by dancing with them to favourite songs, or getting them to clap or tap out to a particular beat. Our own children love joining in with a raucous version of 'YMCA'; don't worry, they will get bored once they hit their teens.

The main idea here is that whole-body movement is good, the more, and more varied, the better. Even games of 'Simon says…' can be used, as well as impromptu games of hopscotch along a pavement – watch out for the cracks! More high-tech electronic games, dance mats, etc. are another good stimulus although they are inevitably limited. Supplement with some running round a large field to taste.

Finally, we must mention the most neglected of childhood skills, tree climbing, and its more sanitised cousin, the adventure playground. Both offer all sorts of opportunity for positive development – of strength, balance and have a go-ness. Don't worry, children will rarely do something too far outside their skillset. Just in case they do, however, be close *but don't hover*! Part of the game at this age is to test limits, yours as well as theirs. So when observing, just try raising the stakes a little: 'Do you think you can do that on the other leg/with only three touches/etc.?'

Fine motor movements

At the other end of the continuum from the whole-body gross movements are the more precise, often hand or fingers, movements of fine motor control. Obviously an essential precursor for musical instruments, but a good sense of feel and touch, proprioception as it is known, is useful for other things as well. Old-fashioned games like 'Jacks', learning the recorder, even being able to toss dice from a cup without skipping them off the table are all ways in which this component can be developed. Of course, it is a good idea to help children establish left from right, and which their stronger/preferred hand is – not doing so at the right stage is one pre-cursor of dyslexia. That apart, it is generally a good idea to challenge children to use their 'weak' hand, in an attempt to get it as good as the other.

In fact, in our modern digital age this is one component that should be moving on in leaps and bounds! Nothing wrong with laptop games in this regard, just so long as they are balanced by sufficient engagement with the other categories. After all, no-one wants the title of 'fittest thumbs in the school'!

Rough and tumble

Correctly, we suppose, this is a subset of gross motor stuff. However, it seems sufficiently important for us to mention it on its own. Children need some element of rough and tumble – girls as much as boys, and this can be provided by parents, simple tag games like 'Bulldog' or most conveniently, older siblings. Certainly, as we will explore later, siblings can be very useful for long-term development. In the absence, however, or if you can't find any boisterous cousins or local friends, a tickle fight works perfectly as a starter for ten. The importance here is that children learn how to struggle and use their strength. Let them win sometimes though!

Creativity

As mentioned earlier, rhythm is an important precursor for social activities like dance. Creativity is also important, however, and, although mentioned by many coaches in many sports, is a rather illusive and hard to define characteristic. That's a shame really because most children are really good at it. Encouraging imagination by listening to their stories, asking them to act them out and move while talking have all been shown to help, and inventing games with others is an excellent source.

Mini–plays, or getting children to mime bits of stories, is another great way – you don't need to be developing 'method acting'! Just asking them to pretend walking into a gale, or pretending to be an animal, will work perfectly well – be prepared to let them take charge though!

Team activities

Last but not least, it is always good to give children an early experience of working in teams. Quite apart from the social skills side, there are a whole lot of other elements. Appreciating individual strengths and weaknesses (and allowing for them), taking on a role, following a leader and/or leading, are all learnt well from this. Turn to more conventional team games and you add lots of basic constructs such as making space, goal-side and vision into play.

Note that this latter set doesn't need a formal setting. Simple games such as 'bench ball' or 'end ball' (pass the ball to someone standing on a bench/in an end zone to score) work perfectly well. In fact, these are often better since the added challenge of controlling with the feet or implement (stick, crosse, hurley, etc.) is removed.

Expert perspective on Chapter 2

Joni Harding is the Education Manager, Swim Ireland and has spent over 15 years as an educator in swimming in the UK and Middle East. In her own words, Joni

> *eats, sleeps and breathes swimming and I strive every day to develop a workforce of trainers who are dedicated, relevant, skilled and passionate about giving children the opportunity to write their own story of participating in sport for the rest of their life.*

I have spent the last 15 years as an Educator in Swimming, delivering teacher and coach education for the Amateur Swimming Association in the UK and the Middle East and now managing a workforce of educators in Ireland. As such, I could certainly be labelled an avid campaigner for the development of FUNdamentals or Aquatic Movement Literacy, whichever term you wish to use. In fact, I often have people look at me strangely when I talk about teaching *skills* rather than teaching 'swimming'. The spectator (the parent) measures their child's progress by the number of widths/lengths their child has swum or whether or not they are practicing their arm action or their leg action for a specific stroke. Putting my 'parent' hat on I can understand this – as a parent you want your child to be safe. In a swimming lesson, teaching this safety is perceived to require only the practice of the swimming strokes. We as practitioners or administrators don't educate parents appropriately and, therefore, they tend not to realise that safety in the water is a direct by-product of the development of General Movement Ability and is therefore essential. What *doesn't* go without saying, is that these *essentials* really are essential to developing effective stroke technique in swimming, as well as any transfer of skill to other activities or sports. Without them swimming can only ever be – at the very best – survival. After all, if you can't float, how can you get your body into the correct position to swim any of the four strokes? If you can't manage your breathing how can you coordinate your body and put your face in the water at the same time? This General Movement Ability is what underpins the more complex movement patterns, which form stroke technique and, put frankly, keep you alive when you are in a great big puddle of water.

This chapter discusses the importance of General Movement Ability and certainly highlights the importance to parents in developing psychological and physical literacy, informing in a way which is noticeably absent (or at least rare) within facilities and clubs delivering Learn to Swim Programmes in the UK and Ireland. It is easier perhaps to highlight the importance of literacy on land. As the chapter mentions, there are numerous providers of fundamental movement skills training. In aquatics, a lack of understanding of fundamental movement skills, as well as the misconception that a child should just be practising 'swimming' when they get into the pool, has had a knock-on effect on opportunities within swimming for effective development of General Movement Ability and has created an abundance of programmes which focus on distance and speed rather than quality, efficiency and skill.

If a parent is looking for a programme which will develop a confident, resilient, strong, efficient and safe swimmer, they should be looking for a programme that encourages the development of Core Aquatics Skills. They may be presented as;

- entries and exits
- submersion and aquatic breathing
- flotation
- rotation
- streamlining
- sculling
- movement and propulsion
- coordination and balance.

Each one of these skills, although on the surface don't shout out 'swimming', will lay a solid foundation both physically and emotionally for the journey ahead. More specifically, delivering these skills through structured play, repetitive, quality practice, whilst ensuring appropriate levels of challenge, allow the emergence of individuals with confidence, resilience and determination, as well as the physical capability to then go on and develop stroke technique. In some ways, swimming is completely unique among sports, because making a mistake in a swimming pool can be so costly. Bearing in mind it only takes an inch of water to drown, being faced with 375,000 litres of water can be daunting – and perhaps gives the perfect opportunity for the development of the more 'subtle' or 'softer' skills mentioned in the chapter, which can be a determining factor in achieving *personal* excellence, whether that be on a podium or in a local pool. I guess I am lucky to work in an industry which (without much effort) gets children involved because parents see it as a life skill. However, because of that we often forget the other benefits of this activity, and as such as soon as a child can swim they often drop out and focus on another sport. This chapter highlights the importance of instilling these core skills, no matter whether the activity is on land or in water but, perhaps more importantly, that these skills lay the foundation physically and emotionally for the journey ahead – no matter what direction that journey may take.

Coaction of psychological aspects in physical literacy

So, hopefully the sections above will have given you some ideas and structure for developing your own 'superstar'. In fact, apart from swimming and some sort of gymnastics, we wouldn't see any one of these elements as essential. Far more important, and what should really be the focus of your efforts, are the psychological benefits you target. Getting these right will go a long way to giving the child a great start, whether for high-level achievement or a lifelong participation habit. In fact, as other sections will show, getting the psychology right can equip for excellence in a very wide spectrum of activity. Even non-physical domain success can be enabled through an early physical focus. So what are the key considerations here?

Well, it mostly comes down to an appropriate balance of challenge and fun. Let's take the obvious one first. Very few people will persist at something which they don't enjoy (more of this in Chapter 4). Accordingly, one key outcome is that children actually enjoy their physical experiences. Of course, this can be more subtle than one would think. Watching videos of, say, a six-year-old golf champion can lead some to recoil in horror – what are her/his parents thinking of? S/he can't *possibly* be enjoying all that practice. Well, we would agree but with a slight caveat. The child may actually enjoy the practice, especially if the prescribing adult is positive and considerate. Different cultures may also play a part here. You only need to wait a few years and see if the behaviour survives that great leveller of all things parental … adolescence! So, the main thing is that *the child* thinks s/he is having fun and, if so, all is fine and dandy … so long as no common-sense health guidelines are being broken, such as double bodyweight squats with a prepubescent child. As later sections will show, eventual superstars look back with pleasure at many happy hours spent practising their skills, whether with parents or siblings. The point is, they enjoyed it and kept coming back for more … not pulling the plug as soon as they had the opportunity.

The second challenge element is also a subtle one. The point here is that children need to get used to trying and failing, *then trying again*, quite early in the game. As teachers, coaches and psychologists we are often 'picking up the pieces' of children who have 'enjoyed' almost constant success, thanks to (usually) Mum and Dad manipulating the situation so that they always succeed, or at least feel like they do. As a very simple example, consider your reaction if your young toddler knocks into the sofa because they weren't looking where they were going. Many will say 'naughty sofa' and give it a smack for getting in the way! We really can't understand this – surely, the child needs to learn that they control their destiny – at least on this scale! Take this up a notch or two, and parents will often try to protect their child from the negative consequences of losing. Once again, more on this later. For the moment, please recognise that the ability to enjoy physical activity, and the challenges it involves, win or lose, are key targets for developing any youngster.

References

Centre for Longitudinal Studies (2012). The age 11 survey of the Millenium Cohort Study. Available: www.cls.ioe.ac.uk/page.aspx?&sitesectionid=1330&sitesectiontitle=MCS+age +11+initial+findings.

Giblin, S., Collins, D., MacNamara, Á. and Kiely, J. (2014). The Third Way: Deliberate Preparation as an evidence-based focus for primary physical education. *Quest*, 66, 385–395, doi:10.1080/00336297.2014.944716.

MacNamara, Á., Collins, D., Bailey, R. P., Ford, P., Toms, M. and Pearce, G. (2011). Promoting lifelong physical activity AND high-level performance: realising an achievable aim for physical education. *Physical Education and Sport Pedagogy*, 16(3), 265–278.

3

THE CHILD'S IDEAL APPROACH TO SPORT

Establishing a growth mindset

Ending the 'nature versus nurture' debate

A key question in talent development is the extent to which the individual's skill is a product of innate ability or learning and experience – the age-old 'nature versus nurture' debate. Although this nature/nurture debate has been discussed ad nauseum, there is still not complete consensus on the matter. Indeed, considerable dispute continues about the balance of genetic inheritance and environmental factors that might contribute towards the manifestation of talent, and this manifests itself in how coaching and talent development is done. Even though there is anecdotal evidence of 'untrained talent' emerging, this occurs too infrequently and is too poorly documented to count as serious scientific data. Likewise, even though some physical and physiological variables are clearly advantageous in sport (tall basketball players tend to have a leg up on the competition, for example), there is little evidence for 'hardware' advantages amongst elites bar obvious preclusions (e.g. 20-stone marathon runners or 6-stone shot putters are rare). Indeed, there are many examples of athletes with seemingly the perfect physical makeup to excel at a sport not realising their potential and either dropping out of the sport completely, or competing at lower levels than would be expected. If you examine 'superchamps' and 'almosts' in your sport (and more on this later in the book) it is impossible to distinguish between elite and non-elites based on physical and anthropometrical profiles (Baxter-Jones and Helms, 1996). For these reasons, those involved in TID are sceptical of the belief that differences in those who make it and those who don't can be attributed solely to the presence or absence of physical attributes – the nature stance. Instead, talented performers are the result of the interaction of genetic factors, psychological factors, *and* a favourable practice environment, rather than on the basis of one of these factors in isolation (Abbott *et al.*, 2005).

In this chapter we focus on the start of the pathway – what sort of attitude to learning and development do you want to foster in your performers so they make the most of their ability? Given the importance of fostering positive attitudes to challenge and development, this chapter will provide practical guidelines about how to develop, refine and reinforce appropriate attitudes that set young people up for a lifetime of involvement in sport. To quote an Irish proverb, 'Tús maith, leath na hoibre'; in English, 'A good start is half the work!'

Differentiating between potential and performance

As we discussed in Chapter 1, it is important to distinguish between determinants of *performance* and determinants of *development*, especially when we are selecting and coaching young performers. Unfortunately, there is a tendency to emphasise determinants of performance, what makes a performer good right now, rather than fostering what helps them *become good*. This has significant implications for 'who gets what' in terms of access to coaching, resources and competition, for example, as well as longer-term repercussions; attempts to identify talent at early stages of development have been found to be particularly ineffective given that the majority of young performers identified as talented do not ultimately achieve success at elite or even sub-elite levels of performance. There is little evidence to suggest that elite performers show significant signs of promise during their early involvement in their chosen domain. Indeed, many elite performers were not identified as talented during their formative years but still managed to succeed at elite levels of competition (Abbott and Collins, 2004). So, if exceptional performances at a young age is 'neither a necessary nor a sufficient prerequisite for later success' (Vaeyens *et al.*, 2009, 1370) why is this the focus of early TID? Vaeyens *et al.* (2009), for example, reported that the majority of the German athletes at the Olympic Games in Athens (2004) made their first international appearance at senior levels of competition. These facts have important implications for the (misplaced) emphasis we place on current performance (how good young performers are right now) compared to a longer-term focus (how well they will perform in the future). Focusing on the factors that both encourage young performers to engage in, and then persist at sport would seem the most useful starting point in terms of talent development.

Talent isn't a fixed capacity

The one-off measurements associated with TI approaches that were introduced in Chapter 1 (selection into TD pathways based on how big, tall or strong a young performer is or on their current performance level) fail to capture any understanding of talent as developmental or multidimensional. Reflecting this limitation is the suggestion that certain behaviours only emerge when the supporting subsystems and processes are ready. What does this mean for how you select and coach young performers at the start of the pathway? First, it points to the importance of considering, identifying and developing those factors that, over the course of time, may promote development. You might have selected a young athlete who has all, or some, of the 'obvious' qualities associated with success in your sport, but once in the pathway, that athlete's progress stalls. For example, a lack of commitment will almost always hinder the development of a young, but otherwise 'talented', athlete. Certainly, the subsequent development and deployment of this characteristic can result in unexpected and sudden changes in development and performance, reflecting the multiplicative conception of talent described in Chapter 1. If these psycho-behavioural skills (and we will explore these in more detail in Chapter 6) act as catalysts of development, it seems reasonable to tease out and deliberately promote the individual skills and characteristics required to meet developmental challenges and transitions as a focus of your coaching. We will return to these ideas later in the book; for the moment the important point is that we need to consider what helps young athletes make the most of the developmental opportunities they are given in their talent development environment. Let's start with examining the importance of attitude as an important predictor of engagement in sport.

Growth mindset: an essential precursor to development?

Given the considerable buzz surrounding the phrase 'growth mindset' in the popular media, it is more than likely you are familiar with the term; but what does it mean, why is it important and what is your role in encouraging this approach for the young performers you work with? In her seminal work, Dweck (2008) suggests that there are two types of mindsets: a fixed mindset and a growth mindset. An individual with a fixed mindset views ability as permanent and judges situations in terms of how they reflect upon their ability; if s/he plays badly, s/he is a bad player; if s/he does badly on an exam, s/he is not clever. This type of mindset has important implications for talent development; individuals with a fixed mindset will rarely seek out opportunities to learn or be challenged because failure would be reflective of their ability. Instead, they choose activities that are 'safe' and where achievement is easily attainable; performers with a fixed mindset fear failure and withhold effort as a means of self-protection against this failure.

In contrast, an individual with a growth mindset views ability as developmental and reflective of the effort they exert on the task. Challenge is viewed as an exciting part of learning and rather than fearing failure, failure is seen as a necessary part of the learning journey. An individual with a growth mindset views a poor performance as an opportunity to learn and sees that subsequent performance is contingent on exerting more effort: if I try harder, I will get better. Dweck describes the difference between a fixed and a growth mindset:

> a belief that your qualities are carved in stone (fixed mindset) leads to a host of thoughts and actions and a belief that your qualities can be cultivated (growth mindset) leads to a host of different thoughts and actions, taking you down an entirely different road.

A young performer with a fixed mindset will not exert effort because s/he believes that if s/he were talented he would not need to try and that effort is a bad thing because it is reflective of inability. For young performers with a growth mindset, effort is the lynchpin that allows them to realise their potential. A growth mindset allows young performers understand that their talents and abilities can be developed through effort, effective coaching and persistence. Of course, not everyone is going to be an Olympic champion but individuals with a growth mindset believe they can get better if they work hard. The key point here is that mindset, or the attitude that young people bring to achievement domains, has a large impact on our understanding of success and failure and subsequent engagement in developmental activities.

How does mindset influence behaviour?

Research has repeatedly shown that a growth mindset fosters positive attitudes towards practice and learning, leads to a hunger for feedback and a greater ability to deal with setbacks (Dweck, 2008). Critically, given the demands of both high-level participation in sport and lifelong engagement in physical activity, a self-regulated performer who possesses a growth mindset has the ability to initiate and persist at tasks that are not inherently motivating or interesting, though nonetheless important for development. We will talk about Deliberate Practice in the next chapter, but the message here is that an appropriate attitude to practice might be the key to optimise the experience. This might be even more significant as your performer improves and the demands within the activity increase. The ability to effectively cope with the stressors of development and adapt to the challenges faced, specifically increased autonomy and responsibility over one's development as one moves along the pathway, is a key component of successful development. Fostering this attitude early, at home *and* in the performance domain, is an essential starting point in the development journey.

As we introduced earlier in this chapter, viewing talent as a gift, something that someone innately has or does not have, is problematic for a number of reasons. First, it suggests that talent is a fixed capacity that can be identified early and remains stable over time. If this is the case, our role as coaches or teachers must surely be questioned! Second, the belief that abilities are innate will have significant impact on both coach and athlete behaviour and their engagement with the talent development pathway. Individuals who view abilities as having innate origins often attribute someone else's performance, good or bad, to their innate level of ability. Conversely, those that believe abilities are 'developable' attribute performance to their level of effort (Dweck, 2008). Performers who believe abilities are innate and ultimately unchangeable – a fixed mindset – are more likely to react to failure and negative feedback with decreased effort, persistence and increased negative emotions. This leads to maladaptive behaviours on the part of the performer; an increased risk of cultivating learned helplessness, a form of self-handicapping behaviour, or forms of complacency wherein individuals believe their natural talent will lead to success and subsequently decrease their effort and motivation to improve. These responses are not conducive to learning and performance, and as a result can compromise talent identification and development. A warning to parents and coaches – be careful about the label you give young children as it can have significant implications on their attitude to learning.

There may also be a dark side to growth mindset; those who believe talent to be predominantly developable are more likely to respond to poor performances with increased effort and persistence. While generally viewed as a positive characteristic, over-persistence may also be a maladaptive response and itself a form of helpless behaviour (Dweck, 2008). In short, believing that talent can be developed with enough effort or practice may not be healthy or realistic. Simply, believing in either perspective too rigidly can be damaging and it is more useful to view mindset as a continuum of behaviour.

How do you use this information when you interact with young performers? In summary, labelling young people as 'talented' can create the expectation that they will be successful at later stages in the development pathway because their ability is innate. However, it is a given that hard work and high-quality training are important to becoming a high-performance athlete. Moreover, creating unrealistic expectations can be damaging to young performers given the low correlation between underage success and success at higher levels of competition. Similarly, creating the expectation that increased effort and persistence will inevitably result in success may also place unfair expectations on young people. Practice is clearly necessary, but it may not be sufficient: genes, resources and luck do of course all play a part. That being said, a self-regulated performer who possesses a growth mindset will likely have many advantages and be able to maximise the opportunities they are given. The rest of this chapter will provide coaches and parents with an understanding and practical guidelines about how to develop, refine and reinforce appropriate mindsets.

Instilling a positive attitude

Dweck (2008) suggested that growth mindsets can be induced with messages from the environment that talent can be developed over time with effort. This has important implications for coaches and parents. What you say, the feedback you give, and how you praise success and failure all influence young performers' attitude to sport, the effort they exert and how they react to success and failure. The rest of this chapter will outline some guidelines on effective practice and on how coaches, parents and other stakeholders can foster appropriate attitudes to development.

How to praise the right way

Dweck (2008) suggests that 'many of the things that we do to motivate our kids are sapping their desire to learn'. Therefore, careful consideration must be given to how we praise young peoples' efforts and performance in sport. It seems that praising ability – how smart, fast, 'talented' a young person is – can foster a fixed mindset. It may be that our enthusiasm for praising children for their ability, even at very young ages – 'what a clever girl' – is instilling a fixed mindset. Instead, praising the process, the young performer's effort and the strategies employed is a more effective method. Praising effort gives the young person a variable they can control – 'if I try harder, I will get better'. In this manner they are in control of their success and they have a means of responding to challenge, failure and mistakes. Indeed, Dweck found that praising children for their intelligence ('You must be smart at this') as opposed to their effort ('You must have worked really hard') has a massive detrimental effect on performance. Over a series of tests, children praised for effort as a whole tried harder, worked at a task longer, and enjoyed challenges more than those praised for intelligence. In the same study those praised for effort improved their test scores by 30 per cent, while those praised for intelligence saw their scores decline by 20 per cent. We clearly need to pay attention to how and what we praise as this plays a key role in fostering the positive attitudes to learning that are central to effective talent development. If you can get your performer (or son or daughter) to share this focus, even better.

Young performers need to understand that taking on a challenge, sticking to the task and trying different strategies to be successful are fundamental to development. Again, the earlier this can be reinforced, the better. This is important because we know that those with a growth mindset are more likely to take on more challenging tasks, and succeed, than those with a fixed mindset, even when other variables (skill level, for example) are accounted for. This may be because mindset influences individual perceptions and development of 'self'. A fixed mindset is typified by feelings of powerlessness and learned helplessness that leads to a self-defeating identity – 'I can't do this'. Having a growth mindset is more likely to encourage feelings of empowerment – young performers understand that they can influence their own development and learning through their actions. Encouraging this attitude is important given the inevitable setbacks encountered on the pathway, and the need to react positively and adaptively to challenging situations. Not getting too caught up in 'wins and losses' is an important consideration for all *if* the focus (as it should be) is on the long-term development of the performer.

Empowering the performer

As suggested earlier in the chapter, promoting concepts that are within the control of the young performer, such as hard work, effort and practice, seems to be the way to promote a growth mindset. It seems that young people learn better and achieve more if they believe that they hold the key, rather than it being down to how intelligent/quick/good they are, or perceive themselves to be. This is especially important when you consider the length of the TD journey and the inevitable 'ups and downs' experienced along the way. For a young performer at the beginning of their journey, adult success can seem a far away and, at times, unattainable goal.

The same can be said for young performers faced with developmental challenges such as injury or deselection; the delayed gratification required to stay with the process, especially in times of adversity, is often a defining feature of those who make it. Coaches, parents, and other stakeholders need to encourage the young performer to understand that development takes time and success rarely comes right away or without overcoming challenge; sticking with a journey rather than giving up at any sign of unrest or difficulty is vital. Again this emphasis on the process, and the effort required to improve and progress, should be a central component of the coaching environment; praising effort, perseverance and progress against long- and short-term goals, rather than emphasising how 'talented' the performer is, will help them understand success is achieved and recognised through factors they have control over, rather than through an innate ability over which they have no power.

Ever tried. Ever failed. No matter. Try again. Fail again. Fail better!

The words of Samuel Beckett – 'Ever tried. Ever failed. No matter. Try again. Fail again. Fail better' – have a lot of resonance for how we should design our coaching practices and talent pathway *and* our interactions with young people. If we examine the biographies of some of the most successful performers, failure and setbacks are common features. In order to encourage a growth mindset and 'gritty' developers, coaches need to cultivate an environment where young performers are comfortable in making mistakes. In this way mistakes are seen as indicators of areas for growth and as an opportunity to learn, grow and succeed. Unfortunately, this is not always a feature of the pathway. We will return to these ideas in Chapter 14, but consider how you exploit failures and mistakes within your coaching practice; a growth mindset sees failure not as evidence of being unskilled or 'untalented' but as a catalyst for future development.

We mentioned earlier in the chapter about the importance of self-regulation in helping young people make the most of the opportunities they are given. Self-regulation involves processes that enable individuals to control their thoughts, feelings, and actions and is described by Zimmerman (2000) as the extent to which individuals are metacognitively, motivationally and behaviourally proactive participants in their own learning process. Self-regulatory skills develop as early as two years of age and by the age of 12 young people use these skills consciously in their performance environment. As such, the development of self-regulatory skills would seem a sensible focus for early years TD pathways since these are the skills that help maximise learning and also help young people balance the various demands of the pathway. Self-regulation skills are prerequisites for learning; the lack of these skills may explain why some performers don't make it the top of the performance ladder.

During early exposure to sport, coaches (and parents) play a major role in regulating learning – they are the ones who set goals, manage the learning environment, support and praise the young performers and so on. However, as performers advance, coaches should reduce that support and expect performers to take ownership over their learning and development; the young performer should take responsibility to self-regulate their learning and decide where, when, how, why and what to do. Unfortunately, this isn't always the case. Coaches, and parents, often try to do too much to support the young performer, hoping to accelerate progress. Although this approach might give some short-term success, it is unlikely that the aspiring elite is developing the self-regulatory skills that they need when the going gets tough. If self-regulation is important, how might you do it?

Self-regulation does not occur naturally but as a result of quality coaching where feedback and goal setting are used as prompts to develop these skills. There are a couple of important things to think about here. First, the development of self-regulation skills take time and should be purposefully embedded into coaching from early years. Foundational skills for self-regulation are developed in the first five years of life which means parents, teachers and coaches play an important role in helping young children regulate thinking and behaviour. Good parenting, for example, is associated with the development of self-regulation skills. A particularly good predictor is support for autonomy; letting your toddler complete a task as independently as possible, for example by providing suggestions only when the child is stuck, seems to be a good basis for later self-regulation. As children increase their ability to act independently, coaches should turn over more of the regulating responsibilities to the children's control, while monitoring their progress and intervening when necessary to provide appropriate support. Though this can be frustrating at the time (for the parent and coach more than the child!), the long-term benefits would seem to be worth it.

Of course, teaching self-regulation does not require a separate curriculum or approach; good 'teachers', whether that is in the classroom, on the football pitch or in the home, do this as part of their everyday interactions by modelling and scaffolding it during ordinary activities. Think of developing self-regulation skills in the way you would help a child learn to read or ride a bike – you want to bridge the gap between what children already know and can do and more complex skills and knowledge. By demonstrating and modelling appropriate behaviour, coaches (and parents and peers) show young performers how to accomplish a task and use the self-regulation needed to complete it. Doing this as part of their everyday experiences can strengthen children's self-regulation, even more so if parents and coaches are on the same page. It is also important to hold developmentally appropriate expectations for children's behaviour, after all they are not mini-adults! Called the zone of proximal development (ZPD) (Copple and Bredekamp, 2009), it is the 'growing edge of competence' and represents those skills a child is ready to learn. Expecting children to demonstrate skills outside the ZPD is ineffective and often detrimental. For example, young children will only be able to sustain attention for short periods of time so training should be designed accordingly or else skill development is unlikely to occur. Likewise, failing to provide challenging opportunities for children to advance their skills can hinder their growth. Of course, this is a moving target based on the child's age and individual ability, necessitating an individualised approach to how you organise activities and manage expectations.

Expert perspective on Chapter 3

Tynke Toering is an Associate Professor at the Norwegian School of Sport Sciences in Oslo, Norway. She conducts research on learning, psychological skills and performance in sport. Tynke also works as a consultant for the Norwegian Centre of Football Excellence, where she helps develop evidence-based tools that can be used by elite football practitioners, gives workshops for football coaches and helps translate data into meaningful information for elite football practitioners.

This chapter gives practitioners a lot of information about the importance of self-regulation and how to develop this in young performers. As described in the chapter, self-regulated learning involves metacognitive factors such as planning, monitoring, evaluation and reflection. In addition, it contains motivational aspects such as effort and self-efficacy (the belief that one can successfully execute a certain task). To develop self-regulated learning skills, it seems favourable to have a growth mindset because the core of self-regulation is that learners take responsibility for their own learning process. That is, if one believes that ability is fixed, one will not take charge of one's learning process because the expected outcome will be the same regardless, while people with a growth mindset will be proactive and seek challenges.

The role of the coach is key to this; in my role I spend a lot of time getting coaches thinking about how to develop self-regulation in their players. To learn self-regulated learning skills, young athletes must gradually develop an understanding of what is required of them to reach a particular level of performance, as well as learn strategies for how to get there. Young athletes will not necessarily have the capacities to create an impression of the skills they need to develop, meaning that quality coaching is important, especially at an early stage. One simple example of this is to explain to athletes why they are doing a given exercise. After the exercise, the coach could ask them to what extent they feel that the goal of the exercise has been reached and why they believe so. When athletes grow older, they themselves can gradually be more involved in the goal-setting process, and the coach can help them see the connections between exercises, training sessions, development goals and longer-term goals. Involving athletes in their development process will help them take responsibility for it and it will facilitate adaptive forms of motivation, such as intrinsic motivation. The athlete will feel more control over the process and have more mastery experiences, both of which are beneficial for effort and self-efficacy.

Additionally, good feedback is essential if we want to develop athletes who can reflect on themselves. They must get the opportunity to make their own mistakes and learn from those, rather than being told what to do in specific situations or being shouted at for making mistakes. The development of athletes' self-regulation skills can therefore be facilitated by coaches who ask questions rather than give answers right away, and who give the athlete space to think for themselves before commenting on their performance. In my experience this is not always the case! As athletes mature, it is also possible to gradually introduce self-initiated feedback, where the coach only gives feedback when the athlete asks for it. My experience is that shouting at athletes for making mistakes tends to cause defensive responses in the athlete because he or she often already knows that an error was made, and/or anxious responses because the athlete gets scared. The athletes' maladaptive emotional response may in turn frustrate the development process in terms of self-regulated learning, because it diminishes the opportunity to reflect on mistakes, learn from them and use better strategies next time. Moreover, it causes maladaptive forms of motivation, which means that the athlete may expend less effort, have lower self-efficacy and eventually even drop out altogether.

A third and final manner to help develop athletes' understanding of performance requirements and self-regulation strategies is to have them evaluate their own skills. The coach can do the same, and differences in opinion as well as skills that the athlete is very good or not so good at can be discussed between coach and athlete. Parents could also be involved in this. When working with very young athletes, coaches must define skills as concretely and simply as possible, and really make sure that the athlete understands. Sessions like this, should also be short in time. My experience is that the younger the athletes are, the more they overestimate their skills compared to the coach's evaluation. However, it is not only about helping the athlete create a realistic self-image. It is just as important, if not crucial, to not kill the athlete's dream. This means that the athletes' age and maturity level are important to take into consideration. Furthermore, it is essential that the coach knows his or her athletes very well in order to be able to 'push the right buttons', and that the coach is aware of the impact of his or her own behaviour on the athletes.

As they develop, and as long as the foundation work has been implemented, most children begin to use self-regulation skills without prompting or assistance. They develop strategies to manage incoming information, choose appropriate responses and maintain levels of arousal that allow them to actively participate in learning. When children routinely self-regulate without adult assistance, they have internalized self-regulation. Thus, to develop self-regulation skills, children need many opportunities to experience and practice with adults and capable peers. When coaches deliberately teach self-regulation, they help children become actively engaged learners, laying the foundation for years of future success in school and life.

In conclusion

In this chapter, we highlight the importance of establishing an appropriate attitude to learning as an important determinant of engagement in sport and physical activity.

Fostering a growth mindset and the self-regulatory skills to maximise learning would seem a sensible focus for coaches (and parents) at the beginning of the talent pathway. This approach, in parallel with a focus on general movement ability as outlined in Chapter 2, ensures that young people have the best foundation for making choices about their long-term engagement in sport and physical activity whether that is in the elite world or recreationally. If we don't get it right at the start, it is likely that young people will miss out on a lifetime of physical activity and sport engagement.

References

Abbott, A. and Collins, D. (2004). Eliminating the dichotomy between theory and practice in talent identification and development: considering the role of psychology. *Journal of Sports Sciences*, 22(5), 395–408.

Abbott, A., Button, C., Pepping, G. and Collins, D. (2005). Unnatural selection: talent identification and development in sport. *Nonlinear Dynamics, Psychology and Life Science*, 9(1), 61–88.

Baxter-Jones, A. D. G. and Helms, P. J. (1996). Effects of training at a young age: a review of the training of young athletes (TOYA) study. *Pediatric Exercise Science*, 8, 310–327.

Copple, C. and Bredekamp, S. (2009). *Developmentally appropriate practice in early childhood programs*. Washington, D.C.: National Association for the Education of Young Children.

Dweck, C. S. (2008). *Mindset: the new psychology of success*. New York: Ballantine Books.

Vaeyens, R., Güllich, A., Warr, C. and Philippaerts, R. (2009). Talent identification and promotion programmes of Olympic athletes. *Journal of Sports Sciences*, 27(13), 1367–1380.

Zimmerman, B. J. (2000). Attaining self-regulation: a social cognitive perspective. In M. Boekaerts, P. R. Pintrich and M. Zeidner (Eds), *Handbook of self-regulation* (pp. 13–39). San Diego, CA: Academic Press.

4

DELIBERATE PLAY, DELIBERATE PRACTICE AND DELIBERATE PREPARATION

Introduction – the story so far

Reading through the chapters so far, you should have received 'loud and clear' the message that early activities should be broad rather than deep, catering for as many different aspects of movement as possible. The slightly more subtle message was that this breadth will usually benefit from *some good* coaching or teaching input. Please note the italics – these two qualifiers are important and it is worth our while to consider them in more detail. Let's look at them together, however, as they often (and should) go hand in hand. To do this, however, and to make sure that you understand the various arguments which rage around this topic, we first consider the two theoretical perspectives which commonly dominate this debate, before giving you our own, hopefully more moderated, position.

The 'big three' theories of development

1 Deliberate Practice

This idea has been misunderstood and, perhaps as a consequence, somewhat maligned of late. It is, however, still a key building block in how we develop expertise. Importantly, the principles are proposed to apply to development in any activity; sporting skills, more everyday movements such as driving and cognitive expertise, such as writing essays – all might be useful sometime in your or your athlete's/child's life.

Deliberate Practice (hereafter DPrac) is often credited to K. Anders Ericsson, who published the idea in 1993 with colleagues Krampe and Tesch-Romer. As we have already said, there has been a lot of confusion around the idea – often because others have misinterpreted, misquoted or just simply selectively hijacked parts of the paper. Ericsson and colleagues were very clear on what DPrac consisted of:

deliberate practice is a highly structured activity, the explicit goal of which is to improve performance. Specific tasks are invented to overcome weaknesses, and performance is carefully monitored to provide cues for ways to improve it further. We claim that deliberate practice requires effort and is not inherently enjoyable. Individuals are motivated to practice because practice improves performance.

(Ericsson et al., 1993, 368)

A few things to note: DPrac is specifically focused on improving performance and will often focus on weaknesses. It often requires someone else to help by directing practice (such as a coach or teacher) and is not inherently enjoyable.

But ...

That doesn't mean that you always need a coach *or* that doing DPrac isn't enjoyed by those who do it. Go down to your local skate park, or watch kids practicing dribbling, shooting or dance moves and you will see DPrac in progress. This is often done without a formal coach (aka adult!), although mates will often provide useful feedback. Note also that the kids are enjoying it, often sticking with practice in the face of repeated failure until they master the trick! It is important to note this deliberate *but less formal* species of DPrac; children will do this very naturally, albeit that their practice might be restricted to computer games! In short, DPrac is an important part of getting good at something, providing lots of direct and indirect benefits. As in our example here, it may also include lots of social interaction and avoid some of the negatives which have been associated with adults driving kids in sport. DPrac is not the enemy.

A few caveats are worth mentioning, however. First, many have 'credited' Ericsson with the now infamous 10,000-hour or ten-year rule – the idea that it takes this long to get expert at anything. Ericsson did mention the number in his paper, recognising that earlier work on chess masters by Simon and Chase (1973) had been subsequently supported in other domains. This idea was (in our opinion) later hijacked by popular authors to suggest that this was *all* that you needed. In other words, that anyone who was well motivated to work hard enough for long enough could become an expert. Unfortunately not true – it takes all sorts of other things, such as support, luck and appropriate body shape, as this book will later show.

Second, it is worth thinking about the amount or volume of practice which is apparently prescribed by the theory. This apparently clear statement has, in turn, led to all sorts of other misinterpretations. One leading football academy suggested that young players should aim for 10,000 touches a week, pushing players to spend almost every waking moment outside of school hours practising their ball juggling in the garden ... when they weren't at the club! Of course, the numbers are merely guidelines, and there is little or no evidence to support this, just like your 10,000 steps per day on your Fitbit. The number has a nice round ring to it but, as a value, is completely meaningless. Indeed, more recent research has shown people attaining world-class performances in less than 3,000 hours, whilst other work has challenged the primary importance of DPrac as *the* factor in attaining expert status. Notably, a recent meta-analysis (a way of combining the result of many different studies) by MacNamara (not Áine!), Hambrick and Oswald (2014) has shown that the contribution of DPrac to eventual levels of performance is rather variable, with differences apparent between activities and individuals. In fact, they suggested an average DPrac contribution to the level reached of about 30 per cent – in short, an important contribution but far from the whole story suggested by many authors, and certainly perpetuated by social media!

Finally, it's worth thinking about what the deliberate practice-er needs so that s/he can optimise the returns from however many hours of DPrac are completed. As a first step, what is being practiced must have some quality to it. As most coaching texts would acknowledge, practice makes permanent – an important distinction from the more commonly used adage that practice makes perfect. Repeating poor technique will make you much more effective at … you've guessed it … poor technique. Only perfect practice makes perfect, so there needs to have been enough pre-training and/or someone watching to ensure good technique to optimise the return on your investment of time. In parallel, young athletes will need to 'learn how to train', as it is unlikely that they pop out of the womb with this skill (even if it was a difficult birth of longer than 10,000 hours!). Of course, as we highlighted above, they can learn this from their mates; good role models are fantastic at communicating values, including a good work ethic. Of course, the opposite is true as well, so coaches, teachers and parents need to keep an eye on exactly what approaches are being learnt! In any case, however, it is usually the case that some well timed and subtle adult intervention can help to build both skills and confidence in the practice process.

So, taking all this into consideration, our take on DPrac would be summarised as follows:

- It is important, in different ways at different stages of the development pathway.
- It often but not always involves a coach, teacher or other adult.
- It isn't 'inherently enjoyable', but is very often enjoyed.
- It does need some sort of preparatory work, both motoric and psychological (physical and mental) to optimise the benefits.

2 Deliberate Play

Deliberate Play (hereafter DPlay) is a more recent idea. This may have arisen as a 'backlash' to the somewhat mechanistic model of DPrac (you have to do this to be successful), as a counter to the inferred (at least for some people) central role required of adults, or merely because the social psychologist who invented it placed a higher weighting on the values of social interaction and unstructured play! In any case, this idea was the brainchild of Canadian psychologist Jean Côté (1999) and it has been very influential since.

Jean might not agree, but we would suggest that DPrac and DPlay were very much presented, and seen, as opposing ideas, especially in the early years. Of course, all things refine with age (well most – it hasn't worked for Dave!) and the two theories seem now to be a little more reconciled. There are, however, still key differences and Table 4.1 offers a summary of the DPlay characteristics which show many of these differences.

As you can see, DPlay is a lot more child-led, with the role of adult coaches very much more limited. Enjoyment is a primary aim, whilst leaving setup and rule development to the players themselves makes for a much more child-centred approach. Developing creativity is inherent within this approach, as is the social interaction between the children involved. The emphasis on inclusion is much more representative of how things work when adults aren't about. Children will usually tweak the game, the rules and the teams to 'make it fair': inclusion is another guiding principle. Finally, this approach is built on the premise that 'the game's the thing'. Coaching (at least in a formal sense) is minimal and playtime is maximised.

On first sight, there is a lot to like here. The approach brings a welcome alternative to the early specialisation, adult coach-directed environments which have been seen as typical across youth sport. The DPlay approach is typified by an 'early sampling' style, whereby children try out lots of different sports in a non-competitive and (the authors would suggest) non-threatening environment. Family involvement is another positive feature, with encouragement, role modelling and full positive involvement implicit within much of the work. Over the years, Côté and colleagues have assembled an impressive array of research, demonstrating a variety of benefits from DPlay including physical (less injuries), mental (less burnout so less dropout), social (better interactional skills) and, even, final performance levels achieved.

As a separate but, many would suggest, embedded further advantage, the approach claims to enhance creativity in participants. Clearly, this is a much sought after attribute in adult performers but one which many suggest is often eliminated in youngsters by the adult coach's insistence in 'doing things the right way'. Indeed, many recent initiatives are built around play, seen as a neglected or even dying art for today's 'sit insider' digital generation.

TABLE 4.1 The distinguishing characteristics of Deliberate Play

- Regulated by flexible age-adapted rules
- Set up and monitored by children or an involved adult
- Little intervention for skill instruction and feedback during the activity (i.e. maximise time on task)
- Requires minimal resources
- Designed to maximise enjoyment
- Promotes inclusion

Source: adapted from Côté, 1999; Côté *et al.*, 2003.

As this chapter will suggest, however, things are not quite as black and white as the DPlay approach may suggest. This has led us to develop and apply the DPrep idea described next. For the moment, however, the DPlay approach can be summarised as follows:

- It is seen as the best way to introduce sport, and is proposed as the essential element for the early part of the pathway.
- The role of the adult/coach is minimal, with children left to 'get on with it' as the style of choice. Adult involvement from a social point of view, or as role models, is encouraged, however.
- Enjoyment is a central tenet, pushed hard by all concerned.
- It is something which requires minimal preparation, with spontaneous involvement and child-driven evolution central.

3 Deliberate Preparation

As we read through the literature and tried to apply the often competing and contradictory ideas from DPrac and DPlay, it occurred to us that both had missed an essential precursor. We referred to this as the 'Play or Practice Trap'. This is best explained by an analogy – the process of learning to read.

Imagine, on the one hand, a Victorian school-like setting, in which children were drilled every day on how to shape their letters, required to chant out loud the alphabet and made to learn word spellings parrot fashion. A few reading this may have experienced some of these elements; certainly Dave is *that old*! Our point is that such DPrac of reading would be unlikely to motivate kids with a love of reading, especially since they might get so fed up with the early drilling that they never really get into the 'free reading' cycle that our schools justifiably see as so important. In contrast, consider a school where children could choose whatever they wanted to read, whenever they liked but without *any* prior teaching on the basics of how to do it. Such a DPlay approach would also demotivate the children and, however much fun it was at the time, leave them frustrated and uninterested in reading as a lifelong habit, owing to the difficulties which all but the 'naturally brightest' might encounter. In short, neither approach would work. Some basic instruction would be needed in the latter case whilst some guided and structured play would undoubtedly help the first.

This was what led us to the idea of 'Deliberate Preparation' or DPrep. The design and deployment of a regime that provides a robust foundation of psycho-motor and psycho-behavioural skills so that kids are equipped to both practice and play, as desired and/or appropriate. The idea is that, through a common core DPrep package, children are prepared to make the choices described in Chapter 2 without being limited or inhibited by a lack of *actual or perceived* skills. DPrep is the essential precursor which your child should ideally experience from before primary through to around Year 3. Parents can do a lot of this themselves but, unless they happen to be qualified coaches or teachers, they are likely to want some outside input as well.

Chosen well, this will also provide the important social interactions which are also important through this stage.

Finally, just a word in passing on creativity – a current 'hot topic' across a number of sports and also, conversely, a factor often raised by the DPlay lobby as an argument against overly structured coaching. And, once again, an analogy to help explain our point. Most children draw, and they can be very 'creative' in their interpretations when painting Mummy and Daddy! This can drop off very quickly, however, if the child perceives that s/he lacks the skills to make the creative piece look good. Furthermore, we would usually expect creative adults to display some underpinning skills through which their creativity can be demonstrated – even if that is cutting a cow in half and sticking it in a jar! So, in similar fashion, providing children with some basic skills (and confidence in them) is likely to encourage and facilitate creative solutions and ideas rather than limit them. In simple terms, DPrep supports and increases creative drive, whilst *just* play becomes rather limited. As this is written, we are working with youth sport coaches to test and develop these ideas. For the moment, however, there is a lot of anecdotal evidence to support the idea. After all, it's hard to be creative on a musical instrument if you don't know how to play it! Using your body works pretty much the same way!

Putting them together?

Hopefully, this is clear to all and readers will avoid the extremes of DPrac and DPlay, physical drilling and banal, un-coached play (aka child sitting) which can easily be seen in your area. But before we proceed to considering what such a programme might look like, a couple of qualifiers on what is written here, so that you the reader feel comfortable with exactly what is being said.

We do acknowledge that the two 'opposing positions' of DPrac and DPlay are often much closer and well integrated in practice. In fairness, Côté sees the need for DPrac, albeit later in the development pathway once children have opted for specialisation in a few or single activities (Côté *et al.*, 2009). In similar fashion, Ericsson's DPrac model has often been unfairly stereotyped as 'merely drilling'. This is particularly noticeable around the 'not inherently enjoyable' confusion we discussed earlier. The need for DPrep becomes obvious, however, when one considers current Primary PE provision. For many schools, this is provided by sport-specific coaches (Community Football Coaches are very common in the UK, for example) or exercise specialists qualified to work with adults. Both have a tendency to teach a limited range of skills in a limited way (see the next section), whilst at the other extreme, playtime activities alone (as described above) also fail to meet the need for effective DPrep. So, given that you have accepted these ideas, either as a parent or a coach aiming to work with this age group, how can effective DPrep be structured? What would sessions look like and what outcomes should you expect?

Effective DPrep – what to look for and/or what to do (and why!)

As a guiding structure, let's again use the reading and writing analogy. How this works is shown in Figure 4.1. We developed earlier stages of these ideas in conjunction with sportscotland and colleagues from the University of Edinburgh. Both are gratefully acknowledged for their roles in supporting and shaping this thinking.

DPrep is based on the careful development of basics (what we will call MOVES or WORDS) as the building blocks for more complicated executions later. So, as Figure 4.1 shows, simple basics are taught and developed to a reasonable degree, before gradually combining them into sequences or combinations (SKILLS or PARAGRAPHS). These SKILLS are deliberately varied within a simple structure, as children are coached to develop understanding and capacity to apply the skills to different challenges. Finally, the skills get used in context, such as simple games or, eventually, age-appropriate versions of sports (STORIES). As things progress, the DPrep principles (teach, coach and structured varied practice, coach/play and free varied practice) gradually give way to the children getting involved in DPrac ('I like this, I want to get better at it') and/or DPlay ('It's really fun to try all these different games and invent some myself').

So imagine this process in the build up to playing bench ball; a simple game where you score by passing the ball to one of your teammates standing on a bench, which is often used as an introductory activity for games such as rugby or basketball. Children start with a basic catch (the MOVE), with adult or older children providing some useful teaching points, such as 'thumbs out to catch low – thumbs in to catch high'. They practice the different types of catch with structure to show the differences. Questioning can help to develop the MOVE towards the next stage

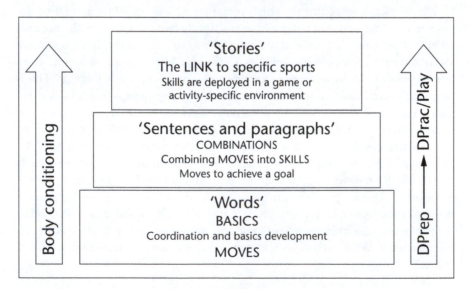

FIGURE 4.1 The three-stage model of movement development

– 'so how high would the ball be for you to do a thumbs-in catch?'. As we move to the SKILLS stage, children catch and pass/throw the ball. Structured variable practice gets them catching in a variety of ways, then throwing for distance or for someone else to catch. This might start as a contrast between an overarm throw (for distance) or an underarm throw to make catching easier. Finally, children can use the catch and throw skill to play a game (tell a STORY) which can be more or less sport-like as needed.

There are several important points to make here. First, without some basic teaching to develop catching skills, children just can't experience the fun which is the central tenet of DPlay. Second, how important it is for progress to be monitored. The teacher/parent/coach can watch for problems (closing your eyes and/or looking away as the ball arrives) and take the challenge down a notch until success is more frequent. Third, and *however*, some challenge is always kept in there so the child gets used to failure being an OK thing to be overcome, not a shameful thing to be avoided. Finally, watching a DPrep session will show individuals being challenged at appropriate but often different levels across the session – hard to do but essential! Two lines of children passing back and forth isn't really preparing them for the variations in a game *but* might be a useful early step or later reminder.

What should be included?

Based on our experience, and our ongoing research work with colleague Susan Giblin, we have the following components as the DPrep 'curriculum'. In each case we offer some suggestions for the 'Moves to Skills to Sports' development process.

1 *Interceptive timing:* anticipating ball flight, then putting a limb (hand, foot, body, head) or object (bat, racquet) in the way. As things progress, the limb or object is used to direct the ball in another direction.

    Pat a ball onto the floor or into the air – catch or strike the ball – catch and throw/strike in a new direction – most games.

2 *Locomotion and agility:* good body control whilst walking, running, jumping, changing direction and varying speed.

    Run/walk – run/walk/dodge/dodge in reaction to someone else – TAG – most games.

3 *Spatial awareness and balance:* maintain a stable centre of mass, then move from and to balance positions.

    Stand on one leg – hop – hop from one leg to another in a sequence (e.g. two on the left, two on the right) – run, land then jump high – Long Jump – Triple Jump.

4 *Rhythm and sequencing:* awareness of and ability to follow a rhythm.

    Hand/finger tapping – both hands – both hands different (e.g. L-L-RRR) – same for feet – simple dance moves on dance mat or simple sequences (Macarena) – complex dance moves (follow a leader).

This isn't a comprehensive coverage of all the components involved (these are often listed in a taxonomy) but does offer a simple checklist for things you are doing with younger children. In an ideal world, this sort of DPrep starts well before school, and even before nursery. You don't need to have any special training to provide your child with an excellent movement base. In similar fashion, most coaches and teachers should be able to develop some imaginative ideas for how this could work. The main thing is, however, that the children are challenged and supported as they move through the MOVES – SKILLS – GAMES sequence.

Next steps – what and why

As they get better, children should be encouraged to try out their new skills. Our suggestion would be that a combination of taught/coached DPrac and open play DPlay will work well. In either case, however, doing some 'home practice' is very useful; the child gets to practice in a different environment, with different people and often, with a different emphasis on the quality of movement. For us, doing this sort of thing with your child is as important as home practice of 'real-life' maths, reading, etc. A serious lack of physical ability (real or imagined) can be a real 'social isolator' for children, especially once in school where their abilities can be on show. As with any skill, practice will help so long as there is challenge and support. We aren't talking champion gymnast, Usain Bolt speed or fantastic footballer juggling skills; the aim is for sound basics and, as per Chapter 2, confidence in them.

Body conditioning – what and why?

Just a word about the left hand arrow in Figure 4.1. We cover physical fitness training in more detail later on. For the moment, however, it is worth acknowledging the importance of establishing an early fitness habit. Once again, we aren't talking about Mo Farah endurance or World's Strongest Child. However, it would be difficult to have genuine movement skill without an associated basis of the other four S's of fitness. So, looking at some activities to test and develop Speed, Strength, Suppleness (flexibility) and Stamina (endurance) should also be part of your DPrep curriculum. Clearly in fact, the four areas highlighted above will all contain some elements of these.

Just to stress: we are not talking about a major fitness regime for your six-year-old, even though some parents and coaches may push this with varying degrees of logic, reasoning and rationale! Simple checks such as the following, with practising associated to build strengths and counter weaknesses, can be incorporated in a fun way and offer a good basis for a healthy lifestyle later on. They might even help you if you join in. So, a simple but not exhaustive list, based around our expectations for a normal (i.e. not in specific training) six-year-old:

- Can your child sprint effectively and fast for 40 metres?
- Can s/he jog without stopping for 800 metres?

- Can s/he hold a press up position without sagging in the middle?
- Can s/he hang from a bar (use your local park playground) for ten seconds?
- Can s/he reach down and touch her lower shins/ankles without bending her knees?

For each of these simple tests, there may be a good medical reason for not trying to reach the standard. But if not, then it is worth checking, and working to address shortcomings where you can.

Expert perspective on Chapter 4

Erin Sanchez's ballet career included training with the American Ballet Theatre, Boston Ballet School and the Alvin Ailey School. She is currently Head of Student Welfare and Dance Science, London Studio Centre, Vice Chair of Council for the Imperial Society of Teachers of Dancing (ISTD), the Healthier Dancer Programme Manager at One Dance UK. Erin is also a Registered Provider and Quality Assessor at Safe in Dance International (www.safeindance.com); Manager of the International Dance Psychology Network and has lectured in dance science in the United States, UK, Egypt, France, the Netherlands, Malta and Serbia.

Based on my experience as a dancer, dance teacher and a programme manager for dancers' health, I can see a lot of valuable information here. Although evidence from other domains, such as the information presented here, has more profile in vocational dance training, implementation in development domains is exceedingly rare. Overwhelmingly, if evidence is considered it is balanced against a sense of responsibility to tradition and a commitment to aesthetic, stylistic or physical measures of performance. Training environments in dance assuredly need thoughtful, expert and consistent application of these principles to support thriving talent development and reduce long-term negative consequences, including injury risk, burnout and dropout.

Some things to consider when applying these principles to dance:

1 'Dance' is not a single activity, it is an umbrella term for hundreds of movement styles, representing a diversity of training, traditions and physical or artistic challenges as different from one another as golf is from Greco-Roman wrestling, so identifying an ideal training route for dance is problematic. Further, regardless of the style of their initial training, most dancers will perform a variety of movement styles within their careers at the discretion of choreographers or specific performances. (Just suppose professional hockey players were the last-minute substitutes for the Olympic figure-skating team!) In light of this, the structure of deliberate preparation proposed here, both in the early years and throughout

training, would be enormously beneficial to support the diverse professional challenges dancers are likely to encounter.

2   Training methodologies likewise vary, based on history, movement demands and codification (whether there is a written description of movement and progression). However, most 'theatre' dance training (ballet, contemporary, jazz) is led by deliberate practice: a regular, supervised repetition of fine motor skills to condition for very specialist movement tasks. In addition, training specifically focused on early talent development is usually characterised by two traditional and fundamental beliefs: (1) more specialised dance practice will always create better performance, and (2) the earlier specialist motor skills are mastered the better the dancer will be. Timetables in these styles leave little or no room for other movement skills or for unstructured play, and thus child-led dancing (deliberate play) can be especially limited in early vocational training. In less codified styles, such as hip hop forms, movement vocabulary is loosely fixed but evolving with the movement of individual dancers. Early specialisation may be equally (or even more) common but may include a more diverse early movement experience. This training integrates deliberate play and improvisation as fundamental building blocks for developing and refining motor skills before a progression to the kind of repetitive deliberate practice (though possibly less structured or supervised) described above.

3   Across styles in dance, there is an acceptance of fatigue as a normal, and sometimes desired state. It may be unsurprising that overtraining and injury are common among young dancers in pre-vocational training environments given the intensity of deliberate practice expected. However, many dancers I know feel that they perform best when they have exhausted themselves on the task. Young dancers may also be actively discouraged from trying other physical activities for fear of injury or building muscles that would be disadvantageous to the desired aesthetic. Fundamental physical skills and conditioning that are not directly addressed in dance technique may not be developed without integrating the deliberate preparation discussed in this chapter, possibly leaving fatigued dancers at greater risk of injury.

4   In my experience, dancers strive to embody an *impossible, ephemeral and subjective* standard of performance. Excellent performance in dance cannot be measured in hundredths of seconds to the finish line, nor in goals, nor the besting of an opponent; rather it is the constant chase for the limits of expression and aesthetic in movement. It was interesting to note that another part of deliberate preparation was largely missing from my own early dance training – I lacked a sense of my own ability to take the rules and manipulate them. I had no sense of what skills I might need to 'play' as a dancer, nor did I have any sense of how I good I might be at those skills. This may be especially challenging for adolescents, as a sense of

competence and confidence may only be available from teachers' opinions or uninformed physical comparisons with others. Instilling young dancers with basic physical competencies and confidence in their abilities will support them as they continue into this highly competitive and perfectionistic career.

In conclusion

In this chapter, as with many others, we have offered you a bit of the underpinning theory, as well as some practical tips. The knowledge base is important here since you need to be able to critically consider the various ideas and initiatives which are on offer. As we said earlier, a bit of careful thought and commitment can offer a lot of benefit to your child, or those under your care as a teacher or coach. It is always worth trying, so long as you approach it all in a positive and light-hearted manner. After all, sport and physical activity are supposed to be fun!

References

Côté, J. (1999). The influence of the family in the development of talent in sports. *The Sport Psychologist*, 13, 395–417.

Côté, J., Baker, J. and Abernethy, A. B. (2003). From play to practice: a developmental framework for the acquisition of expertise in team sports. In J. L. Starkes and K. A. Ericsson (Eds), *Expert performance in sports: advances in research on sport expertise* (pp. 89–113). Champaign, IL: Human Kinetics.

Côté, J., Lidor, R. and Hackfort. D. (2009). ISSP position stand: to sample or to specialize? Seven postulates about youth sport activities that lead to continued participation and elite performance. *International Journal of Sport and Exercise Psychology*, 7(1), 7–17.

Ericsson, K. A., Krampe, R. T. and Tesch-Romer, C. (1993). The role of deliberate practice in the acquisition of expert performance. *Psychological Review*, 100(3), 363–406.

MacNamara, B. N., Hambrick, D. Z. and Oswald, F. L. (2014). Deliberate practice and performance in music, games, sports, educations and professions: a meta-analysis. *Psychological Science*, 25(8), 1608–1618.

Simon, H. A. and Chase, W. G. (1973). Skill in chess. *American Scientist*, 61, 394–403.

PART III

Pre-academy

What to do till you select your chosen sport

As the next three chapters demonstrate, there is a lot of generic stuff still to do as your performer starts to think about specialising, or takes the first steps onto their chosen sporting pathway. Coincidentally, as we emphasise across this section, doing things right at this crucial stage will equip the youngster for a number of different pathways, some in sport but many outside, together with the kit needed for lifelong physical activity. So, performance *and* participation; what's not to like!

As you will see, we 'split' content rather crudely between the physical and the mental – or as we put it, below and above the neck. This is, of course, a separation of inconvenience, as any good TD specialist will tell you. The two are as inextricably linked as your head and body! So as you read one of the chapters, please make the links to the content in the others.

In the final chapter, we provide lots of ideas about the integration of parents and coaches. No doubt here that the performer is benefitted when parent and coach are in accord, so 'stronger together' as the saying goes. Note that this is always best as a two way relationship, rather than one telling the other what to do. We have seen this attempted from either direction (COACH to parent and PARENT to coach) and neither is satisfactory; and *certainly* not beneficial to the performer who can get caught in the middle. It's worth remembering that both are collaborating to prepare the performer so that she or he can overcome the upcoming challenges, not working to eliminate or smooth out the bumps which are an essential learning and development experience.

Once again, readers are encouraged to reflect the wide variation in age at which developing performers may hit this stage. It means that our content is also quite broad, with lots of complimentary ideas presented. So please read critically, use what you want but take note of the rest.

5

NEXT STEPS IN DEVELOPMENT – BELOW THE NECK STUFF

Introduction – what should we be trying to do at this stage?

Well, this might be the most controversial chapter in the book. It was certainly the most difficult to write! Not because the concepts are any more complicated than elsewhere; as stressed in Chapter 1, the golden rule of 'it depends' applies throughout, with consequent importance placed on individualising what is going on at every age and stage plus, *most* particularly, across individuals.

No! This chapter is the most challenging because it addresses physical conditioning – an area which has more experts than you have muscles! At the elite level, there are lots of ideas on how to train; some directly conflict with each other, whilst others might just be slight variations, new 'wrinkles' on the same approach. Whatever the degree of difference, however, there are a lot of differences apparent in what is presented by some as an 'exact science'. Of course, many of these differences may well be down to individual variation in the athlete; whilst this is a sensible explanation, however, you will find rather a lot of 'my way or the highway' presentations in the area of fitness training.

Add in the complications of maturation, training age and avoiding early specialisation, all of which we cover later, and the picture is even more confused. As a result, whilst we try in this chapter to continue with our stated aim of offering practical advice, things will be a little more general than elsewhere, and a little less specific than readers might like. Apologies in advance, but what we do offer are a series of guidelines which parents can use to evaluate coaching setups and coaches can use to design them. We also take care to present the reasons why we think what we do. Once again, as stressed in Chapter 1, this is often the best guidance for parents – ask why and note the response. If you are met with a barrage of 'Do you know how many county champions I have coached?', 'Trust me … I'm the expert' or 'Don't you know who I am?' then you know all you need to. Move away quickly! If, however, you receive a carefully considered and rational argument, then you can compare it to the logic presented here and in other texts.

For practitioners, our advice applies in reverse. Think how and why you do what you do, use the principles rather than the exact practices used by others (remember to ask *them* why as well) and take the trouble to explain this to parents and performers who you work with. As later chapters will show, it will reap you some big benefits in the long term.

Finally, and also as with previous chapters, we also offer a few references where those committed readers can follow up on the ideas presented. So, with that Health Warning in place, let's get to it.

Building on the GMA base

In the earlier chapters, we stressed the importance of developing a broad movement base or movement vocabulary. Not only does this provide the right preparation for children to choose which development pathways they want to follow (remember DPrep?); it also gives them the confidence and capacity to take on new challenges. Well, the same ideas apply into the next stage; indeed, as this chapter will show, it might be important across the lifespan as well. The importance of maintaining and enhancing a good General Movement Ability (GMA) base is explained in Figure 5.1.

The tower on the left represents the all too common, sport-specific development route taken by many clubs and academies. For a start, many children start from a narrow GMA base. The combination of restricted play opportunities (child safety plus availability of space for tree climbing, adventures and so on) and weaker

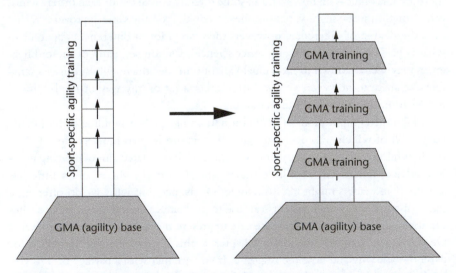

FIGURE 5.1 A narrow, sport-specific development line, in contrast to the 'regular enrichment' approach of the Christmas tree

PE provision result in a limited movement experience. In fact, the situation can be made even worse if the child 'self-specialises' early! Even though being mad keen on a sport or activity sounds like a positive, if that is all the child does, they may limit themselves for later. Once in the club or academy, the young performer does lots of activity-specific skills, resulting in a comparatively narrow 'skill band'. Of course, some sports or activities will be broader than others – games will generally involve a broader range of challenges than, say, a single athletics event or rowing. Irrespective of this, however, if the child's activity is focused solely or substantially on a single set of movements, s/he will end up with some limitations.

Of course, this specific training will work very effectively in the particular sport or activity selected. There is little doubt that kids today are better younger than the children of a generation ago. Accordingly, everything looks good unless and until the performer needs to execute movements which lie outside his or her 'normal diet'. When we discuss these ideas with coaches, many will point out that this isn't really a problem, so long as junior stays with the sport. Unfortunately not so! There are three big reasons why a young player must be able to operate outside this sport-specific skill band and, unless they have received some broader experiences, such a challenge will necessitate them falling back on the base they had much earlier, or even not at all.

First, children grow! This means that they must constantly adjust their skills to fit the new body. When the growth spurt kicks in (more on this in a later chapter), the challenges step up significantly. As a result, children need to adapt to their new body shape and size quickly if they are to avoid a performance slump, a loss of confidence and/or potential injury. Second, young performers get injured. A broad movement vocabulary seems to help with the quality and even speed of rehab: there is even some emerging data to suggest that it may also help to prevent injury in the first place. Finally, the movement requirements of the sport may change. For example, age bands in athletics are associated with different sizes of hurdles or weights of implements. As a result, the young athlete must execute a subtly but significantly different movement pattern. In games, the size of the pitch, the number in the team and even the rules change with age. In any case, coaches have been known to ask players to change position, whilst the 'musical manager' situation in football (when the music stops, the boss changes clubs) means that players must be more adaptable and flexible than ever before. All these variations require the player to have a broad skill base which s/he can deploy to meet the new challenges.

In an attempt to keep things broad and provide children with the adaptability they will almost inevitable require, we have developed the enrichment process shown on the right of Figure 5.1 – what we call the 'Christmas Tree' programme. The idea is that the activity- or sport-specific training blocks are interspersed with much broader sessions of GMA work. In general, this is usually non-sport stuff – for example, footballers may play badminton or basketball, do some tumbling or judo groundwork, or even play simple but different games like crab football. As a result, each individual's movement vocabulary is kept broad, keeping them equipped for the different challenges which they will inevitably encounter. This approach is particularly useful around the growth spurt, when GMA can help to counter the movement challenges and perhaps even help with injury prevention as well.

In closing this idea, it is also worth mentioning that a similar approach can also benefit older athletes. You will see several references to this later in the book. Even well after the TD process has finished, a regular dose of GMA work can be effective in keeping the performer adaptable and even injury free. We have seen some beneficial effects with 'mature' rugby players, helping to prolong their careers and even (in the opinion of their coaches) enhance their ability to play different positions and fill various roles more effectively. So the message is, keep some variability in your training throughout but also, as the next section suggests, be aware of when it is a particular concern.

What else do we need to be doing, when and why?

The key message to take from the previous section is that GMA is important, and that this seems to continue through the pathway. But what else should youngsters be doing from a physical point of view? In this section of the book, we are focused largely on pre-puberty, up to the age of around 11 in girls and 13 in boys, which is technically referred to as the Tanner Stages 1 and 2. For clarity and in simple terms, pre-puberty relates to before the development of breasts, pubic hair and periods starting for girls, and voice breaking, pubic hair and body shape changes in boys. Obviously, the ages are just guidelines, as there is often considerable variability in the onset of puberty. Importantly, this can vary across gender and race: one good guide is when the same sex parent went through these changes, but nothing can beat keeping a close eye on the individual athlete. For obvious reasons, this is yet another aspect where close communication between athlete, parent and coach/ teacher is extremely helpful!

Key issues at this age and/or stage

In dealing with pre-pubescent children, there are lots of important constructs to understand and cater for, plus a few rather contradictory or confusing ideas. So, before getting into some ideas around the what, it is worth covering the key constructs and addressing head-on some of the ideas that can confuse.

1 Training age versus chronological age versus developmental age

The internet is full of wonder kids, performing marvellous physical feats. The temptation is to think 'if that 9 year old can, why can't mine?!' Well, of course, a moment's thought will tell you why – their phenomenal performance is down to training – a block of work that your young performer/child has yet to complete. This is what underlies the idea of 'training age'. Many will be thinking, 'Ruby is tall for her age, she should be able to cope with this', or 'Joe is 10 already – why can't he train as hard as the other kids in his age group?' The important factor is how long has the child been training for and what has s/he been doing. So, any 'expert' worth the name will want to see what sorts of activity the child has been doing and for how long, before starting any new process or writing a training programme. For similar reasons, sharing ideas between parents or coaches from athlete to athlete is likely to lack impact or even cause damage in the short or long term. Accordingly, chronological age (in simple terms, how many birthdays) is likely to be relatively unimportant, apart from fixing school year or competition entry.

2 Critical windows of opportunity

We cover this idea for two reasons; first, because a system called the 'Long-Term Athlete Development' (or LTAD) Model was a dominant idea up until a few years' back. Indeed, many sports and coaches will still use LTAD to describe what they do, often not realising exactly what the Model says should be involved. Our second reason relates to the increasingly accepted idea that starting some things early is a good idea; in other words, that starting the 'training age' clock can benefit later performance. We are fine with the second but have some severe issues with the first! The challenge is around the term 'critical windows of opportunity', which was pushed by the originator of LTAD, Istvan Balyi. The idea was that certain components of fitness had specific time periods in which they should be developed. So, there was an aerobic or stamina, window, a strength window and so on. Work in the appropriate window would generate better gains on that component than at other times. Going even further, if the benefits of that window were not taken advantage of, for example by less or even no attention to that component, then the benefits would never be realised.

In part, our issues may be down to terminology. The 'critical window' idea suggests some unique, special and otherwise unobtainable advantage to the effective exploitation of the period so described: as we said above, the idea that if you don't do it now you never will! Certainly, and after much debate, this idea has been severely questioned, if not kicked into touch (cf. Ford *et al.*, 2011). This is important because, as a coach, teacher or parent, you may come under some pressure from LTAD disciples to get kids specialising early, so that the critical window can be fully exploited. *Resist this temptation!* For lots of reasons, early specialisation is questioned, whilst the arguments for the critical window ideas, whether applied to aerobic, strength or power, are at best unsubstantiated.

That said, there are some good arguments for getting kids into the training habit early. We will examine this later in this chapter, and later in the book. Once again, however, beware the use of watered-down adult programmes, whichever champion athlete is said to be associated with them. *Children are different* – in fact, one of the clearest pieces of guidance to come out of the research might be that children are even more different than adults. And Lord knows they are pretty different. So, individualising programmes and sessions to optimally meet the needs of each individual, including allowances for his or her developmental *and* training age, is far and away the best policy. Growing is a complex issue and generic guidelines are inevitably going to suit some but be wrong for others. Indeed, you will note that our suggestions at the end of this chapter are deliberately vague for just that very reason.

3 Health-related versus performance-related versus developmentally focused

Let's carry on the message from the previous paragraph. One of the biggest problems at these ages is when coaches just 'download and apply' training ideas from senior athletes. It should be obvious but we will say it anyway … children are not just small adults! Accordingly, individualising training is key. However, another important dimension is the difference between performance-related and health-related training. As the name implies, the first is likely to be focused on improving performance today. This sort of training approach will display a similarity to adult programmes in the same sport. As we hope this books shows, there are *all* sorts of problems with this approach, relating to both the training age and developmental stage difference between children and adults.

Accordingly, the main aim of work at the pre-pubertal stage is more 'building the engine' and 'strengthening the structure' than raising performance *now*. This is a bit more specialised than what is normally called health-related fitness or HRF – the sort of thing that mature adults get at their local gym or health club. In fact, though not as harmful as a schedule based around adult performance, an adult HRF schedule is also going to be severely sub-optimal. The bottom line of all this is that specialist input is needed. Parents need to look for well qualified and experienced practitioners with a specialism in training the young, whilst coaches and teachers need to be up with the literature in the area and staying abreast of developments in this evolving area. We come back to this in more detail in the last section of this chapter.

4 The different natures of 'fitness' at ages and stages

As a final consideration in our whistle-stop tour of underlying theory, it is worth considering how and why performers benefit from different sorts of training, at different ages and at different stages of their development. At the top level, things are a bit simpler. Mo Farah can run fast because he has done lots of miles; Lionel Messi plays well because he keeps practising the basics and Jessica Ennis-Hill has a body toned by long hours of gym training.

Things are different for younger and lower training age performers, however. For a start, most of the early gains made when you start doing an exercise are neurogenic rather than myogenic: in English, your nervous system gets better at controlling the muscles involved than the muscles themselves get stronger. Of course, this doesn't last too long, and the size of rugby players today shows you that a lot more than the nervous system or brain have been developed! In the short term, however, early gains are both quite noticeable *and* largely down to the body learning *how* to do the movement rather than being *stronger* at doing it!

This same argument applies, and perhaps even more so, to pre-pubescent athletes. Much of the benefit they get is due to better movement control rather than being fitter at that specific movement. So, functional strength (how much the young performer can lift or how much load s/he can handle in a sport-specific sense) may be much more related to their level of psychomotor development than their absolute strength (what they can do in a very simple movement and/or the size of their muscles, what the specialists call hypertrophy). This distinction becomes even more important around the dreaded growth spurt, when youngsters may lose functional strength even though their muscle strength (as measured by very simple movements or even what they look like) can stay constant or be improving.

5 Psychosocial considerations

'Oh yes', we hear you cry. Psychologists have to get their bit in, even in a chapter on physical conditioning. Well, sorry, but it is one of the important considerations in what training should be like and how it will operate before and during puberty. For a start, as Áine stressed in Chapter 3, establishing a healthy level of self-esteem around physical issues is an important factor in the child's early life. This factor becomes even more important with the onset of adolescence, as the young performer's point of reference switches from parents to peers. After all, no-one likes to look silly in front of their mates and this becomes an even bigger factor as puberty kicks in. Accordingly, all adults concerned with youth sport participation, let alone excellence or development, need to be very aware of how their athletes are coming over to, and considered by, their peers.

There are several important considerations around this. First, as we consider from a practical point of view in the next section, there is the change of reference pre-puberty from parents to social/absolute comparison. In simple terms, you can hear this in the way the child speaks. A response to the question 'How do you know that you are good at this?' will shift subtlety from 'Because Mummy says I am' to 'Because I am the best in my class' or 'Because I can do … [so many reps in a time/jump three lines on the pavement/beat twelve seconds at this drill]'. This is an important but powerful transition which all need to be aware of and exploit. We will address these 'self-presentational' challenges (simply, how do I present myself to gain maximum acceptance from my peers) later. For the moment, recognise who is important to your child/athlete and, therefore, who we should use as the 'reference for success'.

Once puberty hits, Impression Management (see Chapter 11 for more details) becomes a common concern for youngsters. The simple definition is that 'I am more concerned at what other people think of me than what I think of myself' is especially powerful for the growing athlete, and trying to modify this to achieve and retain acceptance becomes a real worry for adolescents. To summarise this section, what your performers do from a physical perspective is significantly moderated by what they think that makes them look like – even more so when the physical shape required (or assumed to be required) for the sport is 'less than acceptable' to their peers. As an example, Dave used to coach female weightlifters, rugby forwards and throwers. To be accepted by their peers, however, most of these talented and committed youngsters would describe themselves as 'javelin throwers' because, at the time, there was a 'perceived as attractive' role model that they, or more crucially their peers, could relate to! As a youth sport coach, teacher or parent, once your athlete hits puberty, take care to consider who they aspire to be like, who they aspire to look like and how they present themselves to their friends!

So, building on this overview of key concepts, and remembering our warning earlier about the need to individualise, we next offer some exemplars of the sort of physical training which might go on through these important stages.

So what does that look like? Exemplar sessions for aspirant performers

Hopefully, our brief coverage of the key terms will have equipped you to develop your programme or ask some probing questions of those who offer one. As a crucial addition, however, and whatever your role, you should be attending and observing sessions. Another simple measure, over and above the 'Why do you do what you do?' test mentioned above, is to check whether 'You do what you say you do'. Passing both tests is not a complete assurance for parents, nor is ensuring that you would pass this as a certain mark of quality for coaches, but they serve as pretty good initial markers!

So, assuming that you/your coach has passed the initial test, what else is there to look for/provide as you seek out some specialist help? Well, once again we must reiterate that no one prover will offer the complete answer. However, some simple check marks are as follows. For a more complete, 'next step' answer, you might want to start with a very readable article by Myer *et al.* (2013) or the Healthy Children website (www.healthychildren.org). However, assuming that, having bought *this* book, you would like some answers now, what guidance can we offer you for physical training at the pre-pubescent and through–puberty stages?

In simple terms, the main change as the athlete matures and gains training age will relate to a change in balance from general agility and 'total body' fitness, to the more 'normal' components such as aerobic capacity, strength and power. In short, things should start with multi-joint bodyweight exercises and a mixture of activities designed to develop and reassure the young athlete, through to the initiation of more 'adult-like' training sessions in which components like strength, flexibility and aerobic capacity are often developed separately, in a balance determined by the demands of the sport. Some suggested structures and exemplar exercises are presented in Table 5.1.

In using and applying the information within Table 5.1, we would stress again the need for individual treatment. For example, by the age of ten, some children will be in specialist sport or activity programmes (for example, gymnastics, football or dance) and will have been training in specialist mode for a few years. Others will be still at the experimentation stage, trying out a variety of different activities *but* building on their DPrep base. So, as the essential first step, look at the child in front of you, considering her/his developmental and training ages, plus specific involvement. The availability of expert help with physical training/development is another important factor. So remember, the ideas above are just that: ideas to be used as a base, not a strict prescription for growing your superstar. Hopefully, Table 5.1 is self-explanatory. What should be obvious is the gradual move from integrative to distinct activities, the progression of challenge and the balance across the fitness components. Pursuing these principles is much more important than slavishly following this, or any other programme.

After puberty, training becomes much more adult-like, presuming that the necessary base has been built from these sorts of activities – we offer a bit more on this later. Whenever the athlete chooses to specialise, however, this should never mean an automatic switch into adult-like, performance-focused programmes. There is always a need to ensure a sound base, so sensible coaches will ensure specialist support, or ensure that they themselves develop and evolve the skills and knowledge to provide this.

Anything else?

An important additional factor to be considered in this chapter is whether extensive training during childhood and adolescence can have a negative impact on both health (e.g. injury) and long-term performance in sport (Demorest and Landry, 2004). One essential need is for regular and careful monitoring of training; specifically, what is it doing to the young athlete in terms of general tiredness? Once again, there are lots of ideas on how this might be done, and you could spend a lot on the modern methods available, including heart-rate variability, blood or saliva tests for immune function (how well the body systems can withstand infection). Before you reach for your cheque book, however, there are much simpler methods available, most of which relate to the athlete's personal perceptions, or subjective experience, of what the training is doing to him/her. Without getting too technical, parents and coaches can do a good job of monitoring by asking about three or four simple subjective markers, as follows:

• How hard was the training today (against how hard it was designed to be)?
• How well did you sleep (how long, how deeply and how refreshed did you feel on waking)?
• How sore are your muscles?
• How lively and 'up for it' do you feel now?

Of course, clever athletes who are really committed to punishing themselves can learn to fake this. If you see this happening, get specialist help from a medic and psychologist as soon as possible. In the vast majority of cases, however, these four simple questions, scored on a 1–10 scale and recorded, will offer you all you need at this level. Changes in mood and vitality (which is what these constructs are

TABLE 5.1 Suggested principles and exemplar activities at different stages of physical development/training age

Age (chronological/training)	Component of fitness	Aim	Exemplar activities
3–7/0 (shouldn't have started yet)	All (integrated activity)	• Fun fitness! • Build skills and confidence • Encourage work ethic ('grit') and competitiveness with self and others	• Simple pursuit and/or timed circuits on playground equipment or a purpose designed (and matted) gymnasium circuit • Family walks • Tag and chase games • 'Simon says' or 'copy my movements' games • Ideally with mirroring and matching contrasts • Hand/eye work with a variety of different size balls – catch and throw games • Swimming and diving
7–10 (female), 7–11 (male)/0–3 (sport-generic training preferred)	Aerobic/anaerobic	• Develop work ethic (can you keep going?) • Build personal reference (can you improve on what *you* did?) • Introduce different fitness components (and idea of personal strengths and weaknesses)	• Steady state runs/races over 800–2,000 m • Swims for distance (up to 400 m) • Hill walking • Tag games over short intervals (e.g. bulldog)
	Strength/power		• Handling bodyweight (e.g. monkey bars) with repetitions • Low box jumps on to mats • Dynamic lunges • Single leg Romanians
	Flexibility		

	Agility/GMA	• Whole body movements, such as crab walks • Build balance through static and dynamic exercises (e.g. stork balance for time challenge, hop-hop-freeze, etc.) • Change of Direction (CoD) challenges (e.g. shuttle runs) • Forward and backward rolls, plus cartwheels and balances
10–13 (female), 11–14 (male)/3–6 (ideally multi-sport)	Aerobic/anaerobic	• Steady state runs over 3,000 m • Longer walks/bike rides/swims • Sprint games (starting from different body positions – sprint start, on the back, on tummy, etc.)
	Strength/power	• Press ups into raised leg/clap push ups • Hangs into pull ups/dips • Increasing height depth jumps • Ground plyometric (i.e. run then hop for distance)
	Flexibility	• Squats with good form (back hollow and feet flat) • Squat snatch balance
	Agility/GMA	• Varied movements outside experience • Tumbling and/or trampoline work

measuring) will occur for a variety of reasons, not just the physical challenge. Changes will occur around the growth spurt, school exam time and in association with the relationship issues which are 'just part of the fun' in adolescence. Whatever the reason, however, paying attention to these markers is a good idea, with adjustments to training/activity load as appropriate.

The other key element in the injury avoidance equation is for appropriate prophylactic (preventative) training at early ages and stages. Reflecting these considerations, and reiterating our messages above, training at pre-pubescent and puberty stages should address flexibility, strength (particularly lower limb) and proprioception (balance and agility) as generic and sport-/activity-specific concerns. An appropriate balance of activities to address these factors can reduce injury by around 40 per cent (Soomro *et al.*, 2015), a significant factor whether the young performer wishes to purse a high-level career or just stay healthy.

Expert perspective on Chapter 5

Kevin Mannion currently works as the Academy Athletic Performance Manager at Gloucester Rugby club. He is an ex-professional rugby league player and has spent the last 16 years working with academy age athletes across a variety of sports including rugby league (at Wigan Warriors), rugby union (Leicester Tigers) and tennis (LTA).

The biggest message that can be taken from the chapter is that children should not be treated as adults – in terms of both prescription and specialisation. As a society the behaviours of children have changed dramatically to the point of some becoming the best athletes in the world, but on a console. Green spaces are now no longer used for deliberate play activities and the overpopulation of cars restricts games being played in the street. In essence, children no longer climb trees, play knock and run/hide and seek, Skilly, 3 and in, all the games that we played and assisted the child to learn all the key actions of: Push, Pull, Flexion, Extension, Rotation and Bracing. As a result of this, children are partaking in organised sport, where they learn to play the game, whilst coaches get occupied by short-term match results, at the expense of developing the athlete over the longer period. For this reason physical development is impacted!

Physically more literate children would be/are able to transfer and adapt to new skills more successfully and at a faster rate, as they already have the underlying patterning to adapt. Example: If a child can't pass off their left hand do you keep passing? Or do you work on the ability to rotate at the hip, look at their shoulder flexibility *then* try the pass again? In short, fundamentals are key.

The elements raised through this chapter are all details that parents of young sports people should consider and take note of. There are not a lot of new things going around in the world of S&C, at present. We just have the means to investigate and research those methods in greater detail. Unfortunately though, because of this there is a lot of rhetoric thrown around to get people to take up certain programmes and ideas and, assisted by the media attention, some gain, the most attractive are usually bought into.

For me there are some key messages that need to be re-iterated from this work and can be used when identifying the needs of your child both in sport and general health.

1   To quote a very famous person, 'not everything that can be measured matters' – children grow at different rates and at very different timescales. The only information you are concerned about is what impact the work being done has on your child's development. Their rank or grouping is an indicator of their performance at that time, not where they will end up.

2   GMA is essential for both sport and life, due in no small part to the reduction in PE in schools and deliberate play. Partaking in organised sport leads to early specialisation: keep the base broad for as long as possible, until you *have* to commit. In any programme you should be looking for key elements that will help them as they choose which sporting path they want to go on.

3   Put your child first, not the club, or the school, or the team.

And finally don't get baffled with bullshit! If a coach cannot articulate to you what your child is doing, and the potential benefits it will have in straightforward language that is easily understandable, then they don't understand it enough themselves!

In conclusion

In closing, we return to the caveats we expressed at the start of this chapter. We have attempted to offer an overall, generic picture whilst stressing the need for specific to sport, training/developmental age and individual characteristics. The main take-homes are that young children should be encouraged to develop an activity habit which is wide-ranging and challenging. Notably, this is never a wasted effort since this will set them up for lifelong physical activity whether or not they choose to go for high-level sport – the ERE route we identified in Chapter 2.

Of course, our advice must also be considered against the realities of whichever sport you/your child are involved with. Whatever the rights and wrongs (and both exist!), the reality is that, by the age of 8, a significant minority will be committed to a single sport or activity. Consideration of the ideas in this chapter will help to ensure maximum rights and fewer wrongs will accrue!

References

Demorest, R. A. and Landry, G. L. (2004). Training issues in elite young athletes. *Current Sports Medicine Reports*, 3(3), 167–172.

Ford, P., De Ste Croix, M., Lloyd, R., Meyers, R., Moosavi, M., Oliver, J., Till, K. and Williams, C. (2011). The long-term athlete development model: physiological evidence and application. *Journal of Sports Sciences*, 29(4), 389–402.

Myer, G. D., Lloyd, R. S., Brent, J. L. and Faigenbaum, A. D. (2013). How young is too young to start training? *ACSM Health and Fitness Journal*, 17(5), 14–23. Available: http:// journals.lww.com/acsm-healthfitness/Fulltext/2013/09000/How_Young_Is_Too_ Young_to_Start_Training_.6.aspx.

Soomro, N., Sanders, R., Hackett, D. and Cobley, S. (2015). The efficacy of injury prevention programs in adolescent team sports: a meta-analysis. *The American Journal of Sports Medicine*, 44(9), 2415–2424.

6

NEXT STEPS IN DEVELOPMENT – ABOVE THE NECK

Psychological Characteristics of Developing Excellence (PCDEs)

In this chapter, we turn our attention 'above the neck'. In terms of TD, a range of psychological factors have been shown to play a key role in the realisation of potential. We (MacNamara *et al.*, 2010a, 2010b) term these Psychological Characteristics of Developing Excellence (PCDEs), a term encompassing both the trait characteristics (the tendency to …) and the state–deployed skills (the ability to … when …) shown to play a crucial role in the realisation of potential. PCDEs are not just the mental skills, such as imagery or goal setting that are a traditional part of a Mental Skills Training (MST) package, but also include attitudes, emotions and desires such as commitment (see Table 6.1) that are essential for negotiating the TD pathway. PCDEs allow young performers to optimise development opportunities (e.g. first time appearances at a new level of competition, significant wins and losses), adapt to setbacks (e.g. injury, slumps in performance) and effectively negotiate key transitions (e.g. selection, demands for increased practice) encountered along the pathway to excellence.

TABLE 6.1 Psychological Characteristics of Developing Excellence

- Commitment
- Focus and distraction control
- Realistic performance evaluation
- Self-awareness
- Coping with pressure
- Planning and self-organisation
- Goal setting
- Quality practice
- Effective imagery
- Actively seeking social support

You are probably familiar with examples of athletes with seemingly the perfect physical makeup to excel at a sport not realising their potential and either dropping out of the sport completely, or competing at lower levels than would be expected because they did not possess or appropriately deploy these skills. The potential to develop depends on physical ability, an appropriate physical profile *and* other determinants such as commitment, motivation and determination. Even if a young person looks like the 'real deal' and is performing at a high level as a youth, they must possess and systematically develop the PCDEs that allow them to interact effectively with the developmental opportunities encountered along the pathway.

Of course, equipping young performers with these developmental skills will not necessarily result in high-level performance since there is a wide range of variables that influence the likelihood of reaching the top. However, it will provide aspiring elites with the capacity and competencies to strive to reach their potential, at whatever level that is. You can probably name some athletes in your sport who didn't seem to have the physical profile to be successful – 'too small', 'not tall enough' – but were able to compensate for these weaknesses through increased effort, determination and commitment to the learning process. It seems that PCDEs, and the ability to deploy them appropriately, might be the difference between who makes it and who doesn't.

Without PCDEs, and the ability to deploy them effectively ...

As you read this section, think of some performers you have encountered who had a promising junior career but couldn't translate that to the senior stage; the young performer who showed all the 'promise' and potential to be successful but couldn't produce a performance under pressure. Let's look at a couple of case studies and consider how PCDEs help young performers cope with the development pathway.

Early promise collapses under pressure

An overly smooth pathway may be the worst preparation for senior success. Why? If a young performer hasn't had to cope with any setbacks or deal with disappointments during their early years, it is unlikely that they have developed the skills, work ethic or commitment to cope with the ebb and flow of development, especially when they start to compete in more serious competitions or against more able performers. If things have been too 'easy' then the performer might be unprepared when faced with challenges and setbacks. PCDEs appear to be the mechanisms for achieving success and dealing with the inevitable challenges of development. If so, systematically developing these as part of your coaching practice seems sensible.

Athletes can perform but are extremely delicate

In Chapter 3, we spoke about the importance of self-regulation as a factor in TD; self-regulation seems to be a distinguishing factor in who succeeds and who doesn't. Self-regulated learners have the skills to self-monitor their progress, manage their emotions, focus on self-improvement and seek help and support from others when necessary. Conversely, young performers without these skills do not take personal responsibility for their own development but instead rely on others and attribute failures to maladaptive reasons that they cannot control. Unfortunately, few TD models systematically encourage the development of self-regulated learners, despite the support for its benefits. Providing early opportunities to develop and refine PCDEs that help performers overcome developmental challenges and stressing the process of learning of how to cope independently should be one of the key aspects of TD. Helicopter coaches, or snowplough parents, tend to try and soften the journey for performers, removing challenges, doing things 'for' and 'to' the athlete in an effort to expedite success. Teaching PCDEs, and providing opportunities to deploy these appropriately (even if that process is messy or delays progress), appears to be an appropriate way to prepare performers for what is ahead.

Our suggestion here is that PCDEs play a crucial role in translating potential into performance and, unless they are systematically developed as an integral part of the TD pathway, your sport will lose out on considerable amounts of talent.

Defining PCDE behaviours in *your* context

As elsewhere in this book, we want to provide some guidelines about the practical application of these concepts. So, how might you do this? Incorporating PCDEs into your TD environment is a key step in encouraging performers to behave like champions and make the most of the opportunities they are afforded. To begin, what type of behaviours do you want your performers to display? The first step in this process is to understand exactly what these 'champion behaviours' entail and what performers should be doing to demonstrate these both generally *and* in response to specific events and challenges.

First, PCDEs must be defined as clear and observable behaviours. By doing so, you are telling the performer exactly what behaviour is expected of them, and coaches/teachers can effectively monitor and reinforce appropriate actions. An example might help, so let's use one PCDE, 'commitment', to illustrate this point. Commitment is likely to be defined by different coaches, athletes and even sports in a variety of ways. For example, a committed athlete may be one who never misses practice, or who engages in lots of independent training or someone who 'never gives up' (see Table 6.2). In order to avoid ambiguity and increase clarity, break down each PCDE into observable and objectively defined behaviours, important for your athlete(s) at particular points in development. By doing this, the coach and parent (and of course the performer themselves) can easily assess, monitor,

TABLE 6.2 Commitment behaviours

- Arrives early to training
- Keeps going hard in practice
- Trains independently away from the rest of the team
- Shows a consistent effort and good preparation
- Works hard at their own level
- Understands and is responsible for both training and rest where appropriate
- Is resilient when faced with obstacles and setbacks

Source: adapted from Abbott *et al.*, 2007.

measure and reinforce progress and behaviour. This joined-up thinking is critical to make sure everyone is on message; all concerned must understand what behaviours are important for their particular activity and consistently model and/or reinforce them. Make sure that PCDEs are defined in a manner that is meaningful both to the individual performer and in the context in which they perform. The main consideration here is that each PCDE must be operationalised with the specific needs of the individual in mind.

Now, consider what behaviours, using the guidelines above, you would like particular sets of athletes in your sport to engage in to demonstrate each of the PCDEs presented in Table 6.1. What does commitment look like in your sport? How might it differ for athletes at different stages or different ages? How does an athlete behave if they are engaged in goal-setting behaviours? What actions would a young athlete take to show they are seeking social support? Some examples are given in Table 6.3; go through the list and think how these might apply in your sport and for particular groups of athletes. The key points to remember are that the behaviour should be *visual* (something that can be seen and measured), *behavioural* (something that can be promoted) and *positive* (i.e. not a lack of ...). Simply, you need to specify very clearly how you want your athletes to behave based on aspects that will strengthen their performance and mental skills profile.

Reinforcing, encouraging and refining PCDEs

Once key PCDEs, and the behaviours associated with them, have been identified, what can you do to promote and reinforce these in training and competition? You can do this by designing coach behaviours and systems that encourage, prime and reinforce the desired behaviours. A number of guidelines can increase the effectiveness of these behaviour modification techniques. First, as previously suggested, it is important to target and define the behaviours that need to be addressed. It is essential to limit this focus to only a couple of behaviours at a time, otherwise both the performer and coach can get overwhelmed by attempting to change too much too quickly. Furthermore, if only a few behaviours are targeted at each stage, it becomes easier to reinforce these effectively and consistently; as with lots of aspects of coaching, not trying to do too much, too quickly is likely to be the most effective way to establish change.

TABLE 6.3 Defining behaviours associated with PCDEs

- *Commitment*
  - Arrives early to training
  - Works hard at own level

- *Focus and distraction control*
  - Remains focused under distraction
  - Displays a consistent pre-performance routine

- *Realistic performance evaluation*
  - The ability to analyse what you do well and what you don't
  - The ability to attribute success and failure appropriately

- *Self-awareness*
  - Awareness of adaptive and maladaptive influences on performance

- *Coping with pressure*
  - Reacts appropriately to mistakes and criticism
  - Shows confidence to thrive under pressure

- *Planning and self-organisation*
  - The ability to balance lifestyle commitments
  - The ability to prioritise different activities

- *Goal setting*
  - The ability to set short-, medium- and long-term goals
  - The ability to set appropriate goals

- *Quality practice*
  - The ability to maximise understanding in training
  - Shows an understanding of why you are doing what you are doing

- *Effective imagery*
  - Using imagery to rehearse new skills
  - Using imagery to simulate new environments

- *Actively seeking social support*
  - Knows when and how to seek out support from others

Second, coaches, teachers and significant others must provide feedback and reinforcement that clearly indicates the individual's progress towards achieving the desired behaviours. These *coach behaviours*, provided within a supportive environment, not only increase motivation but also the likelihood of the desired behaviour occurring again in the future.

Finally, athletes must have a clear understanding of what behaviour is required and coaches must clearly state the outcomes of performing, or not performing, these targeted behaviours. Essentially the coach/teacher employs *coach systems* to clarify what behaviours are expected and what the consequences are of engaging or not engaging in those behaviours. These systems act as 'setting conditions' that encourage, teach and promote the desired behaviour. It is important to keep these principles in mind as we now consider what these coaching practices might look like in your environment.

Coaching behaviours and coaching systems

This section will discuss how a combination of *coach behaviours* and *coach systems* (see Figure 6.1) can effectively promote the PCDEs in your talent environment. It is important that coaches consider how both their own behaviours, and the system within which they work, promote desired (and, unfortunately, dysfunctional) behaviours. Coaches must carefully consider their interactions with athletes if these specific behaviours are going to be promoted and strengthened and thus likely to re-occur. For example, if a coach wishes the athlete to behave in a *committed* manner by 'addressing weaknesses in training' they must reinforce this through coach behaviours such as goal-orientated feedback based on individual performance and progression related to their goals. It is also important to consider how the coaching system increases the likelihood of the desired behaviour occurring. In this case, the coach system could take the form of regular goal setting and progress meetings between the player and coach. Through the interaction of coach behaviours and coach systems (see Table 6.4) the athlete is encouraged to engage in the desired behaviour. If these practices are continually adhered to, the athlete will accept and internalise these behaviours to the point where they occur as a matter of course, to the benefit of athlete's performance.

Using the example in Table 6.4, pick out some PCDEs that you would like to focus on with a particular group of athletes. First, identify the behaviours associated with this PCDE. Then think about what coach behaviours and coach systems can do to encourage athletes to act in the manner desired and then positively reinforce 'good' behaviour.

An important point here is that all three aspects – athlete behaviour, coach behaviour and coach system – must interact with the coach reinforcing appropriate behaviour and providing appropriate setting conditions that support the development and deployment of PCDEs. Let's use another example to illustrate this. The coach has identified that their athlete would benefit from using imagery to correct

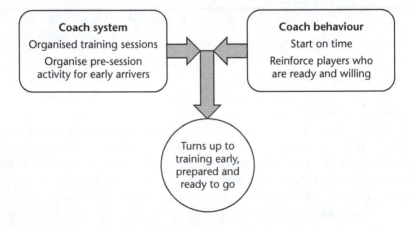

FIGURE 6.1 Interaction of coach systems and coach behaviours

TABLE 6.4 Coach systems and coach behaviours

PCDE behaviour	Coach system	Coach behaviour
Supports others' efforts	Buddy system of support Feedback on individual goals	Knowledge of and active input into 'buddy system' (who, goals, feedback style preferences)

mistakes and deal with difficult situations – a placekicker missing their first shot at goal in a match, or a high jumper failing to clear an opening height in competition (see Table 6.5). What coach behaviours and systems could be used to encourage and reinforce this behaviour? The example in Table 6.5 describes how the coach system could be regular meetings that upskill the athlete in terms of imagery use, while also discussing the feelings and emotions associated with performance and how to cope with these. Coach behaviours could include encouragement from the coach to the athlete to engage in imagery, providing time for this in training and reinforcing the role of imagery through questioning and discussion. It is important that the relationship between the coach behaviour and coach system is consistent, otherwise the likelihood of the athlete engaging in the desired behaviour is small. For example, if you don't provide time for the athlete to incorporate imagery into their training and competition routines, or positively reinforce its use, it is unlikely to become a feature even if you say it is important! Tweaking the approach to suit your particular situation is key; PCDEs must be defined, and coach behaviours and systems developed with the needs of the athlete in mind.

As you work your way through the different PCDEs, it should be becoming clear that similar methods (e.g. coach systems and coach behaviours) can be

TABLE 6.5 Example from a PCDE curriculum at a football academy

Topic	Support	Challenge
Grit (determination)	• Session on combining imagery and goal setting to improve performance • Coach selects and player presents good practice	• Cross-country run four times per season • Timed skills tests four times per season • Keepy-uppy challenge (home practice/group performance) • Behaviour goals for school and home
Coach-led goal setting	• Session on SMART goals • Coach models use in games and training	• Coach works with players to set goals for grit challenges • Three levels goals at Under 10

employed to encourage a range of behaviours. This has a number of benefits – it simplifies the coaching process and increases the probability of each system and behaviour being appropriately implemented. By embedding the development of PCDEs into coaching (rather than as an added-on extra), the athlete is more likely to accept and internalise these behaviours to the point where they will automatically engage in them. In fact, when we go and watch 'good coaching' we see this exact process. Effective coaches design their practices and environment for 'explicit' (improving a technique, working on a game-plan, improving fitness) reasons but also for 'implicit' outcomes (increasing confidence, self-regulation, commitment – PCDEs). Doing this systematically both as an individual coach, and as part of a cog in the TD system, is the goal and goes a way to ensuring no piece of the puzzle is ignored.

Teach–Test–Tweak–Repeat

So how do we ensure that athletes have the necessary PCDEs and ability to deploy them appropriately? We propose a 'teaching, challenging, evaluating and refining' cycle, what we will term 'Teach–Test–Tweak–Repeat'. Using this approach, young athletes experience a gradual development of skills, which are then tested against realistic (rather than contrived) challenges along the TD pathway. After the challenge, coaches and other practitioners engage the athletes in review, developing their own capacity to evaluate and self-manage in tandem with structured feedback. Given the need for reflection and refinement, this approach is built around a periodised use of challenge, allowing sufficient time for athletes to learn from, develop and refine and, crucially, secure confidence in their capacity to use the skills. Keep this in mind when you get to Chapter 13 where Dave talks in more detail about the use of the 'rocky road' as a developmental tool.

For the moment, it is important to note that this approach is a *lot* more than merely the provision of mental skills training. Unfortunately, it is our experience that sport psychology provision in TD is often ad-hoc, group workshops delivered in isolation from the actual development environment, by practitioners who are not embedded in the pathway. This might explain the negative reputation that sport psychology has among some performers, coaches and parents! As a more effective system, the PCDE approach we propose becomes central to coaching rather than an 'extra' part of the TD system. As we said, good coaches develop PCDEs as part of what we do. The guidelines offered here offer a systematic way of including PCDEs in coaching, ensuring that they are developed purposefully and appropriately at different stages. We propose that work must be one-on-one as much as possible, to help the individual to explore, discover and build confidence in the particular blend which works best for them in their particular environment. This, in turn, raises the need for regular and ongoing refinement or even revision as people grow and situations change.

PCDEs in practice: some important considerations

In this section we provide some guidelines about how you might incorporate PCDEs as part of your developmental agenda. As you read, start to consider how this might play out in your environment, identifying both challenges and opportunities that must be accounted for.

In most sport, young athletes progress through a series of age-groups as they move towards senior status. The aim therefore should be that young athletes have experienced input and application of all PCDEs (see Table 6.1) by the time they reach the tail end of the pathway. This developmental curriculum prepares the young athlete for the sharp end of the development pathway when pressures really come on. In football, for example, this would be around age 16 when young players are likely to get signed to a professional contract and there is a real pressure on their performance. In an early specialisation sport such as gymnastics, these pressures are likely to come into play at a much younger age and the implementation of the PCDE curriculum should reflect this. The point to note here is that the deployment of PCDEs may be complicated by the specific demands faced by athletes within different domains. Early success in track athletics (e.g. sprinting), for instance, may be achieved with comparatively little effort (or even Deliberate Practice) if the athlete possesses natural ability, relatively greater physical maturity and/ or an appropriate physique. In contrast, the same early success is less likely to be evident in more technical team sports (e.g. hockey) if the athlete hasn't yet developed the necessary technical and tactical skills to engage successfully in that activity. As an even more extreme case, young gymnasts must engage in highly technical and demanding practice before they can even begin to perform. In short, given that different performance environments require different levels of Deliberate Practice at different stages of development, it may well be that there are activity-related differences in the set of PCDEs required or at least in the timing of them on the pathway. The relative timings of these challenges are an especially important concern given the importance of positive early experiences as precursors of prolonged engagement in sport and physical activity.

What do you need to consider in order to implement a PCDE curriculum in your sport? A number of principles apply. First, the approach is skills-based, using a careful periodisation of challenge and support to Teach–Test–Tweak the skills, then Repeat in a positive spiral. In Chapter 14 we provide more detail on the importance of challenge, but for the moment think how you could exploit 'coachable moments' to reinforce and refine PCDEs.

Second, the skills are taught through a combination of formal, informal and procedural methods and then tested against realistic challenges. In best practice, PCDEs are integrated as part of your coaching; athletes will have to deploy PCDEs in response to challenges in their environment, and 'coach behaviours' such as feedback will refine and reinforce the application of the skill. After each coaching episode, coaches and other practitioners engage the athletes in review – what happened and why, developing their own capacity to evaluate and self-manage in tandem with structured feedback. Given the need for reflection and refinement, and recognising that this will differ depending on the age and maturity level of your athlete, you must allow sufficient time for athletes to learn from, develop, refine and, crucially, secure confidence in their capacity to use the skills.

Third, the formal part will usefully involve (if available) psychologist and coach (at the least) in presenting the skill. Of course, if you coach in a team sport situation this is challenging since the provision of support is a complex issue and a range of individual differences mediate the impact of this type of training. As such, the need for an individualised and gradual approach to the development and deployment of PCDEs is another important feature of this approach. This is backed up by a variety of informal interactions, with coach, psychologist, parent, other support specialists and even fellow players modelling effective application of the skill to realistic challenges. The procedural part – the coach systems – also helps to keep the skills at the forefront, and embed them within the culture of life for the young player. For example, post-game debrief procedures will expect 'Realistic Performance Evaluation' as a normal feature.

Fourth, the skills are taught, deployed and culturally encouraged as part of everyday practice. As we stress elsewhere in this book, this does not mean that the young performers are not encouraged to deploy the skills in other areas of their life. Indeed, getting this to happen becomes a rare problem as the performers gain confidence in their mental expertise. We do feel, however, that presenting the skills against the environment they are to be used in helps to maximise transfer. In simple terms, athletes see the skills as part of their sport, rather than a peripheral that only *might* be useful.

To contextualise these principles, Table 6.5 presents a section of a PCDE curriculum aimed at Under 9s and 10s in a football professional academy. The guidelines espoused in the preceding section should be clear within the activities suggested. Players at this age will only be working on a subset of the full PCDE curriculum. At later stages, formative evaluations are completed at regular intervals, twice a year, using a self-report PCDE Questionnaire (PCDEQ; Hill, MacNamara and Collins, in review). The PCDEQ2 provides a self-rating on different elements (both positive *and* negative) of the PCDEs. We stress here the formative use of the questionnaire – it is not a selection tool but rather one way to gain a picture of what is happening. You will want to triangulate these self-ratings with coach evaluations, performance data and school reports, providing a comprehensive picture of each player's development and a useful resource for reviewing and refining the player's Individual Development Plan in conjunction with key stakeholders. Action plans can then be contextualised against genuine performance challenges, further promoting application and enhancing motivation. We suggest that a well planned, well managed, periodised and individualised challenge strategy has strong merit in the long-term development of more psychologically robust athletes.

A captive audience? Physical education as a means of developing PCDEs

Of course, relatively few young athletes participate in a structured TD pathway such as a professional football academy. In Chapter 4 we emphasised the importance of the foundation of the TD pathway. Therefore, physical education (PE) and youth sport would seem to be prime environments to impact TD since all young people experience compulsory education. Indeed, an important consideration is that the focus should be on *education* rather than *activity* or *identification*. This reflects the importance of Deliberate Preparation, where participation and performance in sport and physical activity can both derive from a common, robust foundation of psychomotor and psychological skills. It would seem to us that PE presents an important environment to consistently and coherently focus on and promote these precursors that enable all children to readily participate in physical activities at the level they eventually choose to pursue. Unfortunately, it is our experience that the quality of the PE experience, often focused on bouts of physical activity and participation, doesn't equip young people with the mechanisms for prolonged participation.

We offer here one example of a TD initiative that recognised the importance of Deliberate Preparation (see Chapter 4) and the role of psychomotor skills and PCDEs as essential precursors of long-term engagement in sport and physical activity. The Developing the Potential of Young People in Sport (DPYPS) programme was developed in conjunction with sportscotland (Abbott *et al.* 2007). The DPYPS approach utilised a dual curriculum encompassing both psycho-behavioural and psychomotor skills, and was aimed at pupils in primary school and the early years of secondary school. Essentially, the skills offered within the DPYPS programme are those psychological and psychomotor fundamentals that underpin learning, development and performance across performance domains.

The psychomotor activities within DPYPS were designed to initially promote a basic moves vocabulary (e.g. the ability to catch) before encouraging the combining of basic moves into increasingly complex coordinative structures (e.g. the ability to run, catch *and* throw a ball). In Chapter 4, Dave spoke about these ideas when he presented the idea of Deliberate Preparation. By providing for learning experiences in fundamental components such as jumping, running, hopping and balance, it was hoped that DPYPS would offer young children the basic skills they need for successful early experiences and subsequent development in sport, be it at elite levels, participatory levels or as health-related physical activity. But, just as importantly, taking these activities forwards into 'full games' serves to empower and enthuse youngsters to get and stay involved. Their own perceptions of confidence are crucial in this respect.

The interlinked psycho-behavioural curriculum provided children with the PCDEs (e.g. goal setting, imagery, realistic performance evaluations, focus and distraction control) that have been shown to facilitate learning and performance across all sporting domains and beyond. While some schools and teachers develop such skills as a natural part of their pedagogical approach, the need for systematic education and practice is clear. The PCDE curriculum was presented to children developmentally, and in practice worked both as classroom activities and as an integrated part of teaching methodology. This included a series of activities presented across and within three levels to allow them to be matched to the students' capabilities. At Level One, children were encouraged to realise their level of competence and to self-reinforce. At Level Two, children were encouraged to begin to take responsibility for their own development. At Level Three, children were encouraged to aspire to excellence by achieving autonomous development. In order to illustrate how this worked in practice, exemplars of imagery activities at each of the three levels are presented below.

- *Level One imagery*: children were presented with practical tasks that promote the use of imagery and highlights how imagery, if used alongside practice, can help build confidence and improve performance (see Figure 6.2).
- *Level Two imagery*: At this level, children were presented with practical tasks that promoted the use of controlled imagery during practice and competition (see Figure 6.3).
- *Level Three imagery*: Level Three was presented as a sport-specific level that provided coaches with guidance on how to promote the PCDEs developed at Levels One and Two within their sport-specific context. In this example, the

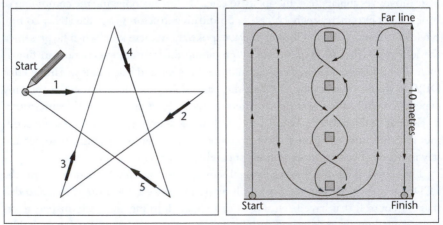

Using imagery to improve confidence and performance

Part one

Pupils look at the star shape below and 'image' following the route to successfully draw the star in one movement. The pupils are told to have a go drawing the star and reflect on how imagery helped.

Part two

Pupils watch a video of an athlete who is imaging running around a slalom course (the Illinois agility run) and then reflect on the athlete's use of imagery:

The pupils then image successfully completing the slalom course below before running the slalom course and reflecting on whether imagery helped them.

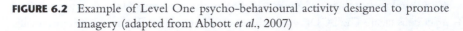

FIGURE 6.2 Example of Level One psycho-behavioural activity designed to promote imagery (adapted from Abbott *et al.*, 2007)

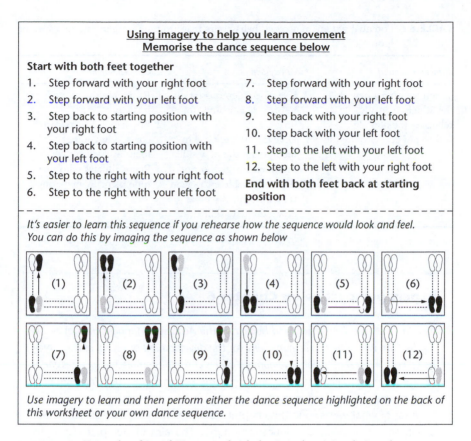

Using imagery to help you learn movement
Memorise the dance sequence below

Start with both feet together

1. Step forward with your right foot
2. Step forward with your left foot
3. Step back to starting position with your right foot
4. Step back to starting position with your left foot
5. Step to the right with your right foot
6. Step to the right with your left foot

7. Step forward with your right foot
8. Step forward with your left foot
9. Step back with your right foot
10. Step back with your left foot
11. Step to the left with your left foot
12. Step to the left with your right foot

End with both feet back at starting position

It's easier to learn this sequence if you rehearse how the sequence would look and feel. You can do this by imaging the sequence as shown below

Use imagery to learn and then perform either the dance sequence highlighted on the back of this worksheet or your own dance sequence.

FIGURE 6.3 Example of Level Two psycho-behavioural activity designed to promote imagery (adapted from Abbott _et al._, 2007)

coach identifies the behaviours the athlete in their sport need to show in order that they use controlled imagery (i.e. athlete behaviour; what will we see your athlete doing during training and competition to show they are using controlled imagery?). (See Table 6.6.) Systems and coach behaviours that can be employed to promote imagery use are then developed.

The impact of the DPYPS programme were felt not just in the sporting context; the carry-over benefits of the DPYPS approach to other dimensions of excellence were also reported. For example, following the intervention the children were able to transfer the skills acquired though the DPYPS programme to other arenas and challenges – they got better at doing homework, concentrated more in class and at home, or were able to seek out solutions when things got sticky (Abbott _et al._, 2007). This was a particular strength of the curriculum since it encouraged children to adapt the PCDEs that they acquired to various sporting and non-sporting activities.

TABLE 6.6 Potential systems and coach behaviours that promote imagery use in a specific sport

Athlete behaviour	Coach system	Coach behaviour
When learning a new skill, the athlete mentally rehearses the new skill before physically trying the skill	1 Use video/demonstration to provide a prompt for imagery 2 Give the athlete time to incorporate the new skill into their imagery script 3 Allow the athlete to spend time imaging as well as doing the new skill	1 Reinforce the role of imagery 2 Emphasise that to learn effectively you need to focus on relevant cues 3 Praise athletes who spend time mentally preparing

Source: adapted from Abbott *et al.*, 2007.

Expert perspective on Chapter 6

Neil McCarthy, a former England hooker, is the Academy Manager at Gloucester Rugby Club where he has responsibility for the development of young players. Neil has a keen interest in talent development and is currently completing a Professional Doctorate in Elite Performance examining some key principles that underpin progression and development in sport.

A lot of what was said in this chapter resonates with how we structure the development pathway at Gloucester Rugby. The aim of our pathway is to develop young players with the capacity to play first-team rugby at Gloucester; we place a strong emphasis on all facets of the game but central to the academy programme is the development of psychologically robust athletes. To do this, we have worked with the PCDE curriculum discussed in the chapter, integrating it into our coaching and ensuring that it has both a Rugby and a Gloucester 'feel' to it to make it relevant to our players. Of course, this approach is hugely individual and one of the difficult parts of organising our pathway is to ensure this individualised approach in a team environment. We have to cater to the particular needs of each player while also maintaining a balance with the needs of the club.

We believe that the academy environment should not be (or at least should not always be) a comfortable place to be; players need to be challenged so that they grow from the process and develop the skillset needed to play professionally. For some players this happens naturally, for others (sometimes the high-flyers) we have to 'put the bumps in the road' to make sure they get exposed to, and benefit from, challenge. These 'challenging periods' might be as simple as either encouraging or holding back athletes to compete at levels above or below their current age grading, either through training or exposure in competitions. The challenge doesn't have to be complex and the closer it is to the demands of the pathway, we find the better. For example, we often drip feed players into senior-level competitions or training for short periods of time, or send them away to play in lower leagues to gain exposure to different environments. Even simply warming up at a senior game with senior players is an effective way of developing and refining PCDEs. Recently, we got our academy players to do a skills session during half-time of a premiership game – the pressure of doing this in front of a real crowd and in that sort of atmosphere had a significant impact.

The Teach–Test–Tweak–Repeat cycle is a key part of how we approach this work. Before we expose players to challenge, we make sure they have developed PCDEs to, at least, survive in that environment – we want them to swim rather than sink! When the players come back, and at regular intervals through the season, we do a review of what went well and 'work-ons', with players encouraged to self-evaluate and self-reflect as well as effectively use the structured feedback from coaches. This allows the players sufficient time and space to learn from, develop, refine and get confident in their capacity to use the PCDEs. For us, PCDE development isn't something extra that we do, it is just part of the coaching and development approach we have and is reflected in what happens day-to-day at the club.

In conclusion

So, given that there is considerable evidence for the role of PCDEs as a key mechanism of development, what are the key 'take-aways' for applying this in your context? You need to define PCDEs as clear and observable behaviours relevant to your athlete, in their context, at particular points of development. The behavioural component of each PCDE may look different across different contexts, in different performance domains depending on the specific challenges faced by athletes at particular moments in development.

You must also consider how coach behaviours and coach systems promote desired and dysfunctional behaviours from your athletes. If coaches want their athletes to engage in specific behaviours, they must offer a consistent and supportive environment (coach systems) and consistently reinforce the athlete when they engage in the desired behaviour (coach behaviour). It is important to remember that there may be many coach systems and coach behaviours that contribute to the effective promotion of a set of behaviours. Likewise, a single coach system (e.g. goal setting meetings) may be an effective means for encouraging and developing a number of PCDEs. Finding what works for you, your performer and your context is the important bit.

The overarching philosophy of the TD pathway is also an important consideration here. It may be that promoting and reinforcing PCDEs may not result in short-term success since the coach is working on a longer-term agenda. As such, the 'meta-coach' and system that the coach works in plays a role; if coaches are reinforced for winning and short-term success they are likely to make short-term decisions that lead to this immediate success, regardless of the long-term development implications. Therefore, coherency and consistency from all involved in the talent development pathway is a crucial consideration.

The generality of PCDEs is also a positive feature of this approach – the same PCDEs seem to be important regardless of domain or stage of development. From a talent transfer perspective this is important as it enables the cross-fertilisation of talent; athletes will have the skills to successfully transfer from one domain to another. Even if the athlete remains in their sport, they will have the skillset to cope with developmental challenges and the range of 'other stuff' challenges that are a feature of growing up.

Developing PCDEs, as well as other essential precursors of participation, such as perceived and actual competence, should enable young athletes to overcome the various roadblocks and de-railers they encounter as an almost inevitable feature of development. This approach to TID should facilitate the effective pursuit of excellence in sport at the individual's chosen level of achievement and, serendipitously but very positively, achievement in other non-sporting domains. This 'win-win' outcome should be used as an important selling point, helping 'buy-in' from key stakeholders such as parents and schools.

References

Abbott, A., Collins, D., Sowerby, K. and Martindale, R. (2007). *Developing the potential of young people in sport*. A report for sportscotland by University of Edinburgh.

MacNamara, Á., Button, A. and Collins, D. (2010a). The role of psychological characteristics in facilitating the pathway to elite performance. Part 1: Identifying mental skills and behaviours. *The Sport Psychologist*, 24, 52–73.

MacNamara, Á., Button, A. and Collins, D. (2010b). The role of psychological characteristics in facilitating the pathway to elite performance. Part 2: Examining environmental and stage related differences in skills and behaviours. *The Sport Psychologist*, 24, 74–96.

7

CONCERNS AND CONSIDERATIONS FOR PARENTS AND COACHES

Introduction

As we launch this, the final chapter in the pre-academy section, it is worth revisiting what parents and coaches are trying to do. Certainly, if your child/athlete is going to 'make some noise' at the top level, many of the signs will already be apparent. *However*, these signs will be much more positive, and supportive for their next steps on the pathway, if the signs are process rather than outcome. In other words, young performers at this age and/or stage are better to be doing things right and showing that they have the tools for future progress and success. Too many talent systems are identifying children on current performance rather than these key attributes. Often as a result, the young performers get promoted beyond their true level and end up dropping out of the pathway – and, maybe, even out of the game.

So, for long-term success and enjoyment, plus an optimally developing experience (remember the ideas in Chapter 2), parents, coaches and teachers should be most focused on equipping the youngster with all the tools s/he will need. Importantly, this equipping stage is best accomplished by doing certain things *but not* doing others. The most effective processes at this age/stage will be based on a subtle balance, which will change as the child changes. Age, circumstance, ambitions – all will play a part and need careful watching for and thinking about to keep the process as effective and beneficial as possible. As before, we address these ideas by considering a series of questions which are often asked by those involved.

How hard is too hard? How much is too much?

As parents, we all want the best for our children. Furthermore, the vast majority of teachers and coaches want only good experiences and outcomes for the children they work with. Despite these good intentions, however, there is a growing wave of 'anti' posts on social media and the like; many are built around the excessive demands being placed on children at too young an age. Accordingly, getting a well thought-through and accurate answer to the questions above would seem to be an important issue for all concerned in young people's sport and physical activity.

Understanding how to place appropriate demands on young athletes is an important consideration for coaches and parents. We have already discussed some of the evidence around the risks of early specialisation. The message should be coming over 'loud and clear' that, for the vast majority of children in a western society, thoughtful moderation is the best policy. Of course, there are lots of stories surrounding today's superstars on how their parents were pushing them to train and practice from a young age. What is less publicised, however, is how many kids ended up hating the sport, the coach and their parents and gave up completely. As with almost everything else in the book, the crucial rule to apply is 'it depends'!

That said, it is important to stress that children need challenge and that almost all will thrive on an optimum balance of challenge and support. My favourite example is always taking the 'trainer' wheels off a child's bike. They fight for balance as you run along beside them holding tight to their clothing to prevent the inevitable tumble and tears. The trouble is that it *is* almost inevitable! Stay hanging on and they remain safe and yell-free *but* they don't learn to ride the bike. So the bottom line is that some challenge and, indeed, some failure is not only inevitable but crucial for progress. Furthermore, the long-term impact of such failure, so long as the child sticks with it and (hopefully) overcomes it, is even more important to generating a resilient, 'takes the knocks but keeps going' young person that we all want to see. As we said above, the trick is finding and using the right balance.

One big question here is the level of challenge quality versus quantity – literally, how hard against how much. It is increasingly understood that high-quality and challenging experiences are critical developmental tools, whilst high-quantity experience is a major contributor to mental exhaustion and burnout, plus the distinct possibility of longer-term problems. In an attempt to see what were the most common (and presumably beneficial) experiences, we interviewed performers compared across triads (Collins *et al.*, 2016). So, we would recruit a 'Superchamp' from a sport and country, defined as someone who had won five or more Olympic/World medals or (if a team sport athlete) 60 or more caps. All of these were senior internationals of long-standing (no more than two medals at any one championship) or senior players with experience across multiple premiership clubs and/or leagues. We then recruited 'Champions' (one or no medals/three or less caps but a seasoned high-level performer) and 'Almosts' (successful as a junior, but semi-pro or lower as an adult) to make up trios of participants, all with similar backgrounds (age, nationality, ethnicity, etc.) and, of course, from the same sport. This chapter is open access; we will mention more from it in Chapter 14. For the moment, however, a very short summary for some pertinent results is shown in Table 7.1. Given that we are talking about challenge, it is worth looking at this to see what did and didn't work for these now adult performers, looking back on their past experience.

TABLE 7.1 Some key points from the Superchamps study

Supers	Almosts
1 Slow, often bumpy progression	Smooth ride – 'the next XXX'
2 Supportive, encouraging but 'staying distant' parents	*Very* high levels of parental interest and drive
3 Strong but challenging coaches – *personal* standards emphasised	Vocal support ('you are *great*') then *much* less
4 *Very* high personal drive – athlete often causes the 'bumps' through personal standards	Committed early – enjoying the attention but very 'other' referenced. *Real* problems or even dropout later
5 Positive reaction to challenges and setbacks – 'uses to stimulate'	Negative reaction – 'why me?', 'I am unlucky' or 'It's not fair'

Superchamps versus Almosts

One big finding that comes out straightaway is how bumpy the ride was for the Superchamps, in comparison to the 'this is easy … look at me' experience of the Almosts. There is an American expression 'snowplough parents'. The idea is that these people push away any difficulties for their child, offering encouragement, resources, car rides, etc. to smooth the path to the top. As parents ourselves, we can completely understand this – as we said earlier, everyone wants the best for their children. We can also understand this approach as a method for youth sport coaches. For a start, keeping things simple for the learner is a way to quick improvement, which keeps the performer motivated and the parents (who are often paying for the training) on board. Unfortunately, this rapid progress is often an illusion – a point we return to in Chapter 9. For the moment, however, please note that skill learning is much better in the long run when it is made more difficult. This isn't a linear relationship of course – make it too difficult and even the most committed young-ster will give up. With moderate difficulty, however, rising to the challenge will usually end up giving you a better, more flexible, robust and adaptable set of skills. The other reason why coaches are often attracted to 'smoothing the pathway' is because that is what is done at the top level. Most high-level performers will sur-round themselves with a 'Team Me' which exists to support them and keep every-thing else running smoothly whilst they, the performer, get on with the hard job of elite sport. For a senior performer, perhaps even for any harassed adult, this is a good option which enables them to focus on the most important parts of their life. But not, we suggest, for a developing young person!

So, as shown in Table 7.1, line 1, Superchamps had an early life which was pretty packed with a variety of challenges. As a result, they learnt to balance dif-ferent demands, learning personal organisation, focus, goal setting and planning skills along the way – all rather important for high-level performers and all part of the PCDEs which this book sets out as the key mental skillset for success. In their sport/activity sphere, they were not seen as a rising superstar, nor pushed as one, nor (most crucially) seen as one by themselves. Rather they (mostly) enjoyed coping with the challenges.

Lines 2 and 3 in Table 7.1 offer some direction for parents and coaches. Importantly, most parents of Superchamps that we interviewed tended to take a 'back seat' with their children's sport involvement. They were certainly encouraging but helped to keep things in perspective by being interested in all aspects of their child's life. School work, and the push to keep focused on it, was a consistent thread across parents of Superchamps. Likewise, the first coaches these athletes had (and all moved on to other coaches as they got older) set, demanded and (as others reported) got high standards of behaviour and commitment. Interestingly, standards set were for the individual; 'You can do better' or 'That was a good performance under the circumstances' were typical comments. Coaches of Superchamps were also very aware of everything else that was going on in the young athlete's life, with adjustments to demands made as appropriate. In simple terms, the child athlete was kept aware of what s/he could do and how much effort was required.

In contrast, parents of Almosts were *very* involved – committed to supporting their child but also pushing her/him forwards at every opportunity. Other activities tended to be forgotten, whilst the parents were frequently in contact with the coach, demanding the very best extra special treatment for their child. In somewhat similar fashion, coaches of Almosts heaped praise, time and attention on their young superstars. This lasted so long as the young athlete was doing well, then all of a sudden the attention stopped! Interestingly, some Almosts made a recovery with another coach, but the sudden lack of interest was certainly debilitating for many. The clear messages are that keeping things general and helping your child/athlete to overcome challenge rather than helping them to avoid it are key elements for future super success.

Keeping a balance – some tools to use

The balance we talk about is not just an actual thing; rather, the young athlete's perceptions are key as well. They also need to see how things are progressing and have a perceived sense of control over all the things they do rather than feeling swamped by the sheer volume, or pushed into things by others. In addition, however, because of the dynamic and individualised nature of development, personal needs rather than just chronological organisation must be recognised. In other words, coaches can make good use of a variety of monitoring tools and means of presentation to help the young athlete appreciate where s/he is, what is happening and where things are headed. Using goal setting and profiling approaches is very helpful. For example, see the discrepancy method shown in Table 7.2.

The whole point of ideas like this is to ensure good communication: to ensure the young athlete, parents and coach are on the same page. The idea here is that the coach (better at this age) develops a list of what is needed for performance in that particular sport. The athlete then ranks him or herself on each factor, using a 1–10 scale, with 10 as perfection – the Current Rating. Athlete and coach then work

TABLE 7.2 The 'discrepancy' method of profiling – an example for a young kart driver

Factor	Current Rating	Importance Rating (I)	Discrepancy (D)	$D \times I$
Aerobic fitness	6	9	4	36
Neck strength	8	6	2	12
Nice hair	3	1	7	7
Reactions	4	9	6	54
Track knowledge	5	7	5	35
Braking	3	9	7	63
Commitment	7	7	3	21

together to score how important each factor is for overall progression – the Importance Rating. Next a quick sum, taking the athlete's current rating from 10 to generate the Discrepancy. Finally, Discrepancy is multiplied by Importance to give us the $D \times I$ column. This number is really useful as it gives us an importance factor for that particular individual. The higher the number the more time s/he needs to spend on that factor. You might notice that we have included a spoof factor … hair style isn't really crucial! The main thing here is that profiling, and the goal setting which goes with it (more of this later in Chapter 14) keeps everyone on the same page, so avoiding the pulls in different directions which can really derail progress – at this or any age.

Note that parents can use this approach with their children, although probably not quite so formally! On a serious note, it never does any harm to portion out the week and keep an eye on the balance of activity. So your son or daughter may be football crazy, but keeping some balance is always a good thing. Most of you will have switched onto the reward idea…. 'So if you do 30 minutes reading for homework, then you can go play'. Notice that, whilst rewards work well, doing things the other way around with punishment is far less effective. So please avoid 'You haven't done your homework so you aren't playing'.

Talking back and forth – the best tool of all

Chats with your young athlete are another important way to keep things balanced and moving in a positive direction. A few years ago, we did a study of tennis coaches' behaviour when working with young up-and-comers. Amongst the few conclusive differences which we found (style and emotional contact were far more important) was that more effective coaches picked up the balls *with* their players whilst others went to the other end of the court. Although more efficient time-wise, this didn't seem to be appreciated by the players. Later we found out why. The best coaches were chatting to their players about everything and anything – getting to know the players as individuals so that they could relate to their needs.

Forging and enhancing relationships is almost always a good thing. As a coach you will not necessarily be their best friend but you can provide a very positive role model. That was another conclusion from our tennis coach study. When asked who should demonstrate, most coaches would respond technically – 'I do, because I want them to see the shape of the shot'. The best coaches, however, attached a whole lot more to the same action …

> Well I demonstrate; so they can see the shape of the shot but more importantly so they can see how I expect them to behave: how hard I work; how I cope with making mistakes, with frustration and so on.

The point here is that the good coach will use as many means as possible to communicate standards and behaviours to his/her players. Telling is only one option, and rarely the best, especially when used as the only method.

Similar principles apply to parents on how, when and why they chat through sports stuff with their child. Once again, clarity is king, so ensuring that what you say is sending consistent messages: consistent to what you have said before *and also* what the coach is pushing. Even more importantly, however, be careful with the emotions you are sending and what is received (the two might be rather different!). The long car ride home after a game, match, training session or performance can be an accident black spot for your relationship with your child. S/he can be both frustrated and upset with how things panned out. Often, your criticisms, however well-meant or kindly put, can be the last straw on the camel's back. The consequent blow up and stony silence has ruined many a weekend, so be warned.

Communications are often best left for a while and the best clue to when to talk and when to look out of the window is your child him/herself. Get used to asking whether they would like to talk it through, make a positive comment about how much *you enjoy* watching them play then leave it to them to ask for input. Spending time away from the sports setting to set this up is a great investment. Knowing that you appreciate their feelings and that you are there for them when they want it is likely to generate a really positive relationship. Similar 'rules of the game' can be established around what you say/shout at games. Dave always used to get a row from his netball playing daughters until he woke up, smelt the coffee and started to play the game by *their* rules!

Early specialisation versus early focus

So, assuming that communications are well established and working effectively, what should you be encouraging your young athlete to do? Specifically, and this is very much a topic of hot debate, should s/he be specialising early in whichever sport or activity they show potential in?

There is lots of publicity and discussion around the concept of early specialisation. The general agreement seems to be that this isn't a good thing in the long run, with many authors suggesting that it leads to early success but later burnout. What is not mentioned, however, or at least far far less, is the suggestion of early diversification or, more exactly, what the young athlete should focus on in the early stages of their career.

A lot of the work in this area comes from a German researcher Arne Güllich. For example, in 2011 Güllich reported on an excellent study completed with over 1,500 world-class German athletes. With one big caveat (which we will come back to later), he found that as an average, early specialisation did generate early success but was also associated with less senior achievement. In contrast, early and high-level involvement in sport, though associated with less success in the eventual target sport, was associated with high levels of success in that target activity. In simple terms, an athlete who was eventually very successful in, say rowing, would often be characterised by lots of training and commitment to other sports when they were younger. Interestingly, the volume or amount of training these early diversifiers completed was often more or less the same as the early specialisers – just spread across more activities.

In similar fashion to much of the content in this book, Güllich asks where this 'benefit' may come from. Perhaps, he suggests, early diversification offers young athletes a chance to find what sports they are best at (Áine covers this idea later in Chapter 13)? Or maybe the diverse early experience was good for motor skill development (see Chapter 4)? Or perhaps the diverse challenges early on generated positive learning in the youngsters which benefited them later whilst also helping them to avoid the pressures of early commitment to just one activity. Given our PCDE approach (see Chapter 6), this last one seems particularly attractive to us. Whatever the reason, however, (and we suggest that all three might apply) the idea that early involvement in and commitment to a variety of activities might be bene-ficial is an important one. In fact, we would go even further to suggest that such involvement can also benefit non-elites through developing all the tools for a life-time of sport and activity involvement.

It is important to note the big caveat which Güllich mentions, before consider-ing the implications of these ideas. First, the caveat … in his data, Güllich stressed that there were a number of different pathways which athletes had taken on their route to the top. In other words, whilst the overall effects (averaged across many individuals) were in favour of diversification, there were some who specialised early and made it to the top. This variation is important and means that there will always be examples of individuals who started young and achieved elite status. Second, whilst Güllich's data covered a wide variety of sports, there might still be a bit of a grey area in terms of high-skills sports, e.g. most team games or activities such as gymnastics, judo or boxing. Once again, the argument of variation applies. You will always find examples of very successful 'late entrants'. Perhaps the best com-promise is that, especially for skill sports which need a long time to develop, the target sport should be one of those that the athlete focuses on early, but not as an exclusive 'this and nothing else'.

This certainly provides a way to optimise benefits in sports where the economic fact is that early specialisation is a necessity. In the UK, football is the best example of this, with children as young as six getting involved in very structured pro-grammes. Our call would be to maintain balance and diversification by keeping the child involved in a variety of activities. Not too much, of course, or the child *will* end up permanently tired! For a number of reasons, the same few children seem to be good at everything, with them becoming the rope in a tug of war between competing sports. That said, however, good development pathways are increasingly seeing the importance of keeping it broad. Certainly, a breadth of activity is a feature of the academies we work in, and the variation is showing some real benefits. For the moment, however, the message seems clear. Early focus on a variety of activities seems, *on average*, the best way forward.

Are there *really* any early specialisation sports?

Continuing our argument from the previous section, one must ask whether there are any sports for which early specialisation is an *essential*. As with so much else in this book, the answer is complicated! As we suggested above, high-skill sports would seem to benefit from a longer pipeline. There is also a genuine issue for those who start slightly later in such sports, as the inevitable 'playing catch up' can be very demotivating, especially if this takes place at the very impression-conscious adolescent phase! In other words, the need for early specialisation in many sports may be a psycho-social issue, relating to how the individual's need to feel competent may discourage him or her from entering an environment in which everyone else seems way ahead.

That said, with a couple of very notable exceptions, we don't think there is a bio-psycho argument for *any* sport as early specialisation. In other words, a sport where an early start is essential for bio (e.g. body size) and/or psychomotor (e.g. skill development) reasons. Our exceptions relate to the different disciplines of gymnastics, where small size is an advantage to learning moves whilst the early establishment of skills is important, simply because there is 'so much to learn'. The fact that there are always some individuals who, even though they take up the sport later in life, can still achieve elite status seems to support this idea. So what does this mean for parents and coaches?

We cover this in a lot more detail in Chapter 9. For the moment, however, just reflect on the ideas presented above. Parents *and* coaches should think carefully when the youngster has an opportunity to specialise early. In some ways, this is an evaluation of their chances of success: making an informed cost-benefit decision to see whether this is the optimum arrangement. As such, all parties should be looking at the risks, many of which are outlined in this book, as well as the benefits, which are very often quite prominent and pressing. As Chapter 9 shows, beware the ego traps which can entice both coach and parent towards an over-early recruitment. As a key take home from this section, however, please recognise that, whilst there are very few bio-psycho arguments in favour of early specialisation, the realities of the child's self-esteem and the politico-economic situation must also be considered.

The rise and fall and rise of talent

As a final (for many) consideration, it is worth briefly considering other options that might become available. Once again, there is a crucial need to consider each child as a single case. Even though talent development is often, conveniently, spoken about in terms of stages (as we do in this book), the development process is unpredictable, individualised and dynamic. Chapter 9 will examine how effective Talent Development Environments (TDEs) should equip young athletes with the early experiences to facilitate this non–linear development (and the consequences of failing to do so). For the moment, however, what other considerations are there which might play a part in your decisions?

In simple terms, if you are concerned about your child/athlete proceeding to the top, or maybe even just realising their full potential, you need to consider the consequences of dropping out, taking a break or transferring between sports. If there is one thing that *is* clear about talent development, it is the non–linear pathway. Each individual will take a different and almost unique path as they develop. Furthermore, as Chapter 14 will show, the pathway is not only often bumpy; it *needs* to be if the athlete is to achieve at the top level. So, given that the pathway will include a number of rises and falls, what does this mean for staying with the programme?

Such thinking is surprisingly common. It is clearly not an issue for younger ages, but many developing athletes think long and hard on their choice of university. Will this course and location offer me the support and quality coaching that I need? Is there a club close enough that I can join or are the university setups good enough? In simple terms, people often think about an early career break in their sport. The question is, are these really effective? In a lower–level but still often difficult decision, children will often lose interest (or feign losing interest) in an activity which they have apparently enjoyed and done well at for several years. Once again, why might *this* occur and what are the implications?

Of course, in both cases there might be an entirely logical reason and chain of thinking underlying the question. We know of several elites who took the decision to prioritise study over sport, spent a successful few years doing something else (study or career move), then returned to eventual success. Growth spurts, moving house or changing interests are equally valid reasons lower down the pathway. For those less clear-cut arguments, however, are there any real long-term costs of premature drop out *or* drop in?

Well, the short answer is yes! Cases of children 'coming back' to activities are very rare. They are, usually positively, lively and into new things. This isn't an argument to stick at things but the associated skills and attitude (think of what we spoke about in Chapter 3) might be something that you want to engender. Consequently, talking through decisions up front and 'doing some deals' might make the drop out (or desire to drop in) a more positive experience than it otherwise might be. Children will often 'come and go' in their enthusiasm for an activity, just as (although not *always* because) their performance will wax and wane because of all sorts of variables, including growth spurts, 'sticking points' in skill development or 'just because'! Reflecting this, developing some 'rules of engagement' is a good preface to taking up a new activity. 'If you want to join this club, then I expect you to stay for the whole term' would be one such 'rule'. Without it, kids may come and go with alarming speed, leaving the poor indulgent parent with a veritable jumble sale of kit for assorted sports. Whilst this may please those who sell it, coaches will also find it difficult to cope with such coming and going. Indeed, high turnover in a club is usually associated with less than fair treatment for the middle-order kids. The best will get attention because the coach wants to push them on; the newbies will get attention to make sure that they are inducted as soon as possible. Meanwhile, the middle-order performers tend to get ignored. It is worthwhile reflecting on how many of these middle-order children eventually come through as Superchamps (see line 4 in Table 7.1); ignore them and possibly lose them at your peril!

In closing this section, consider the implications of line 5 in Table 7.1. Coping with and pushing through discouraging setbacks is a mark of eventual Superchamps, whilst falling away and whinging at the first hurdle ('It's not fair …') is a sign for concern. We would stress that this is an important message even if your child/athlete is not destined for stardom. Pushing through disappointment is a key life skill which, unfortunately but inevitably, we will all need. So, decisions to give up on or take up, new activities should be a more carefully considered process than it often is. Commitment is another important attribute which children can learn (and coaches develop) as they go through the 'suck it and see' process.

Expert perspective on Chapter 7

Anne Pankhurst has spent her professional career in coach education, including spells as the Lawn Tennis Associations' Coach Education Director 1994–2004, USTA's Coach Education Manager 2006–2009, and Coach Education Consultant to USA Football 2009–2010. She currently consults to Professional Tennis Registry, Virgin Active and the USTA.

This chapter discusses several issues that are highly pertinent to the development and wellbeing of young athletes. As a coach, and also as a parent of one junior and senior international player and of another who was highly successful in several sports, my understanding of the research underpinning the issues in this chapter has been invaluable. As a coach educator in two different nations, I am very aware of the necessity of coaches and parents having quality information about athlete development. However, as a (relatively recent) talent identification and development researcher, I am acutely aware that research outcomes do not reach the people who need them, i.e. coaches and parents. Thus, much valuable information on issues such as those raised never become applied to the next generation of young athletes. This seems to be because coaches of young players tend to apply their experience of a sport and knowledge from their coach education courses – assuming both to be valuable. Yet their experience is simply theirs and coach education courses rarely incorporate up-to-date research information. Parents, however, are frequently new to the sport in which their child is involved, and are unlikely to understand the 'systems' (especially the competitive ones!). Further, parents are usually unlikely to have another child involved at the 'performance' level in any sport – so their experience base is very limited. Parents seek guidance from the coach – and so the low-quality information on talent development in young athletes continues!

My personal and professional experience helps me discuss some of the issues raised in the chapter. I have experienced several large-scale talent iden-tification programmes in different sports governing bodies, for children as young as 7–9 years of age. The apparent (and mistaken) assumption of such programmes is that the capacities needed by adult athletes in a sport can be seen and tested in young children! Further, training them systematically will ensure adult success! Both research (and experience) indicates all of this to be very rarely true. High training volumes and intensity levels are endemic in many talent development programmes and are closely followed by inappropri-ate challenges being imposed on young athletes. This is further compounded by coaches and parents doing their best to make sure young athletes avoid the (very valuable) 'bumpy road'!

The issue is that of giving feedback positively and qualitatively to young athletes is very important. Dave's story of his daughter's netball resonates strongly with me. An Elton John CD was purchased by my son at the beginning of a long car journey home, just to keep me quiet after he lost a final in a tour-nament he should have won!! Cleary applying the research governing feed-back was not a personal strength!

Early specialisation is a very important issue. I would cite the research of one tennis nation that found that every player in that country who became world ranked had been 'on the radar' at 14 years of age – the flip side being that before 14 years of age, the overwhelming majority of juniors 'on the radar' never 'made it'. Further, there is much research evidence (and my professional experience) that supports the notion of very negative effects on the quality of life for young athletes who specialised in a single sport at a young age.

Finally, my own research indicates that positive relationships between coaches, parents and sport governing bodies, together with a sound under-standing and application of the relevant research outcomes by all three parties, are essential for high-quality athlete development programmes and conse-quent athlete success. The challenge now is to dissipate the underpinning knowledge – this chapter goes a long way to help meet that challenge!

In conclusion

Our message through this chapter is that there are a wide variety of consequences, both positive and negative, for the choices taken at this age and stage. Notably, parents should be making decisions based around the longer-term benefits (both sporting and attitudinally) for their children. In similar fashion, coaches can make an enormous 'generic' contribution, even if many of the children they help to develop will 'benefit' other sports, and other coaches. This is just one of the reasons why we fully endorse the idea of specialist youth coaches, people whose expertise is just as recognised and valued as those who work at the top of the performance pyramid. We look at the characteristics of such individuals later in the book. For the moment, however, try to be, or to find, such coaches for your children. They are worth their weight in gold!

References

Collins, D., MacNamara, Á. and McCarthy, N. (2016). Super champions, champions and almosts: important differences and commonalities on the rocky road. *Frontiers in Psychology*, 11 January. Available as free download: http://journal.frontiersin.org/article/10.3389/fpsyg.2015.02009/full.

Güllich, A. (2011). Training quality in high-performance youth sport. Conference Paper. Available as free download: www.researchgate.net/publication/235959251_Training_Quality_in_High-Performance_Youth_Sport.

PART IV

Entering the pathway

In every performer's pathway there comes a stage when they specialise and enter a (more or less) structured pathway. For our purposes, we will consider an academy setting as one which provides specifically targeted TD support to a selected group. In the real world, recruitment and selection of young performers into these academies is as much a strategic and resource issue as a performance one; you want to find the best 'potential' in the hope that these individuals will develop into the best performers in your sport (or club) and you can beat your competitors. There is only a limited amount of resources to go around, so how can you get the best return for your investment? The first chapter in this part of the book examines this recruitment process from the perspective of both those who 'make it' into the system and those who fail to be selected. We offer some suggestions about how sports might do this better recognising the realities of the competitive environment. For example, what do you do if you find yourself working in an environment that persists with early specialisation and early recruitment into the pathway? Professional football clubs, for example, still recruit from as young as seven years of age. If this is the case, what do you need to do to overcome some of the pitfalls of early recruitment? We provide guidance as to how coaches and parents might navigate these realities and optimise the experience for the young performer. Examples are provided of how you might provide a diversified sport experience within a (seemingly) specialised pathway – essentially how you might expose young performers to a range of activities and sports so their potential is not limited by an overly narrow focus on one sport or inappropriate training volumes.

We go on to explore what an effective Talent Development Environment (TDE) looks like and the long-term principles that *should* underpin a quality TDE. For coaches, this should help you evaluate what you are doing against the long-term development of the performer. For parents, this information should help you make informed decisions about quality when choosing academies or talent development environments.

8

THE RECRUITMENT PROCESS

Plusses and pitfalls

The realities of talent identification: what do you need to consider?

The sports and National Governing Bodies (NGBs) that you work for, or your children are involved with, are under considerable pressure to be successful at all stages of the pathway. This may be because of funding, inter-sport competition for athletes or even misinformed stakeholders over-estimating the importance of winning and short-term success. Reflecting this, all sports and clubs focus (to a greater or lesser extent) on the selection of young athletes in the hope that they are unearthing the next superstar. In this chapter, we will present some of the strategic and tactical dimensions to TID that influence recruitment and the decisions made about selection and deselection. Given the financial and resource constraints that are a reality of sport, these have significant real-world *and* practical implications on *how* and *why* coaches and sports select athletes at various stages of the TID pathway. Understanding this, and knowing what to do to counter the pitfalls, gives you a good chance to beat the system! For coaches, it will help inform your decisions about who and when to select. For parents, it should help you understand why, or why not, your child gets recruited and how to optimise either experience.

Even though the limitations of early specialisation are (we hope!) recognised, it is fair to say that there are some good reasons why sports persist with recruiting very young performers. For example, given the financial cost of buying professional adult soccer players it makes sense that professional football academies contract large numbers of players at a young age. This is true for a number of reasons. First, that player may turn into the next Ronaldo and, having signed the player at a young age, the club is making a significant investment for a relatively small initial outlay. Second, in the competitive marketplace, identifying potentially talented players at a young age, and contracting them to *your* club or sport, means that they are not available to other clubs or sports. Of course, the financial resources available to professional football clubs are not mirrored in most other sports and therefore the same issues may not be at play. However, no matter what context you are working in, there are finite coaching resources, money, facilities and even exposure to competition available. Simply, the TID pathway cannot sustain everyone. At some point, you need to select, and deselect, athletes from your pathway. In practical terms, TI is about filtering input in order to optimise resources. How do you choose who will give you the best return on your investment? Indeed, the choices made about *how*, *when* and *what to identify* will have important implications for the efficacy of the TD pathway.

How to select athletes for your pathway?

Most children start in sport because their parents choose their activity and the club or context for them. As they move along the TD pathway and things start to get more competitive, clubs and sports get more selective about who participates. Trials, selection camps and screening days are used to select and stream participants into teams. Unfortunately, a lot of the time we tend to select young performers for reasons that are pretty unrelated to long-term success. You will be familiar with the use of trials, or reaching a certain performance level, as ways your activity selects performers for representative teams, whether that is at county, regional or international level. More formal testing protocols have also been used which attempt to identify individuals with the potential to excel in sport using batteries of physiological and skill testing (e.g. Sport Interactive – Scotland, sportscotland and Sports Council Northern Ireland, 1997; Talent Search – Australia). All of these tools are based almost entirely on current performance (i.e. how well an athlete performs at that particular moment in time) or the possession of anthropometry which matches an ideal template based on current successful elites. They use current performance as a proxy for mature performance and rely very much on the 'coach's eye'. Although performance or anthropometric 'snapshots' might well be useful monitoring techniques for coaches – they give good information about progress and performance in relation to others or past history – they fail to capture the potential for future development. The bottom line is that these TI measures are mistaking potential for talent and are as likely to miss out on potentially talented performers as identify those with potential.

By now, you will have heard the clear message that elite performance is not necessarily preceded by superior performance as a junior and therefore it is almost impossible to predict who will actually make it to the top. In fact, trying to identify young performers based on factors that underpin success at adult levels of performance does not have much merit or supporting evidence. The variables of speed, size and strength, for example, that typify TI models are highly unstable due to the influence of physical maturity and experience during development. Therefore, the earlier you select, the less likely you are to identify someone who will 'make it'. However, given the finite resources at your disposal, you can't keep everyone in your talent system so you have to make choices about who and when you select.

What are the risks associated with TI? These can be broadly understood as follows.

1   *Inclusion error.* TI, especially unidimensional batteries administered with young athletes, may identify and select athletes who, though performing well at the time of selection, do not have the potential to become elite performers. The anthropometric variables that underpin TI models may discriminate performance pre-puberty, but lose their significance once late developers mature and catch up with their early maturing peers. These athletes can be termed *false positives* and once selected can use up valuable investment in terms of time, money and resources that is unlikely to pay dividends at the elite level. Given that every talent pathway has a limited capacity, the recruitment of 'false positives' is likely to take space away from athletes with higher potential but lower levels of current performance (at the time of selection). Of course, it is hard to ignore these athletes who 'look the part' and are outperforming (at the time of selection) their peers. As we will talk about later in the chapter, the TID system that recognises these issues *and* does something about it as part of its coaching is likely to be the most successful.

2   *Exclusion error.* The 'flip-side' is that one-dimensional and static TI measures are likely to exclude potentially talented but late maturing children from development opportunities. Potentially talented performers may be excluded from your pathway because of inappropriate identification measures that are based on criteria designed to identify current performance rather than potential for development. These can be termed *false negatives* as they have high levels of potential not captured by TI measures placing a strong value on current performance, or a current physical profile. For example, it is unlikely that a young Usain Bolt would have been identified as a world-class 100-metre runner based on his physical profile! This 'exclusion error' might not be such a problem if you have a rich and deep talent pool. However, it does become an issue if you are putting all your eggs in one basket and selecting small numbers of athletes onto your pathway.

The important thing to consider here is: what level of risk are you willing to take? Is it too risky for your sport to miss out on potentially talented athletes (false negatives) due to a small initial talent pool? Can your talent system cope with a large number of athletes and therefore is it okay to include false positives in the hope that you have unearthed one gem? We will discuss these points later in the chapter but for now keep in mind that selecting athletes is a risky business so you need to acknowledge these risks and design your system to counter them as best you can.

Talent identification – understanding the butterfly effect

As we have spoken about elsewhere in this book, a child's relative age (Relative Age Effect, RAE) is one factor that influences the likelihood of a child being identified as talented; that is, the relationship of the individual's birth date to the age grouping system of their activity. Children born in the first half of the selection year are much more likely to be perceived and identified as 'talented' using performance and/or anthropometric identification measures as they are more cognitively and physically mature than those born later in the selection year (Helsen et al., 2000). The overemphasis on success at age-group level in sport, where competition is organised in 12- or 24-month age-bands, exacerbates the issue of talent spotting since selection is determined by a child's current physical attributes rather than their potential to develop in the future. If the emphasis within your system is on having the best Under 14 team, then you will select those young athletes that allow you to be successful within that age-group. This leads to a RAE, in youth sport at least, since it is likely that the best performing players are older and therefore more physically mature than their relatively younger peers. We are not suggesting strategic family planning as the way to get your child into the system! However, it is worth noting how making crude selections based on current ability is likely to have a long-term impact on your talent pool.

But what effect do these decisions have in the long term? The selected children are given access to training and development resources such as coaching and competition experiences that accelerate their progress. This is because coaches, parents and teachers are more likely to support individuals whose early successes display promise of potential; it is hard to ignore these apparently obvious signs of 'talent' and, because there are limited resources to go around, the door of opportunity for younger, less physically mature or less successful players is closed. This 'butterfly effect', where the effect of a small ability difference at a particular point in time leads to positive interactions, can have dramatic differing consequences for the individual's development. In turn, relatively younger children within the age cohort find it more challenging to progress and often drop out completely. The bigger player, for example, has a greater chance of progressing based simply on the fact he is physically bigger. In simple terms, if you miss out on the snapshot, it is extremely hard to get back in the picture!

Of course, relative age is not the only factor contributing to inequality in sport selection. Research indicates that if a child hasn't been exposed to similar activities, or lacks the family or social support to engage in the given domain, they are less likely to perform well in TI testing and as a result their ability may well remain undetected. Consider also the number of private-schooled athletes who competed for Great Britain at the 2016 Olympics. The over-representation of privately educated athletes in Team GB (a third of 2016 medallists were educated at private schools) suggest that socio-cultural factors play a role. Family support, relatively high socioeconomic status, schooling and family structure are amongst the variables that mediate the likelihood of a young athlete being identified as 'talented' in the first place. All these factors promote positive early performance and success in sport (and increase the likelihood of selection), but they do not reflect an individual's true potential. Again, given that the aim of TD should surely be on long-term development, acknowledging the inequality of the field during key selection points is an important step. Essentially you need to be aware of, and account for how these issues impact on selection in order to improve the decisions you make about who, and perhaps most importantly who not, to select.

Who to select? The danger of betting on the wrong horse!

So if TI is a matter of weighing up the costs and benefits of who you select, what are the implications? We know that in youth teams the RAE is prevalent. There are consistent asymmetric birthdate patterns in most underage teams – essentially more children born during the first quarter of the selection year are likely to be selected than children born in the fourth quarter. This is generally attributed to significant physical differences in children who are born just before, or after, the cut-off date; relatively older athletes demonstrate a performance advantage at early identification points. The relatively older athlete demonstrates more desirable phys-ical attributes that are generally aligned to senior-level performance markers and this influences their selection.

But is this an issue in terms of long-term development? Interestingly, even though there is robust evidence to suggest RAE is a significant factor for talent identification, the RAE bias is reduced in senior elite-level sport. Simply, when elite-level teams are examined the RAE seems to disappear. In fact, there seems to be an RAE-reversal with players born late in the selection cycle being represented to a greater extent than their relatively older counterparts. So, is being relatively younger actually an advantage in the long term? The answer seems to be yes, but …! If you are relatively young and get into the TD system, the outlook looks good. It would seem that the 'conversion rate' of relatively young athletes is better than for their relatively older peers. Relatively older players have also been shown to have greater exposure to injury than their relatively younger peers and higher salaries have also been observed for relatively younger athletes at the performance level. If this is the case, let's explore how you might exploit this in your TD pathway.

The important question that this information poses is what does the relatively younger athlete experience that results in a relatively high conversion to elite levels of performance? It may be that relatively younger athletes experience greater chal-lenge during the development phases, occurring due to life experiences or the nature of pathway experiences (cf. Collins and MacNamara, 2012), and therefore receive more 'benefit' from the experience. From a coaching perspective, how can we learn from this and implement it with all our performers? It seems that a rockier, more challenging route to the top, as experienced by relatively young athletes, may be a key facilitator for success as it promotes the development of the grit, mental toughness and PCDEs required at the elite level. If this is the case, how do you ensure that the relatively older athlete also encounters the developmental challenges that will aid their long-term development? We will discuss this 'rocky road' and how you might implement it further in Chapter 14. For now, the take-home message is that the factors that influence selection into the pathway are rarely the same factors associated with performance at the end of the pathway. Recognising this should influence not only your selection decisions – who you select – but also the experiences that you give the athletes once they are on your pathway.

Bio-banding: a (misplaced) solution for the RAE?

Recently, there have been a number of innovations that have tried to address the RAE in youth sport. As one example, some football academies in the UK have implemented specific trials and training sessions for late births. Purportedly, this is to allow scouts to view relatively young players in a fairer way as they are removed from relatively older peers. Indeed, many sports and academies have different groups for late and early developers as a way to cater for maturational differences. This categorisation may have beneficial aspects for both early and late maturing athletes. For the former group, grouping similar size players together is proposed to stop them relying on their size and strength to succeed and instead forces them to develop the technical skills they will need when relatively younger players catch up with them.

A further development has been the rise of a phenomenon called 'bio-banding': players are grouped based on their physiological development rather than age. Of course, despite the packaging, bio-banding is not a new approach. New Zealand rugby has for years grouped rugby teams according to weight rather than age because Maori and Polynesian children tend to develop faster than their white counterparts. We would contend that 'good' coaches and PE teachers have always done this where players are moved up and down age-groups so they get an appropriate development experience. Indeed, despite the face-validity of some aspects of bio-banding, it (and the enthusiastic but uncritical adoption of the approach by some clubs and sport) seems to reflect the 'scienciness' that we spoke about in Chapter 1. Categorising based on biological age rather than chronological age does not address all the inequalities involved in youth sport and seems as crude a measure as the one it is trying to replace.

Bio-banding may seem like a way to level the playing field but is it really a good idea? After all, big players play against small players at the elite level all the time. We would suggest that some of the ideas underpinning the approach are worthwhile, but implementing these as part of the wider TD process and ensuring effective coaching and selection as part of that approach would be a more useful way forward. For example, differences in cognitive and emotional maturity, both important determinants of development, are not addressed by this approach. Why reinvent the wheel? Carefully managing the challenge, providing opportunities to be 'big' and 'small' at different stages of the pathway, and addressing all aspects of maturity (cognitive, social, physical, emotional) would seem a more effective and balanced diet. Removing the challenge, as can happen with a bio-banding approach, may lead to taking away the development of the grit, determination and resilience of the late developer. Likewise, perhaps a reduced focus on short-termism would ensure that the relatively older player has a chance to develop the skills needed for long-term success. The TD pathway needs to cater, at every stage, for all players; not just for the one struggling but also for the high-performing (even if it is just at that time) player. We would suggest that effective TD systems, and good coaching, do this as part of what they do and innovations such as 'bio-banding' may be more academic rather than practitioner-focused.

When to select? Understanding the Tiger effect and early specialisation

It may well be that you wish to recruit young athletes into your sport for a host of reasons; if they sign to play football, they can't play rugby; if they join your club, they can't join a league rival. Even if you are aware of, and acknowledge the risks and limitations presented so far, you are faced with a conundrum; if you don't select at a young age, it is likely that other sports (or competing clubs in your sport) that do engage in early talent selection will attract lots of athletes. Essentially, you could lose a pool of athletes to sports or clubs that offer early engagement opportunities. From a parent's perspective, you don't want your son or daughter to miss out on developmental opportunities that others are getting. This drives the need to select in order to remain competitive in the marketplace for young athletes. So, if the system is a driver for early selection *and* you recognise the risks of false positives and false negatives in your selection decisions, how do you maximise your return on investment of those in your system? We offer some guidelines here about how to optimise the experience. Again, as elsewhere in this book, the principles remain the same but you will need to think how these apply in your sport or context.

In general, the pool of players at the foundation of the pathway should be kept as broad as possible; in a culturally popular sport like football, with the potential earnings that may accrue from a successful career, recruitment is not generally an issue. In minority, or less popular sports, the initial talent pool is much smaller and you might have to be even more careful about selection and deselection decisions to maintain this depth. This is especially true when there is competition from other sports for the same athlete and this is often a factor that drives sports to promote early specialisation as a means of 'keeping' an athlete in their sport. It also seems that the decisions about early selection are more often driven by the system (this is how we have always done it!) rather than any evidence to support its effectiveness. If this is the case for you, the important question to ask yourself is whether the selection and deselection decisions are being made for long-term development or short-term success?

There is also a perception that the earlier a young athlete specialises in a sport, the greater the likelihood that they will be successful; this perception is supported by the 10,000-hour 'rule' and success stories like Tiger Woods, Rory McIlroy or the Williams sisters. Of course, and as you can probably account for from your own experiences, for every Tiger Woods there are thousands of individuals who don't make it and are no longer active in sport at all, let alone at an elite level. The case against early specialisation is made in Chapter 7 but consider here how, if you *do* select very young athletes (for the strategic and tactical reasons we have already discussed), how do you provide them with the experiences they need to translate their potential into performance?

Football is a good example of a sport that selects very young players – in fact, one professional football academy in the UK recently advertised a talent identification day for Under 6s! Given that there is little, if any, evidence for the requirement of early specialisation in football, it seems that systemic drivers force clubs to make these decisions – if we don't recruit him, someone else will! If my son doesn't join the academy as an Under 7, he will never make it! There are, of course, some truths in both these examples but as we explained with Hume's Law in Chapter 1, just because something happens, doesn't mean it should! That caveat notwithstanding, if you work in a sport that selects very young athletes what can you do to make the most of that situation?

Hopefully, the need for a long-term agenda in TID is a clear message at this stage. In this case, the focus shifts from the identification of players (with a recognition of the limitations of the selection process), towards a consideration of the development of the players – what experiences are offered to the young players that may counteract the limitations of early selection and specialisation. Paul Waldron, Education Officer and Foundation Phase lead at Chelsea FC, describes the selection process at Chelsea FC and how the foundation phase is designed to provide the most appropriate starting point for development. The variety of opposition (domestic and international), different formats of the game, tournament play, and even international travel all represent some clever ways to develop robust players. Carefully engineered, this pathway helps develop not just the technical and tactical skills required but also prepare the players for the life of a professional player.

Expert perspective on Chapter 8

Paul Waldron has worked for Chelsea FC for over 20 years in both a part time and full time capacity. He has coached players in every age group from Under 9s up to Under 16s and now leads the Foundation Phase. Having spent 15 years as a PE teacher, he also has responsibility for liaising with the players' schools.

Working in a very competitive environment (both in terms of recruitment and performance), I am very aware of many of the issues raised in this chapter. At Chelsea FC, we have addressed some of the 'pitfalls' of selection by ensuring we offer a very rich and varied experience (even before they enter the pathway) that prepares them to progress through each phase.

Foundation Phase overview

At Chelsea FC, the Foundation Phase is comprised of 65 players from Under 9 through to Under 11. The remit is to 'build a player', i.e. provide him with a programme that will develop the technical, tactical, psychological, physical and social skills and ensure that he fulfils his potential. By so doing, the player should be able to continue progressing in the Youth Development Phase (Under 12–Under 16).

Recruitment

The process for finding the best footballing talents starts long before they are offered an Academy registration with the club. A wide scouting network ensures that young players in the south-east of England are identified, monitored and, if deemed gifted enough, offered the opportunity to train in a local CFC Development Centre. At Under 7 and 8, those identified as potential Academy players are invited to train as an 'Advanced Group' and it is from this cohort that the club will offer registrations to form the next Under 9 squad. Therefore, some players may well have had two years of 'Chelsea' training prior to their first season of Academy football. Age bias is very much acknowledged and therefore players who may lack physicality at this stage are still recruited and given the time to develop as 'slow burners'.

The Programme

So how do we go about building the player? The process involves a training programme that is detailed, diverse, challenging and enjoyable! In terms of football-specific objectives, time is spent developing basic techniques to ensure that players improve two-footedness, receiving and attacking skills, ball striking and ball manipulation. They need to put these techniques into opposed situations to nurture their skills and begin developing a winning mentality both as an individual and as part of a team. Players need to be able to comprehend tactical considerations, so playing in every position is a way of developing their understanding of the 'geography' of the pitch. This could also be important further down the line if a change in position is likely to be their best chance of becoming a scholar or even a professional.

A games programme that offers a wide range of formats is also an essential part of their football education. Players need to be able to cope with playing on different sized pitches, with teams of varying numbers, i.e. 5v5 up to 11v11. While the emphasis in the FP is on development, there is a place for competitive experiences to be included in the programme. A number of tournaments are organised within the Premier League games programme, but to offer diversity, the players are provided with the opportunity to play in at least one tournament in Europe each season. The mindset for a tour is different in that there is a challenge to win the tournament and this offers a real insight into the character of each player when playing with this added pressure. It is on these trips that *social* skills (or a lack of them) are evident as players spend a significant amount of time together.

Over the last five years, the programme has incorporated conditioning activities to ensure that players increase their movement vocabulary. This exposes the players to a very wide range of activities and dovetails with our recommendation to parents that players participate in other sports. Developing the ability to move efficiently and effectively off either foot supports the

> player's 'two-footed' technical work and will hopefully provide him with the physical capabilities to meet the challenges of the modern game.
>
> The final part of the programme is the inclusion of psychological challenges. Focusing on a growth mindset and developing PCDEs enables us to create our own 'rocky road' and put the players under pressure. Clearly, some players thrive in these situations while others struggle, and this helps to identify those that need extra support and those that may need to be pushed further.

The varied diet of experiences described by Paul is more akin to the Deliberate Preparation that Dave spoke about in Chapter 4 than the early specialisation pathway that sometimes typifies sports like football. Indeed, even though they select players as young as seven years of age, many professional academies recognise the importance of sport diversification and build this into their offerings. For example, at Ajax Football Club in Holland, often touted as one of the world's best academies, young players spend 45 per cent of their time on activities outside football, with judo, gymnastics, track and field all forming a key part of the pathway. Even though the young player is selected at a very early age, the pathway is designed to give them a diversified sporting experience. What is the message here? If you do select early, you need to think deeply about the experiences you offer at the start of the pathway. The first goal should be developing an all-round, efficient mover and athlete (through a variety of means) before that athlete specialises.

In conclusion: how to do it better?

Given that you have to select athletes onto your talent pathway at some stage, it is important that you acknowledge, and where possible counter, the negative implications of early selection by providing an appropriate development environment catering for both early and late developers. While this may improve the conversion rate of junior to senior athletes for your pathway, done correctly it will almost certainly equip the young athletes with the skills and attitudes to stay involved at whatever level, or in whatever sport they choose. We look at the implications of this in terms of talent transfer in Chapter 13 but for the moment consider the extent to which the choices you make about selection are weighed towards long-term development rather than short-term success.

References

Collins, D. and MacNamara, Á. (2012). The rocky road to the top: why talent needs trauma. *Sports Medicine*, 42(11), 907–914.

Helsen, W. F., Hodges, N. J., Van Winckel, J. and Starkes, J. L. (2000). The roles of talent, physical precocity and practice in the development of soccer expertise. *Journal of Sports Sciences*, 18, 727–736.

9

ACADEMY PREPARATION

What works well (and doesn't)

Introduction

A successful Talent Development Environment (TDE) should nurture young athletes effectively enabling them to realise their full potential. Notably, the best TDEs will develop individuals who will often succeed in other clubs or setups, or even in other sports, by ensuring that each individual receives the optimum support for his or her profile. Even though that club or sport might not benefit, good TDEs do a service for the community, contributing to the general population as well as their own sport. Accordingly, the aim of this chapter is to consider and provide evidence of effective TDEs: what they look like, how they work and what parents and coaches should look for/work at to optimise returns, both general and specific. As a consequence, we try to provide parents and athletes with the evidence-base to make informed decisions about quality when choosing academies or TDEs. For coaches, we provide a checklist of 'things to think about' so that practice, and therefore outcome, is optimised.

The importance of the individualised, often unpredictable pathway that young athletes take as they progress has already been highlighted. Accordingly, we offer an understanding of key features of the TDE and how these should be operationalised to provide a player-centred approach towards the realisation of potential. Based on mechanistic principles, we first focus on the long-term principles that *should* underpin a quality TDE and, second, describe the principles of an effective TDE, and how they are operationalised in practice.

Effective TDEs – what does it take?

So, following this structure, the first thing to do is to examine what the academy setting should do. For our purposes, and reflecting the very varied ages at which various sports commit young performers to such structures, we will consider an academy setting as one which provides specifically targeted TD support to a selected group. In other words, academies generally select talent through some process, have regular evaluations of progress and, sometimes, re-evaluations of potential, and would usually involve some deselection. In our experience, young performers can find themselves in such an environment from as young as 6, right up to a 'first time' experience at 18 plus! The most crucial difference is the clearly stated aim of developing potential, coupled with the identification of the youngster as having some worth developing!

Preparing for and catering for non-linear development

The first thing to recognise is that good TDEs will make allowances for the non-linear nature of development. In Chapter 8, we described how several sports still apply a simple cut for more advanced training, often based on straightforward performance measures such as time or distance. Swimming would be one such sport – some (and we emphasise *some*!) academy setups taking on and dropping kids depending on whether they achieve (or don't) certain target times. As we have suggested in this book, however, this approach is anything but straightforward! Performance will be affected by a wide variety of measures, including maturation, motivation and luck. As another example, consider the data in Figure 9.1, which shows performance on the 'Bleep' or Shuttle Run Test which was commonly used (and still is by some) as a test of potential; in other words, a Talent Identification (TI) tool.

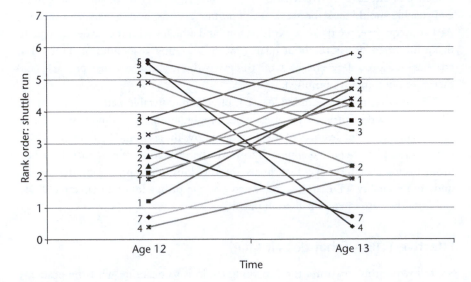

FIGURE 9.1 Repeat scores on the Shuttle Run Test

Remember that these are the same children, tested during a schoolday one year apart. There are several messages here, but the main one for our purposes is how some individuals went from 'hero to zero' or vice versa across the year. Not down to special training, preparation or extra motivation – just the way kids vary across time. *If* development was linear then the same kids would finish high or low in both tests. So the point is that things vary and in a non-systematic fashion. As a result, 'snapshots' of talent identification, a one-day test for example, can rarely if ever be effective. It is simply down to too many confounding variables (sleep the night before, car journey, luck, etc.) how well each individual will perform on *the* day!

So let's be clear. Any good academy or other TD setup will select on more than one observation, will take a longer-term view to ensure that day-to-day 'fluctuations' don't overly colour evaluations and an even longer one to acknowledge that youngsters will 'come and go' almost inevitably as they move along the development path.

Slower and better learning

Another important consideration for Academy impact relates to the styles of teaching/coaching used and how these will differentially impact the learners. This is nothing to do with the stuff on learning *styles*, which has been about for a while, is still part of many coaching qualification courses but has been largely discredited. No ... this relates to the coaching methods used and what they do to the speed and quality of learning.

So first of all, some important concepts about learning and three technical terms that you should understand. Learning can be looked at in three ways; that is someone will have learnt something when ... So what are they?

- *Acquisition*. Literally how quickly someone can get the skill down to a certain level of error. So, for example, someone could be considered to have learnt how to putt when they can get the ball in 7 times out of 10 from a set distance. As we will show below, this sounds fine but is rather limited.
- *Retention*. How well someone can store then remember how to do something. So, using our same putting test, can they still do the 7 times out of 10 performance two weeks later.
- *Transfer*. A very important but rather neglected measure. How well can someone take what they have learnt and apply it (transfer the knowledge) to a similar skill. So if they can putt 7 times out of 10 at 6 feet from the hole, can they quickly do the same from a different distance/on a bumpier green, etc.?

Obviously, quick acquisition is very appealing to coaches, parents and kids. 'Hey look ... I've only just started and already I can do this!' The trouble is that, especially in an academy setting, the young athletes need to remember skills from week to week (no point in having to reteach them every time) and, of course, take the basic skill and apply it to lots of different situations. For example, just passing a ball back and forth between two cones, however accurately you pass and trap/catch, is nothing like the very variable situation you are going to face in a game. The first looks very nice and tidy but the game just will not work unless you can vary (transfer) your new skill to pass and catch quickly and accurately over a variety of distances and in different ways.

Now here is the conundrum and it is shown in Table 9.1. Different coaching tools are better (or worse) for the different purposes.

We have chosen just three tools to demonstrate the differences; scheduling of practice, giving feedback and providing demonstrations: all common methods used by coaches, so a fair test. Crucially, however, all show differences. The basic rule is that making things obvious or 'simple' for the learner is great for rapid learning but not for the 'better' learning which leads to retention and transfer. In simple terms, it is that difficulty, and the effort that goes with it, that helps to establish a better memory for the learner. So scheduling practice in blocks of time lets the learner get into the groove of doing the skill. Offering lots of feedback means that s/he doesn't have to think about how the movement felt whilst providing a perfect (expert demo), usually by the coach, gives them a simple model to follow.

Sounds great, doesn't it? The problem is, however, that quality learning needs the brain to 'get engaged' with the material; to process it, twist it around and understand it. As a consequence, better learning (improved retention and transfer) results from spreading out and mixing up sessions so that the learner is forced to store then retrieve the skills from memory. Each 'retrieve–tweak–store' cycle improves the storage and the retrieval accuracy. Giving less feedback removes the chance for the learner to rely on the coach feedback (the so-called knowledge of results 'crutch') as s/he has to think for themselves what it felt like, how well things went and what to do next time. The coach questioning rather than telling is another support to this. As a consequence, the learner develops a better picture of what should (and shouldn't) be going on, leading to a better internal plan of the skill. The last, demonstration idea works in a similar way. If presented with a perfect demo, the learner just gets on with copying it. By contrast, looking at a number of different 'warts and all' demos makes the learner have

TABLE 9.1 Different outcomes from using different coaching tools

Tool	Coaching method	
	'Rapid' learning (acquisition)	'Better' learning (retention and transfer)
Scheduling	Blocked + massed	Random + distributed
Knowledge of Results (KR)	LOTS!!	LESS
	KR crutching	Reduced KR; bandwidth
Demonstrations	WATCH ME ... LIKE THIS	COULD BE LIKE THIS OR THIS OR ...
	'Expert' model	'Self/coping' model

to think about why the different outcomes occurred. Once again, a richer and more detailed internal picture is developed. The only problem that can occur here is motivation. These methods are harder and require more effort so the learner must stay focused for the benefits to occur. Lose focus and the benefits don't flow. In addition, because progress is apparently slower, getting fed up is a distinct possibility!

So is one method better than the other? Should coaches always stick to one side of Table 9.1 or the other? Well, once again the answer is 'it depends'. If you are in a situation where fast learning is needed, for example on a 'come and try it' weekend or a week-long skiing holiday, then the rapid learning options are best. In most academy situations, however, the young performer is assumed to be a longer-term project. Accordingly, better learning options are more suitable. Unfortunately a choice has to be made: you can't do both and get the best of both worlds; you end up with the worst! So, look for academy situations where the coaching is based on a clear methodology, which links to the stated aims. In short, coaches know *why* they are doing what they are doing!

One more quick word about learning. Many coaches have switched on to a 'constraints-based' approach. We won't go into all the technicalities of this. Suffice to say for the moment that the coach will use changes in the environment or the task to 'encourage' the learner into the desired movement pattern, rather than using long-winded verbal explanations. In itself, this is a great idea. Indeed, there is often a tendency for coaches to be rated (or even rate themselves) on the quantity of detailed information that they offer to the learner. This is, of course, a mistake – following detailed verbal instructions is both difficult and requires a lot of skill in the learner. It also will not promote the better learning which we have spoken about above. So, once again, look for coaches/be a coach who 'shapes' behaviour rather than offering detailed instruction on how to do every little bit of what is required.

Of course, this is covering a vast area with just a couple of paragraphs of content. The main message, however, is not to fall into the 'more explanation equals better coaching' trap. One caveat; we are convinced that better quality learning is associated with *understanding* the basics of the movement. The young athlete certainly doesn't need a degree in biomechanics and a detailed mathematical breakdown of how the skill works! They should, however, understand the fundamentals of the movement and, increasingly, be able to express these in their own words. When you get to even more complicated skills such as tactics, the understanding dimension becomes even more important. So, look for coaches/be a coach who avoids overuse of voice *but* rather predominantly uses a subtle blend of questioning and peer coaching (kids coaching each other) to ensure good levels of comprehension for what is to be achieved and why.

What else do they need?

The pre- and early academy phases are crucial in developing skills which will be needed on the journey, both as the athlete develops and, much later, as s/he peaks then moves on to other challenges. The roles played in shaping these skills and behaviours will vary with age and stage. At younger ages, parents will play the central role; as the athlete matures and progresses, others become more important, with the coach and the TDE (including peers) becoming the most important or powerful influences. This 'peer power' is just one of many reasons why all must attend to the social dynamic of the TDE. Academies are an excellent example of the 'one bad apple' parable. Make sure that standards are high and peers encourage positive behaviours across the group. More of this in subsequent chapters and in the subsequent 'What does it look like?' section of this one.

Good behaviours as their habits

For the moment, a few psycho-behaviours (our term for the combination of skills and attitude which can be observed in how people act) which can be effectively developed at this level. For a start, we return to the role of the parent discussed in Chapter 7: specifically, the need for the young athlete to do things for themselves. The point is that parents can demonstrate or model good behaviours and coaches can require them in supervised sessions but, in the end, the young performer needs to do things for her/himself. The work ethic, commitment and application of PCDEs presented earlier must become a *self*-driven process, not something to be done only when under supervision. Only then will the young athletes develop the confidence necessary to cope with the ever-increasing challenges which they will experience on the pathway to the top. For this and other reasons, we often use covert observation, watching from a distance or when pretending not to watch, as a big part of evaluation, both of athletes and coaches. You learn a lot when watching how the mice play when the cat is away!

Building on this, there should be a clear and well planned movement of authority towards the players. Clearly, this will vary according to the styles prevalent in each sport and country … team sports tend to be more authoritarian than individual, for example. Increasingly, however, athletes need to have a voice in making decisions about how they train, what they focus on and how they play. Accurate self-assessment is an essential precursor to being able to focus your own efforts on your own developmental needs, even if this is happening within a group-focused session. These skills enable the developing athlete to take what s/he needs, whilst also playing their role for the group. Even if the adult environment will involve a coach dominated 'style', athletes must know and be able to address their own strengths and weaknesses. Being both willing and able to address one's own development was a common feature of the Superchamps and Champions we talked about in Chapter 7. Almosts tended to leave it up to the coach whilst their parents tended to dictate/encourage/cajole them into practice.

A sense of proportion – care with sport as the only thing that counts

One other major need at this age/stage is for a balanced view of sports involvement. Now this is a bit more complicated than the work/life balance mantra beloved of lifestyle gurus. For us as committed sports athletes (albeit a few years back in Dave's case), we can quite understand that an athlete will get a bit down after a bad performance. If this happens at a major championships, national/international level or just the most important one to date, that 'bit down-ness' may even approach mild levels of clinical depression – that is a mental health issue for which you might fairly seek help from a doctor or other specialist. This is an understandable part of being very committed to one's sport, albeit that care needs to be taken, and you are just, if not more, likely to see this in a young performer as a seasoned senior international.

Our bigger concern is when sporting success becomes the *only* thing that matters – the one element by which the athlete sees his or her worth as being judged. The saying 'You are only as good as your last game' is pertinent here; this sole and overly heavy investment may well underlie many of the mental health issues in sportspeople which are increasingly making the headlines. In simple terms, if your sporting performance is the *only* way in which you rate and value yourself, self-esteem is likely to be very volatile, whilst retirement will hold all sorts of terrors as you are now clearly, by your own standards, a 'has-been'. This is not an exclusively sporting issue; many different callings show a similar challenge to people when they retire. The situation is even worse when that retirement is forced upon you – by injury or being sacked, for example.

Now you might be wondering why we are talking about this in a book on talent development. Isn't this a concern only for older athletes? Well no, not really, for three reasons. First, getting cut from your academy is an unfortunately common experience for many young athletes; initially identified as talented and signed with much fanfare, but later chopped from the programme with associated loss of face with one's peer group, often at exactly the age when peer approval is most key. Sensible parents and coaches will work hard to ensure that young performers have an informed view on their strengths and weaknesses *outside* the specific sport. For example, athletes cut from one of the academies that Dave works with have gone on to be senior internationals in other sports, whilst many others now work in the same sport as coaches or support specialists. In short, you are more than just what you play.

This also relates to the second reason. This 'sole identity' issue can be even more powerful for those who get through the academy process as a success. Life as a professional performer (in many areas including sport) can be overpowering in its demands and impositions on the athlete as an individual. All other aspects – relationships, preparation/saving for a life after sport, even your identity as anything other than a 'player' – can get buried as you focus exclusively on the challenge in front of you. When that challenge ends, you are forced into a re-evaluation of what you have actually achieved and what sort of future you have … and this can be a *very* challenging look in the mirror! Just as in the previous section, good habits of 'diversification' can be developed at this age by parents, coaches and peers, helping to ensure that the young athlete can develop interests and pride which are independent of their sport. This can be a massive help later when, inevitably, retirement happens or is imposed.

Our third and final reason relates to a construct called 'identity foreclosure'. Developed by psychologists in the US, but quickly seen as applicable worldwide, this idea relates to the tendency for those committed to an activity to 'put their eggs in one basket' and foreclose the development of their identity to focus solely on the one thing. As a result, their friendship group becomes solely about the activity; their self-worth is evaluated solely by how well they do at that one thing and social development (in relationships, for example) just gets lost. Interestingly, many athletes miss out on the experimentation in clothes, style, behaviour, etc. (Dave had long hair in the style of the day and a right plonker he looked too!), only to complete a 'delayed adolescence' in their twenties when they stop their sport – usually to the bemusement of their families! Once again, identity foreclosure can be limited by all concerned encouraging a broader base of interests.

So in summary, these three closely related challenges can all be countered by parents, coaches and peers encouraging interests and involvement outside the sporting arena. Don't misunderstand us – commitment and dedication are crucial, just not at the expense of everything else. Once again, this conscious diversification balanced against obsessive focus was a feature of the Superchamps in our study. It can be done successfully if you work at it!

Is the body ready for the shock of increased training? Preparatory fitness

Our final concern for the pre/early academy phase relates back to ideas in Chapter 2 and the need for specific kinds of 'preparatory fitness'. As we described, this will include a good range of General Motor Ability or GMA, together with a sound base level of fitness. Joint strength is a particular issue, especially in the more gangly youths who can often gain selection to academy structures by standing out physically amongst their peers.

Depending at what age the young athlete starts into specialist training, the 'growth spurt' issue can be a particular concern. Clearly, all young athletes experience growing challenge. Coaches can monitor for this by regularly measuring height or just watching for changes in body shape. Liaison with parents is another good idea as they can apply other tests. We have already spoken about Tanner stages earlier but even just watching for changes in appetite (food consumption goes up in anticipation of growth spurts) can work as an indicator.

The main thing is to ensure that the young athlete can take the training load of the academy, and is prepared for subsequent jumps in load as s/he gets older. Joint strength is a big factor here (physios will talk about 'integrity') and work on this should be a focus both before and during the academy challenge. General fitness to ensure a base for recovery is another good plan. The main thing is that fitness is assessed and addressed as part of the pre-training, induction and academy work processes.

Effective TDEs – what do they look like and how does it feel to be there?

So, given this range of topics, all of which should be apparent in a well run academy setup, how would that look? What should parents look for and coaches provide?

What to look for in a good academy, including whether to make the commitment

Well, for a start, it is worth looking at the culture – what Neil Bath at the Chelsea Academy calls 'what things are like around here'. Just as when visiting a school, parents can learn lots by watching the demeanour of the kids as they walk around. How do they deal with adults, with peers and with visitors? Watching training for some of the ideas presented above is another good idea; *but*, as a parent watching or a coach coaching, recognise that snapshots are never a good idea. Coaches will sensibly modify their methods from day to day and from player to player so that messages are sent and, hopefully, optimally effective. As a coach, you should be asking the 'why am I doing it *this* way' question quite a bit … not too much, as paralysis by analysis is a possible outcome. Certainly often enough, however, to ensure that methods are optimised. Reflecting this, coaches can usefully develop their philosophy of learning and development, what is called their epistemology, and discuss this with parents. Of course, parents can usefully ask about it as well … so coaches, you have been warned!

Watching how the coach coaches/thinking about other elements of your own coaching is another good way to evaluate the environment/raise your own standards. One feature of good practice can be observed in how the coach 'tracks' progress. Good coaching will involve frequent references to how well each particular individual has been doing, and will often set goals for different athletes based on personal improvement. Ideally, athletes will have a variety of different feedback methods for measuring their own progress – coach feedback is an important one (but avoiding the 'KR Crutch' idea from Table 9.1) but variety is the spice of life here. Accordingly, look for young athletes working with each other, questioning from coach to athlete and work on challenges for athletes away from the training centre.

Another important element is timing and how it relates to focus. Young athletes are different to adults; good coaching will ensure session length and changes of activity to match the shorter attention spans that characterise these younger ages. Of course, this isn't to say that young athletes *can't* take these sessions physically. But, if practice makes permanent (only perfect practice makes perfect), then we want to keep sessions at Goldilocks (just right – like the nursery rhyme) levels so that attention stays high.

Is now the right time?

When you have watched enough to evaluate the quality of coaching, or as the coach worked to make things as good as possible, then all parties need to understand the 'trade-off' decision which joining an academy system will involve. So, are athlete, parent and coach all convinced that the time is right? Parents and coach need to be sensible with the enthusiastic youngster; explaining the cons as well as the pros is a good idea if you don't want to end up with a dispirited and disillusioned athlete a few months down the line. Just like buying a pet or taking up an instrument, there are lots of challenges as well as potential benefits. Not considering these up front, and putting plans in place to counter negatives and accentuate positives is just silly. Indeed, this has derailed many a career as the impact of the enhanced training is diluted or sometimes even countered by the young athlete's 'fedupness'!

So, things like 'How will we cope with the extra travelling?', 'What about that youth club you really enjoy?' or 'Will you be willing to do the required training and practice in your own time?' are all issues that need exposing and carefully considering before all rush headlong into the relationship. In most cases, delaying the start of 'committed training' for a couple of years until all are ready for it will generate a much more positive outcome than starting then struggling. Finally, parents and coaches should consider how the ideas on balance expressed within this book can be reconciled with the academy commitment. Keeping some other activities going, having a social life and doing the school thing will all be important complements to the academy if arranged well. Some coaches and parents see these as competition, but we hope that this book offers sufficient examples of how the contribution can be made positive for all elements and people involved. Good honest communication between athlete, parent, coach and (where appropriate) club or organisation is the basis of an effective and productive academy experience.

Building TD systems on mechanistic principles

We hope that this and other chapters have offered a lot of guidance on how TDEs may be best designed. An overview of the principles is shown in Figure 9.2. This figure offers a summary overview of what theory, research and experience tells us are the features of effective TDEs. In this regard, 'effective' means two things: first, that talent and potential are translated into senior performance and, second, that youngsters are not turned off by the process and lost to the sport. Note that these principles will look rather different if winning *now* is your aim. As stated earlier in the book, success today and success tomorrow often result from different approaches. For those interested, we would also recommend the excellent work of Kristoffer Henriksen (2010), completed in Scandanavia but none the less applicable to other cultures. (Thanks to the Danish system, this is published online and is available to download if you wish.)

Key features	Key methods	Nature of model
Long-term aims and methods	• Develop a long-term vision, purpose and identity • Develop systematic planning and implementation • Provide coherent reinforcement at a variety of levels	Integrated, holistic and systematic
Wide-ranging coherent messages and support	• Provide coherent philosophies, aims and methods at a variety of levels (e.g. parents, coach content, practice and reward systems, selection, funding, competition structure, NGBs) • Educate and utilise parents, schools, peers, coaches and important others • Utilise role models at a variety of levels • Set up a variety of support networks over the long term (e.g. peer, coach, sport staff, family) • Provide forums for open and honest communication patterns at a variety of levels	

Emphasise appropriate development *not* early success	• De-emphasise 'winning' as success at developmental stages
	• Provide clear expectations, roles and meaning within the 'big picture' at every level
	• Provide 'stage specific' integrated experiences and teaching
	  • Fundamental physical and perceptual skills
	  • Fundamental mental skills (learning and development; life; performance related)
	  • Sport-specific skills (technical, tactical, mental, physical, perceptual)
	  • Balance
	• Encourage increasing responsibility and autonomy in learning/development
	• Develop intrinsic motivation and personal commitment to process
	• Promote personal relevance, athlete understanding and knowledge	

Individualised and ongoing development	• Provide opportunities and fundamentals to as many youngsters as possible • Provide flexible systems to allow for performance and physical development variation • Identify, prepare for and support individuals through key transitions • Provide regular individual goal setting and review processes • Provide systematic reinforcement contingencies	

FIGURE 9.2 Features of an effective TDE (adapted from Martindale *et al.*, 2005)

Given that there are good and accessible sources of valid information available, designing your TDE/selecting one for your child is more than just luck. There are clear, well researched and understood guidelines that underpin these processes.

But...

If the system is *only* that, it can become a sausage factory: working efficiently on solid principles but lacking the essential spark of humanity which is the essential ingredient to success. We have worked with many elite athletes over the years but they were almost exclusively the consequence of influences from one or two committed and interested individual coaches, who forged strong relationships. These were not necessarily friends (although several became so). Crucially, however, all the best coaches (including those of our Superchamps) were 'strong drivers': people who had the best interests of the athlete at heart but who knew when to push and when to support. Our final point in this chapter is to work on establishing this sort of relationship or, if you are a parent looking at different options, to seek out this as a crucial factor. In simple terms, when all the science is said and applied, coaching is a liveware issue! People count. So take the time to find/be the right coach. Everyone will benefit.

Expert perspective on Chapter 9

Nigel Edwards was appointed as Performance Director of England Golf in 2012 after five years in a similar role for the Golf Union of Wales 2007–2012. Nigel was Great Britain and Ireland Walker Cup Captain in 2011, 2013 and 2015 having represented Great Britain and Ireland in the Walker Cup teams in 2001, 2003, 2005 and 2007.

Talent Development Environments (TDEs) have been a part of my sporting career since I began playing sport without me knowing it! Rugby, football, cricket in school, judo at a local club and golf through club, county, national and international pathway as an athlete and now in my role as Performance Director. My first experiences were stumbling through the world of sport that I was so passionate about; I would watch, read and listen to anything about any sport and truly loved all what sport offered: opportunity, competition, progress, achievement, energy and enjoyment. Memories tell me that my overwhelming desire was enjoyment and I certainly did that and as a consequence of this enjoyment I feel that my progress was accelerated. There were challenges along the way, both physically and mentally but my progress was totally self-driven or intrinsically motivated. I have loved my time in sport and have been very fortunate to experience opportunities that I never dreamt would come my way. As I progressed in my chosen sport of golf the focus did change and competition and achievement naturally came to the forefront of my mind, I loved competition. The environments that I had grown up in certainly shaped the competitor that I was. The learnings on reflection were slow and certainly not what these environments are today – it was a case of trying to find my way by trial and error. Progress has been made, there is now ample research readily available in all organisations who are keen to aid progress but there are also minefields and one should always be aware of the dreaded sales pitch!

Always ask the questions: What? How? Why? For example:

- What is being delivered?
- How is it delivered?
- Why is it delivered?

This chapter raises a number of key issues which can really help and support all involved in TDEs, but especially athletes and parents in finding their way through a system which can be daunting for those who have little or no knowledge. What I like about this chapter is how it details the key learnings or essentials to talent development in a very simplistic manner which really resonates from my own experiences both as an athlete and as someone who is now managing a pathway. I highlight below the key elements:

- communication and expectations
- environment – culture, mindset to learning, responsibility, flexible

- coaching – engaging, communication/dialogue between coach/athlete/parent, challenging, not information overload
- athletes – behaviours, reflection, honesty, commitment, personal skills not just technical skills
- long-term progress not short-term results
- variety.

As detailed in the closing remarks of the chapter, people, communication and relationships are what matters.

One other qualifier to this important advice. Once again, almost all the elites we have worked with, plus many more that we have studied, used a number of coaches greater than one on their pathway to the top. It is extremely rare to find a single individual who will have the right knowledge, blend of skills and experience to take an athlete all the way from 'playground to podium', just as you probably won't have the same maths teacher in primary school and on your university course! We would suggest that good coaches know when to pass an athlete onwards and upwards. At the very least, ambitious coaches will seek out more experienced people who have already taken athletes successfully to the top and fly as co-pilot with this 'mentor' to enhance their own skills. Even better than this, upwardly mobile coaches will spend time watching a range of others, learning from what these role models do *and why* to extend their own skillset.

So in conclusion, this chapter has covered a great deal of information and a number of perspectives which those interested in optimum TDEs may look for/apply. The chapter has also reiterated/revisited a number of messages from elsewhere in the book. The logic underpinning many of these ideas will change slightly with age and stage, but is still fundamentally sound across the pathway. Look for and/or apply it … but don't forget the interpersonal stuff!

References

Henriksen, K. (2010). The ecology of talent development in sport: a multiple case study of successful talent development environments in Scandinavia. Available as free download: http://sportspsykologen.dk/pdf/Henriksen_The_ecology_of_talent_development_in_sport.pdf.

Martindale, R. J. J., Collins, D. and Daubney, J. (2005). A critical review of talent development and implications for sport. *Quest*, 57, 353–375.

PART V

Making the most of your academy apprenticeship

As the next couple of chapters will demonstrate, coaches, parents, teachers and other key stakeholders play a pivotal role in the TD process. The first chapter examines the coach–athlete relationship and how this can 'fly or founder'! Unfortunately, it is often the case that the 'best' coaches work with the 'best' (in terms of status) athletes. It would seem sensible to us that sports consider the type of coach required at every rung of the pathway as the quality of these relationships have the potential to be either a catalyst for development, or a significant factor in both initiation and adherence to the TD process. The importance of quality coaching at all stages of the pathway is far too important a consideration to be left to chance or the willingness of perhaps well intentioned, but ill-equipped volunteers who might lack the skills or abilities to be effective. Quality coaching must not only address the technical and tactical development of young performers but should also be empathetic towards their needs.

The second chapter focuses on the role played by families in the development of talent. How can families support a young performer and keep things in perspective in what is a very pressured environment? Essentially, what is the balance between 'pushy parenting' and under-involvement? In this chapter we provide some guidance as to how the coach–athlete–family relationship can be managed and looks at effective parenting style in youth sport, as well as exploring how siblings can be used to promote positive challenge along the pathway. Suggestions about how this might be done in a coherent manner are offered through a series of case studies from the perspective of key stakeholders.

10

HOW THE COACH–ATHLETE RELATIONSHIP CAN FLY OR FOUNDER

Introduction

Of all the relationships that impact on performance and development in sport, the coach–athlete relationship is considered to be particularly crucial in promoting not only an athlete's physical and technical skills but also in serving to bring about personal satisfaction for both parties. Unfortunately, youth sport is rife with examples of ineffective, unsuccessful and downright inappropriate coaching. You will undoubtedly be able to recount examples of youth coaches verbally abusing players when they make mistakes, exerting their authority and engaging in inappropriate behaviour and interactions. As we have emphasised throughout this book, we need to remember that children are not mini-adults and therefore how coaches interact with young athletes on the TD pathway should differ from their relationships at the elite level. Young athletes are socially, cognitively and emotionally different from adult performers and need to be treated accordingly. Coaches working at the youth level need to take into consideration the physical and neurological changes that occur during adolescence, as well as the psychological and social changes that take place during this stage of development. Simply, if you coach young people you need to treat them as young people!

Traditionally, the coach–athlete relationship has been one of coach authority – focused on what the coach does and what they say. However, and especially relevant to the TD environment, coaching is increasingly seen as a *relational* activity where the coach must balance a multitude of roles – technical coach, mentor, role model – and is often the orchestrator of many facets of a young athlete's life. It is important therefore to consider not just what you coach, but how you coach, the tone you use and how you interact with your athletes. Think of coaching as a series of individualised and unique interactions between a coach and an athlete. Unfortunately, coach education, and especially introductory awards aimed at coaches working on the first few rungs of the talent pathway, rarely emphasise the importance or development of these interpersonal skills. Instead, coaching has been preoccupied with enhancing athletes' physical, technical and strategical skills rather than the interpersonal skills that might be the cornerstone of an effective relationship. When this is coupled with the quest and pressure for short-term success, it is no wonder that many athletic journeys are jeopardised by poor relationships between coach and athlete. The question that we address in this chapter is: 'What makes an effective coach–athlete relationship?'. We present some guidance about what constitutes effective and successful coach–athlete relationships with a particular focus on the TD pathway. As you read, consider what this might mean for how you work with young athletes and what needs to be modified or emphasised in your context to optimise these relationships. If you are a parent, think how this information helps you make decisions about your child's coach.

Unpicking the coach–athlete relationship

What do young athletes value?

If you haven't already, it is always worth checking with your athletes about what they expect from the coach–athlete relationship; simply, 'What expectations do you have from me as a coach?'. The answers you receive might be very instructive and might help you reflect on your own behaviour. Typically, young athletes value a coach they can trust, who listens to them, who cares for them as individuals and not just as athletes, and who makes training productive, fun and enjoyable. What does this mean in terms of building positive relationships? Your interactions, how you listen, talk to and respond to athletes and the respect you show them seems to be critical in making you a successful and effective coach. In fact, for young athletes these factors seem more important than outstanding technical, tactical or strategic knowledge; it seems what you know as a coach is of less importance than how you coach. If you care about your athletes, listen to and value their opinion, and are positive and supportive, you are more likely to positively impact on the athlete and produce motivated and disciplined athletes.

If an athlete is committed to and trusts their coach, then they are likely to respond more readily to the coach's instruction. This is obviously important if you are asking your athletes to push themselves hard in training, work outside their comfort zone or complete challenging tasks. This really comes into play when performers move into the academy system and things start to get serious; time commitment increases, training gets harder, competition gets tougher. Positive coach–athlete relationships are also likely to influence 'spill-over' into other areas of the athletes' lives. Athlete satisfaction, for example, has been correlated with supportive coach behaviours, training and instruction, and positive feedback from coaches. Athletes' sport enjoyment is also influenced by the nature of the coach–athlete relationship, explained by athletes' perceptions of the quality of the relationship. Given the strong relationship between coaching and athlete enjoyment, sport involvement, skill development, performance and motivation, it is clear that a focus on the coach–athlete relationship is warranted. If the relationship can be optimised, it is reasonable to assume that athletes will not only play sports longer, but enjoy them more and play them at a higher level.

A dyadic relationship: the 3 + 1 Cs

From what you have read so far, it is clear that the coach–athlete relationship is dyadic – neither party can exist without the other! The athlete needs to acquire knowledge from the coach, the coach needs to impart expertise to the athlete, and both need to translate this into positive outcomes, whether that is in terms of outcome achievements or personal satisfaction (or ideally both!). In this section, we consider some key constructs that operationalise the coach–athlete relationship and how you might exploit these in your TD environment.

First, the coach–athlete relationship is defined by mutual and causal interdependence between coaches' and athletes' feelings, thoughts and behaviours. Essentially, is there congruence between what the athlete thinks, feels and how he/she behaves and the coach's feelings, thoughts and behaviours? If not, the relationship is probably going to break down due to conflict and a lack of coherence.

These thoughts and behaviours have been operationalised through the constructs of Closeness, Commitment and Complementarity ('3 Cs') (Jowett and Cockerill, 2002).

- *Closeness* reflects the extent to which coaches and athletes are connected and describes the affective nature of the relationship; it is the emotional tone of the relationship. Think of this as how coaches and athletes *like, trust and respect* each other (as opposed to dislike and distrust) and how this impacts on positive interpersonal and affective relationships.
- *Commitment* reflects the cognitive element of the relationship and defines coaches' and athletes' desire to maintain their relationship over time and in pursuit of their mutual goals.
- *Complementarity* concerns the interaction between the coach and the athlete that is perceived to be cooperative and effective; essentially the degree to which coach and athlete behaviours contribute to one another.
- A fourth construct, *coorientation* concerns athletes' and coaches' perceptions about each other and it is suggested that there are two perceptions: direct perspective and meta-perspective. The direct perspective deals with how the athlete perceives the coach in terms of closeness, commitment and complementarity: 'I trust my coach', 'We are working towards the same goals'. The meta-perspective reflects the athlete's ability to infer the coach's 3 Cs; 'My coach trusts me'. A functioning relationship will have a high degree of similarity between what the coach and athlete thinks; if you are both on the same page, it increases the likelihood of an effective relationship. Reflecting this, co-orientation is broken into three dimensions:

- actual similarity: 'I trust my coach' and 'I trust my athlete';
- assumed similarity: 'I trust my coach' and 'I assume my coach trusts me';
- empathic understanding: 'I think my coach trusts me' and 'I trust my athlete'.

High scores on each of these dimensions has been shown to lead to a range of outcomes such as higher levels of satisfaction with performance and personal satisfaction, higher levels of team cohesion, higher levels of harmonious passion for the activity and lower levels of role ambiguity (Jowett and Chaundy, 2004). While understanding the 3 + 1 Cs helps us understand the coach–athlete relationship, it should also help coaches identify problem areas that need to be addressed to improve the functioning of the relationship. For example, identifying points of disagreement, dissimilarity or misunderstanding between the coach and athlete would be a useful starting point for improving the relationship. It could be as simple as the need to clarify what each wants out of the relationship and working towards a shared understanding of various issues. As Dave stated in Chapter 7 this doesn't have to be complex; being available to your athletes, talking to them and ensuring positive communication through spontaneous conversations are very useful platforms to optimise the coach–athlete relationship. When coaches create these opportunities for communication and disclosure they are more likely to develop trustworthy relationships.

What is a successful and effective coach–athlete relationship?

The simple answer is (as always!), it depends! On the one hand, a coach–athlete relationship (especially at the elite level) is often evaluated based on outcome success – has the athlete or team reached a level of normative success such as winning or personal bests. However, if you are coaching young athletes with a developmental agenda, this type of 'success' isn't the most useful way to evaluate the relationship. Instead, the coach–athlete relationship can be described on two interrelated dimensions (Jowett, 2005): outcome-oriented (successful or unsuccessful) and helpful and caring (effective and ineffective). What is the ideal coach–athlete relationship? A relationship that is successful and effective would seem to be the ideal because it includes performance success (the athlete is winning or improving their skill level) and personal growth (experiencing satisfaction as a result of a caring and helpful relationship). A relationship can also be effective without being successful; the young athlete is experiencing some positive outcomes in terms of satisfaction and wellbeing (the effective part) but without performance success. In terms of youth sport, where the emphasis is on mass participation and personal growth, this might be what you and your players desire. Effective relationships include elements such as trust, support, honesty, caring, respect and cooperation (Jowett and Cockerill, 2002) – key ingredients in helping young athletes stay on the pathway. Although an unsuccessful and effective relationship doesn't have positive performance outcomes, the coach and athlete have a strong relationship, with little tension or conflict (as long as their motives are compatible!). Ineffective relationships are characterised by remoteness, exploitation and a lack of interest – even if these relationships are successful, young athletes are likely to soon drop out of the sport as their emotional and developmental needs are not being met. Even if the ineffective relationship is successful, it is the least favourable relationship psychologically because of the negative emotions attached to it. Again, we emphasise the importance of considering the young athlete as a 'whole' and emphasising positive growth and development as a key focus of your coaching. Do this right and success will follow!

How to improve the coach–athlete relationship

Give your athletes a say!

What helps develop an effective and successful coach–athlete relationship? Making sure that there are open channels of communication, that work two-ways, is a relatively simple but important means of establishing co-oriented views. Although young athletes might not have sufficient information to make informed decisions about particular aspects of training and performance, involving them in the discussion can have significant benefits. If you remember back to Chapter 6, we proposed how carefully designed coach systems and coach behaviours promoted the deployment of PCDEs in your environment. The same structure applies here. Even holding informal reviews, feedback or questioning sessions as part of your session can involve the athlete in the process and act as a means of sharing knowledge and understanding. This, in turn, improves compatibility between the athlete and coach as the capacity to understand each other's perspective is increased as is trust and cooperation.

Explain why you do, what you do!

Adolescence is a time when young people seek autonomy and independence and are working towards self-regulation. The coach–athlete relationship needs to acknowledge this and ensure that a degree of interdependence (remember the concepts of closeness, connectedness and cooperation?) is part of the relationship. By giving your athletes a rationale for what they are doing (and the way they are doing it) you are involving them in the process and ensuring there is a shared understanding of what is happening. It might seem obvious to you why a certain training is structured as it is or why you are playing certain games, but it might not be as clear to your players. Coaches should be trying to move athletes from dependence towards interdependence as they travel along the TD pathway.

Acknowledge feelings

One of the things athletes really value is when their coach treats them as an individual, and not just another member of the team or training group. Simply ensuring that you acknowledge athletes' feelings and emotions goes a long way to establishing a positive relationship and ensuring the closeness and connectedness we spoke about earlier. This means that you need to get to know your athlete as a person, how they react to different situations and what makes them 'tick'.

Appropriate use of feedback

In Chapter 3 we highlighted the impact different types of praise and feedback had on a young person's attitude and mindset. The same caveats apply here. Instructional, supportive and individualised feedback helps athletes focus on their own performance and what they can do to improve.

What happens when it goes wrong: conflict in your relationships?

Conflicts, disagreements and misunderstandings are an inevitable feature of coach–athlete relationships at all levels of performance, after all we have all (and some more than others!) come across people we don't get along with or disagree with! As with most things, there seem to be two sides to the coin and the negative consequences of conflict only arise if it isn't managed correctly. Managed correctly, conflict can be a powerful learning tool. Let's explore how you might do this in your coaching environment.

If conflict isn't managed correctly, it can lead to a tense coach–athlete relationship and have a significant impact on coaches' and athletes' mood, motivation, commitment and, of course, their performance. It is also inherently stressful, especially for young athletes who might not have the set of skills and tools (or indeed emotional maturity) needed to manage it effectively. Ensuring constructive strategies are in place to proactively manage conflict is important. These might include:

- Ensuring open, and two-way, channels of communication are a feature of the coaching process. This might take the form of regular review meetings, informal conversations or, in a team situation, the development of a 'leadership' group to feedback to coaches. Although these strategies are relatively common at elite and sub-elite levels of performance, they are equally as applicable for young performers. In fact, putting them in place early provides opportunities for young athletes to develop, deploy and refine the skills so they are well practiced by the time they become senior performers. This Teach–Test–Tweak–Refine approach was covered in Chapter 6.
- Not taking conflict personally (either as the coach or athlete), but focusing on the event or situation in which the conflict arose and find ways to improve the situation.

- Showing empathy and interest in understanding the other's point of view and caring for the other's needs – this reflects the constructs of closeness and compatibility that we spoke about earlier in the chapter.
- Preparing for honest, problem-focused conversations (e.g. knowing what you want to achieve, articulating your side and being flexible to negotiate). This approach reflects the interdependence that is a feature of effective and successful coach–athlete relationships.

If you can succeed in managing conflict effectively, there are a number of positive consequences. The process of managing conflict – problem-focused conversations, for example – promotes self-reflection which is in itself an important skill for both coaches and athletes. Conflict management and resolution also enhances social skills and improves young athletes' ability to understand, appreciate and empathise with other people's feelings. In a coaching environment there can sometimes be a tendency to just 'tick along' and keep doing the same things that you have always done (especially if you have achieved some degree of success). Conflict, and the reflection and questioning that is a part of the resolution process, provides an opportunity to share information, explore each other's opinion, and map a way forward. In fact, carefully managed conflict can leave your relationship in a better place by bringing you closer to your athlete and increasing mutual trust and respect.

What does this mean? Maybe, and we will talk about this more in Chapter 14, you want to have some 'ups and downs' in your relationships with your athletes in order to improve the coaching process and to teach the athlete some valuable skills for the future. As with a lot of TD, an overly smooth experience might not be the best preparation for the future.

Expert perspective on Chapter 10

David Passmore has spent 14 years as a High Performance Coach and Director. During roles with GB and Irish Hockey as coach and High Performance director he has nurtured European, World and Olympic medallists through their critical developmental period. He currently coaches the Ireland Under 21 hockey team and is a mentor on the EHF Top Coach Programme and the FIH Academy programme.

This chapter offers much food for thought to those coaching at all levels. In my experience building an effective coach–athlete relationship takes time and conscious investment on behalf of the coach. When I have coached at my best and built long-lasting athlete relationships it has been because I have consciously invested time in developing the level of trust and honesty required. Too often this is where coaches fall down, especially in team sports where there can be so many players. I try to be the first at training and the last to leave, as this is often when you can have the informal chats when you get to know the athlete better. A chat about what's going on outside of their sporting lives, what their other interests are, their family etc. is one of the best ways to start connecting with them at first. This builds basic levels of rapport that you can build on.

Empowering athletes in their own development helps further build trust and unquestionably serves to increase their self-motivation. We as coaches need to help them to feel they are the 'gate keepers' of their own development and we are there to support, guide and steer. The basis of this starts with finding out what their goals are and then being clear in your commitment to helping them achieve them. In turn, they will commit harder to these goals but will need you to be supportive of their efforts. Similarly, building on what the athletes think and feel is key; using intrinsic feedback is crucial to building that trust as too often we assume things. Trust can be broken when you fail to gain this kind of self-input by the athlete. I remember we were giving video feedback in a post-match debrief and I started to give out to a player who had left his marker in the build-up to a goal we conceded. If only I had asked him first why he had done that I would have realised he was covering another team-mate and had made the decision to leave his marking duties for a more dangerous attacker. Our relationship was never quite the same after that day. I could tell by the way he looked at me.

Athletes need and often seek positive reinforcement about the direction of their development; the best relationships are built on showing self-belief in someone. Openness and honesty are also key. I find those athletes who seek me out to chat something through (even if I haven't coached them for years) are those I consistently gave honest feedback too. What is key in getting the balance is that you similarly have to show the belief in them that any weaknesses they may have can be worked on, and you are there to work with them. That said I would often also invite their feedback on how I was coaching so it became a two-way relationship. We need to listen more than speak as coaches. I would encourage anyone reading this book to think about HOW they are doing what they are doing; in my experience this can be the key that helps athletes flourish.

Some other concerns

Empowering your athlete

You will have gathered by now that interdependence is an important factor in positive coach–athlete relationships. The ability to facilitate the TD journey appears to be characteristic of effective TD coaches; this is in stark contrast to the traditional 'expert' role given to coaches. If this is the case, how might you encourage athletes to take responsibility for their own learning and engagement in the TD process? A good TD coach will facilitate a shift in responsibility from the coach promoting and reinforcing desired behaviours (think of the PCDEs we have highlighted throughout the book) in the early years towards self-initiated and autonomous behaviours as the athlete progresses in their sport. At one end of the continuum, coaches use various means of reinforcement to regulate the actions of the athlete. In what you might term 'helicopter coaching', coaches take responsibility for all aspects of the training and competition environment and the athlete just has to show up, listen and perform! Although this approach might produce some quick results, it isn't the best way to prepare athletes for what they will face later on in their development. In what might be a messier, but more effective approach, coaches will promote and reinforce the development of self-regulation skills as part of their coaching practice – giving athlete's responsibility for aspects of training, encouraging athlete's to give feedback and reflect on performance (both on their own and the coach's performance), for example. The development of self-reliant and independent athletes is an important feature of the TD pathway so systematically developing these behaviours should be central to your coaching. Don't leave this to chance or the luck of a positive home environment.

Knowing when and how to move an athlete on

The needs of young athletes obviously differ from their adult counterparts and there is a case to be made for different types of coaching at different stages of the talent pathway; specialist youth coaches who have the appropriate skillset to work with young athletes and elite coaches who have the expertise to work with mature athletes. In fact, several NGBs in the UK are looking to develop a children-specialist workforce and have tailored coaching qualifications and resources accordingly. This is, after all how the education system works; my primary school teacher did not teach me during my postgraduate study!

But what happens if you unearth a gem? You spend years and countless hours developing a young athlete and helping them reach their potential, and then, what next? Do you pass them on to another coach who has the expertise and experience of coaching at the next level? Do you maintain the relationship and hope to learn as you go? Of course, there are examples of athletes who have achieved at the highest level while still training with their childhood coaches. When gymnast Simone Biles won Olympic Gold in Rio in 2016 she was still under the tutelage of her coach from when she started participating at age seven. Missy Franklin won five medals at the London 2012 Games while being coached by Todd Schmitz, her coach since she was seven. Maybe the *closeness* of the relationship formed over a long period of time is more important than the benefits of changing to a new coach who might have great technical or tactical knowledge. If you find yourself in this situation, how might you optimise the relationship to ensure the athlete is progressing and learning? The willingness to invite other coaches into the environment might be one factor that contributes to success. Making sure that your athlete gets exposure to other coaches, by inviting coaches with particular expertise into your setup or sending the athlete to train in different coaching environments, is another way to maintain the relationship *and* performance. For example, if your athlete gets selected to compete on representative teams they benefit from exposure to other coaches as long as the relationships are well managed. We discuss this management in more detail in Chapter 15, but for the moment consider what you might do in this situation. Is the potential of being associated with the next 'big thing' too much to give up? Or do you have the skills, ability and time to progress the athlete to the next level? A positive coach–athlete relationship will only continue as long as both parties receive awards as opposed to costs (e.g. conflict, lack of performance, dissatisfaction). If you maintain your relationship with the 'next big star' make sure you are doing it for the right reasons and that you can help them take the next step up the ladder.

Parent as coach: a different relationship dynamic?

In Chapter 7, Dave and Anne Pankhurst highlighted the importance of the parent-athlete relationship. But what happens if the parent also assumes the role of coach? It is very common for parents to be involved in coaching their children, especially during the early years of participation, and at the elite level there are examples of parents who coached their children – Richard Williams coached both Venus and Serena throughout their careers. Being a coach and a parent simultaneously is challenging and wrought with conflicting expectations so it is worth considering the dynamics underpinning this relationship.

The benefits of a parent/coach–athlete relationship include a more individualised approach to development where the parent/coach is well placed to give praise, technical instruction, special attention, quality time and motivation. The costs of being coached by one's parent include negative emotional responses, pressure/expectations, conflict, lack of understanding/empathy, criticism for mistakes and unfair behaviour. The inability to separate parent–child from coach–player roles, and the child's difficulty in separating coach and parent roles, is often the main factor that leads to conflict and ultimately a breakdown in relationships. Finding a way to balance the relationship, and making sure everyone knows where the boundaries are, is an important step to making the relationship work.

So, should you do it? Again, the answer is (at the risk of repeating ourselves!) 'it depends!' and many of the caveats mentioned previously will apply: Do you have the expertise needed to bring the athlete to the next level? What are your motives for coaching your child? Can you separate your role as coach and parent? If parents can balance their role, and there is no role ambiguity or conflict, and they have the skills, knowledge and expertise to create positive sporting experiences then the parent/coach–athlete relationship might work. However, there is a lot to consider if the relationship is going to work – tread carefully!

In conclusion

The coach–athlete relationship is at the heart of the TD process and the coach can be a powerful, constructive and positive influence on a young athlete's career. In fact, for some athletes the coach–athlete relationship is what defines and shapes their sporting experience and has a profound impact on both their sporting success and life satisfaction. In this chapter we have attempted to give an overview of what an effective and successful relationship looks like and how you might facilitate that in your environment. One thing to note is that the developing performer will, of course, benefit from encountering a range of different coaches all of whom will have their own way of doing things. This is an important feature of the pathway and ensures that young performers encounter a degree of variability that helps them develop the repertoire of skills needed for eventual success. The young performer doesn't get too used to just one way of doing things and learns to adapt to different situations, methods and relationships. We return to this in Chapter 15 but one thing is for sure, developing young performers is complex and challenging!

References

Jowett, S. (2005). The coach–athlete partnership. *The Psychologist*, 18, 412–415.

Jowett, S. and Chaundy, V. (2004). An investigation into the impact of coach leadership and coach–athlete relationship on group cohesion. *Group Dynamics: Theory, Research and Practice*, 8, 302b–311.

Jowett, S. and Cockerill, I. M. (2002). Incompatibility in the coach–athlete relationship. In I. M. Cockerill (Ed.), *Solutions in sport psychology* (pp. 16–31). London: Thomson Learning.

11

WHAT PARENTS AND PERFORMERS CAN DO TO SUPPORT/SUPPLEMENT OR REPLACE THE ACADEMY

Introduction

As much research will attest, without parental involvement most top performers just won't achieve the highest levels. There are always a few exceptions but, for almost all aspiring elites, optimising support from the family is essential. By the same token, and as already mentioned earlier in this book, parents and families (including the broader family as we will discuss) can get in the way as well. This not only creates hurdles to both the development process and to specific competitions, it can also leave the high-level performer with some key skills missing from their armoury. Concerningly, these omissions can only become apparent a few years later, leaving the pressured athlete up the creek without a paddle!

So, in this chapter we present some ideas on how you can optimally support your aspiring superstar … providing a Goldilocks level of support which is 'just right'. Coaches may wish to read through and, where appropriate, subtly encourage the families of their athletes to use these same ideas. We also cover some key constructs so that parents and coaches can converse, hopefully providing some of the lingo and the ideas behind them.

In providing this overview, we should stress that the nature of the challenge, both quantity and quality, will clearly change with age and stage and there are a wide range of ages and stages in academy-like systems. Accordingly, please sift through what is offered selecting what suits the current and future development of your youngster/athlete.

Finally, it may be that (reflecting perhaps our advice in Chapter 9) you have decided to delay or even avoid the academy-style experience. Accordingly, the chapter concludes with some comments about when this may, or may not, be effective and how to minimise the negatives and accentuate the positives if this is the pathway you decide to follow.

Essential homework for academy/committed athletes

We have already covered what factors to look for in a TDE, and hopefully you will have carefully considered the various options before making your choice. We have also stressed the need for a 'balance' of activity: avoiding an all or nothing thrust on the sport at the expense of personal, social and academic development. Even if you have catered for all this, however, there are still a few things that academy/committed athletes can do to supplement and support their development.

The first is that young athletes should be 'students of their sport'. This should extend to more than just watching it on TV, however. Many scientists underplay the importance of understanding the sport but, in our experience, this can offer all sorts of benefits. In fact, research in the US has shown that tactical understanding can usefully be developed ahead of technique. In other words, knowing *what* to do in a particular situation is a useful 'encouragement' to developing the technique to *actually* do it. Deep knowledge is also a good way to stimulate creativity; if your brain has the necessary concepts, it can work away, overtly and in the background, at solving problems that it understands. In similar fashion, knowing how things work is a big factor in adaptability; and being adaptable is a common feature of top performers. We should stress that, as yet, research hasn't shown whether this is chicken or egg; in other words, are you good because you are adaptable or adaptable because you are good. Whilst the researchers fight it out over this, however, your path is clear. Improve your understanding because, at the very least, it can't hurt but it might …!

Another area for attention, building from our comments above and earlier, is to maintain and develop your young athlete's skills in other areas. We mentioned earlier how important self-esteem (how positive you feel about yourself) is to development. It is always sensible to 'spread your bets', building your self-schemata (literally, the structure you use to think about yourself) on several rather than one domain. So, in an ideal world, your young athlete will be confident in her or his ability as a performer, but also as a student, an individual (e.g. high status in more than just the sporting peer group), and one or more 'hobby' areas. Some of the footballers that we work with are very focused on appearance, social media networking, dance skills and music knowledge; certainly a good start at diversification but we like to encourage even more!

Finally, taking this diversification idea to the next level, we strongly encourage all development athletes to look at a longer-term career. Of course, this is important because, in most cases, sporting careers are short but hopefully sweet. It is only sensible to be developing for the future. Parents and coaches, plus athletes, should recognise that this is also a performance factor. Consider for example, the challenge of coming up to your second or third Olympics, or your 'last club' as a premiership player. The temptation, and natural action, is to switch your thoughts to what happens next; quite literally to lift your eyes beyond the impending sports challenge to fret about what follows it. In such cases, it is supportive of your performance *now* to have everything sorted for what comes *after that*.

You might like to refer to Chapter 12 for more detailed treatment of the transition challenge. For the moment, however, note that this 'looking beyond' phenomenon also applies at the earlier stages of the pathway. Team sports academies have 'retain or release' phases for example, whilst other sports programmes will often review membership of their development groups. Sensible preparation is to make sure that, as an athlete in this situation, you know where you stand (your strengths and weaknesses) and have a clear plan for afterwards whatever happens *well ahead* (say, six months) of the decision point. This enables a tight focus on what needs to be shown in the run-in; a chance to impress at what might be an important time. As a parent, you can do a great deal to set this up, offering optimum support to your performer. Having done this, however, try to make sure that you remain supportive and confident, avoiding communicating your nerves which would just 'add to the fun' for your daughter or son!

Boosting development, avoiding injury and optimising performance – what will training look like?

First of all, it is certainly worth checking with the academy/organisation on the aims of their fitness and conditioning programme. Some, unfortunately in our view, will see only the need for a 'watered down' version of adult performer training. Clearly the philosophy here is to get the athletes fit to win … in short, performance now.

As we suggested in Chapter 9, talent development environments should do just that … develop. As such, and following on from some of the ideas presented in Chapter 5, training provision should always have a developmental component to it. Indeed, arguably this should continue into adulthood as the work becomes more focused on preventing injury. Anyway, your young athlete's schedule should include some elements of building structural strength, which will include basic strength exercises and specific work to build joint integrity. Whether, or indeed, if/when, this will involve weight training is a topic of much debate. For ourselves, we would see this as essential and something that should be started before adolescence. In any case, even bodyweight exercises are effective for younger age groups. We have also highlighted the utility of agility training across the pathway, and this should also be a notable feature.

These general points having been stated, however, there are two more features of 'personal' training which should be catered for. Care is needed of course, to ensure that there isn't too much 'extra' going on. Chronic fatigue can set in very easily, leading to long-term physical damage and mental burnout. Your best bet here is, as stated elsewhere, to consult widely and see what consensus can be found across the different sources. That said, your son's or daughter's coach, and the strength and conditioning (S&C) coach if one exists, should be a primary source. So, that said, what other elements should you be concerned with?

Addressing individual needs

Of course, if your young athlete is in an individual sport, this should go without saying. Even here, however, group schedules can be common. In a team sport environment, this is even more likely. Good systems will not only screen for potential weaknesses, and counter them with remedial training programmes; they will also develop a profile of each individual and ensure that appropriate training is prescribed. Note that such programmes will have most if not all of the following features:

- The schedule will cater for individual weaknesses *and* strengths! It is a big but all too common mistake to only work on weaknesses. As a consequence, the athlete turns from say, average to good average! Building super-strengths in parallel with countering weaknesses is increasingly seen as the best way to develop an individually powerful profile.
- The schedule will have an element of prophylactic (preventative) work, focused according to the particular demands of that sport. Joint integrity is one (see above), ensuring muscle balances such as quads to hamstrings (muscles on the front and back of the upper leg respectively), plus core work attention to the 'core' of the body by developing back and abdominal muscles are others.
- Like any good training schedule, it will be regularly revised, based on assessments together with the need to progress towards longer-term set goals. If your young athlete stays doing the same stuff for longer than six weeks, ask why. This may be OK but …
- The schedule will be a balance of various components: aerobic, anaerobic, strength, power and mobility should all get a mention. Of course, some of these components may be addressed in group session but, once again, it's better to ask if unsure.
- Finally, the schedule should be part of a nested plan – layers of this week we do so that in this six week block we do so that across the season we can. You may well hear the jargon terms micro (short), meso (medium) and macro (long) used. At least now you can join in the discussion!

The last element is likely to vary across the year, often following the principles of 'periodisation'. This basically splits the year into phases, with training volume (how much you do) and intensity (how hard you do it) varied to optimise the training effect. Coaches will often plan to 'peak' (hit best form) for certain competitions or times of the year. In simple terms, peaking involves decreasing volume and increasing intensity, then cutting right back on training to generate the peak. A lot is written about this and some coaches delight in very complex plans – a feature which has recently come in for a lot of stick due to the very complexity and doubts over its ability to consistently generate a peak across a wide variety of individuals! A more common approach now is for a regular monitoring process, using a variety of tests to evaluate 'training readiness' on an individual basis. This approach can allow for variations in work capacity because of different reactions to the training given plus anything else going on in the athlete's life, ranging from menstruation, through exam pressures. A common element of such evaluation uses simple questions on things like muscle soreness, sleep quality, mood etc. This said, you should look for these various features in your son's/daughter's training schedule, and feel free to ask about how things are designed.

'Active' rest or recovery in the off season

As a feature of the periodisation process, the peak is usually followed by a rest period, before the next cycle of work begins. As above, these 'rests' will be incorporated at a micro (e.g. Sunday off), meso (e.g. a one-week lighter schedule) or macro (e.g. month off in the summer) level. Parents are often thrown by the term 'rest' however. For most coaches and in most cases this will be a *comparative* rest, rather than an excuse to veg out in front of the TV and eat hamburgers! That sort of rest, whenever taken, just takes the body to an overly detuned state.

Accordingly, current wisdom is for an 'active rest' phase, in which the body is allowed to recover but fitness is maintained, by use of different activities. So football academy players might go and play cricket or do some athletics. Martial arts athletes might get into swimming and so on. The point is that the body isn't allowed to just go back down to the start point fitness-wise. Rather, the 'recovery and regeneration' process (you may hear your coach talking about 'R and R') is catered for by doing different things so that the parts of the body and system usually impacted get a break.

Some may even use this period to work on a specific factor. It might be quite normal for a footballer to be sent off to work on sprinting speed and acceleration. Others might focus on building muscle size or strength. All fine so long as the activity is sufficiently different to what goes on for the rest of the year!

How the rest of the family can help *and* not suffer – advice for parents and siblings

Whether you have only one or several aspiring elites, this is a genuine challenge which can unbalance the closest and most dedicated of families. Those parents who do best take care to consider and plan for the various challenges, including the whole family in decision making wherever possible. Needless to say (but we will say it anyway), maintaining a balance across siblings is a key part of this process. There are too many stories of relationships wrecked by a lack of 'fairness', whether real or perceived. So, to end up with successful and happy children, there are several factors to which parents must attend.

Parent to athlete

For a start, care is needed in how one communicates with the aspiring elite. As we have already said, parent reaction to success and, even more powerfully, failure is a crucial feature of effective progression at these stages. As psychologists, we talk about 'teachable moments': times when, usually because of what has just happened, an individual is optimally susceptible to advice. Success and failure offer such times, so long as the advice is offered carefully, sensitively and with good timing. So, reiterating advice from earlier chapters, on the car ride home or whenever the moment offers itself:

- DON'T jump straight in – emotions may be running high or feeling raw so gauge your moment.
- DO be supportive – the three 'goods', then three 'to work ons' formula for feedback is a good basic model.
- DO reiterate your love for your son/daughter and avoid the 'Well you know I love you *but* ...' type approach!
- DO be realistic – don't try to avoid blame or try and convince them they played well when they had a shocker – as with so much about human psychology, rationalising emotions but with sensitivity – the loss might BE the worst thing that has ever happened; at least for them!
- DON'T always relate your son's/daughter's performance to what the others did. Rather, match it to them individually, basing comments on what they are capable of. *Please don't* compare them to siblings, the team's star player, your friend's child, etc.!

Of course, *what* is offered as advice is also important, not just *when*. In this regard, it is always important to seek out opinion and input from significant others, most particularly but not solely the coach. After all, even if one or both parents have been successful sports performers in their own right, things have changed. Furthermore, your child is trying to succeed in *this* system so, even if you feel uneasy about the perspective offered, it is really important to ask for it, then consider it carefully. Using other sources (see also the next section) is an excellent idea; other coaches, coaches of other sports and teachers can offer different perspectives although pragmatically, your daughter's or son's coach's opinion must carry a greater weighting. If you feel really uncomfortable, perhaps you shouldn't be there!

One of the biggest 'no-no's' is overemphasising the importance of winning. You might like to refer back to the Superchamps versus Almosts picture in Table 7.1. Parents of Superchamps were most usually distant but supportive, a behaviour that prevented their children developing a morbid fear of failure. It's worth noting that being over-concerned with the result, and the associated need to avoid making a mistake, is often the kiss of death to the young athlete. S/he can keep everything very safe, so avoiding the opportunities to be adaptable and creative by trying new things which is really an essential for eventual success. This over-emphasis on the result also works in the long term to decrease enjoyment, resulting sooner or later in dropout.

Here are a couple of other quick ideas about social interactions around your child's sporting involvement.

- DO try to get to know other athletes and their parents. A sense of community around the academy/organisation is very useful. Remember, it is exceptionally rare that your child will be competing against the other kids for resource, support or attention. Collaboration is likely to do much more for your son/daughter than a competitive relationship.
- As a general rule, DON'T overdo the support. Having your own cheer leading group can be very disconcerting for a youngster, especially if accompanied by chants, banners, etc. It might all be meant with the best intentions but you might end up making your child the butt of some mocking. This is especially likely when they start getting into the adolescence thing. As a general rule, quiet encouragement and positive looking is the safest bet!

As a final thought, please recognise, and allow for, the essential diminution of your role as your child athlete moves to adolescence. Peer perspectives gain in power, whilst being one of the 'in crowd' becomes the most important driving force. Of course these may need questioning, but exerting the same levels of care described in the previous section will be necessary. Effective coaches of adolescent performers are well up on this; sensibly using peer role models (who may be the stars of the team/squad but not necessarily) and subtly tweaking the culture to 'encourage' rather than demand certain standards of behaviour. We know that 'social' power is greatest at adolescence, with this importance starting to kick in from 12/13 years of age. Accordingly, make sure that you adjust your style carefully as your athlete matures.

Parent to non-athlete

Unsurprisingly perhaps, favouritism and all that goes with it is a major potential issue; furthermore, this takes effect whether the favour is real and apparent or just perceived. In short, care is needed. To be honest, this is likely to be an issue within any family with two or more children; it just gets exacerbated when one is seen to be achieving at a high level, whether this is sport, music, dance or even academics. Common sense goes a long way here. Turning your living room into a shrine by displaying all the trophies and medals is unlikely to make the non-favoured peer or peers feel very positive. Balancing time and resource is another pretty basic move. Peers will get hacked off pretty quickly if the answer is always 'You know I'd love to, but your brother/sister needs me to …' when time or support is requested.

A second contributory factor relates to the rapidly changing roles and expectations of both parents. For example, the change in traditional roles of the father as 'sole breadwinner' and mother as domestic queen must be considered against who is best to support the young athlete. In our experience, a sharing of this role is often the most effective. In addition, it can go a long way to countering the green eyed monster stuff we talked about in the previous paragraph.

One very good way around these challenges is to involve siblings in the planning process; in short, make sure that they understand why and are happy to commit to the idea that Fred/Freda gets more time here because s/he needs to do XYZ. But that means that Joanna/John gets time there. If the balance is *shown* to be working, and that parents are very aware of it, then things will often operate much more smoothly. An important construct here is *perceived* equity. Children are not small adults but they are not emotionally immature either. Indeed, children have a very advanced sense of fairness, just watch them sorting out balanced teams for a game … so long as adults don't interfere! So, non-athletes will usually be quite understanding that things might be somewhat unbalanced; just not *too* much. So talk it through, because perception is all!

This involvement approach becomes all the more necessary in the case of single-parent families, or when one parent is incapacitated by temporary illness or permanent disability. Once again, making sure that all concerned appreciate the challenges and can contribute to developing the necessary compromises will help enormously.

Things get even more complicated if the other child/children is/are also involved in sport. This makes the balance thing even more important to achieve. However, as the next section will suggest, there is also a lot of good that can come from this.

Sibling to sibling

Whether one, both or all are the sports nut, well adjusted family units will usually come up with mutually supportive play and discussion, so that siblings give and get support in equal measure … well, at least in a perceived balanced fashion. Our recent research has highlighted the really positive support which siblings can offer; providing challenges, supporting practice and offering subtle emotional support in parallel to parents or sometimes, beneficially 'under their radar'. Remembering the ideas on skill acquisition in Chapter 9, an older sibling can make a brilliant coach. S/he benefits as well – coaches will attest to the benefits of teaching someone else something to your own understanding. So this mutually supportive play is just that … everyone benefits.

Of course, even the most loving of families 'have their moments', but encouraging and actively rewarding mutual interest and involvement is generally a good and effective plan. Big occasions for one family member, whether sporting or otherwise, should be that for everyone. So, once again, make sure that everyone is involved in the planning around attending that cup final, that tournament or that stamp collection exhibition. Many elites in our research have talked about how positive they felt as a result of everyone being there. It can work the other way, however, so be careful. Our 'Do's' and 'Don't's' from above still apply!

A final word

Clearly, in a multi-ethnic society, many different expectations and norms of behaviour apply. Having an understanding for this is essential for the coach, so if you feel that s/he may benefit from increased awareness, please don't hesitate. Similar situations apply if your family background is different from the norm. Same-sex parents, second marriages with different age/ethnicity spouses, or even adopted younger siblings of different ethnicity. All reflect situations which a good coach will appreciate knowing about. Even if no special arrangements or changes have to be made, good coaching usually involves knowing your athlete (remember our tennis example earlier in the book). If in any doubt, just ask.

Similar considerations may apply in reverse. Climbing the greasy pole to high-level success may require your youngster to interact with people of very different opinions and attitudes. Nothing strange about this we suggest. After all, your son or daughter is going to encounter these sorts of differences in their everyday lives. It's just that, in pursuit of success, they might have less of a choice in terms of who they interact with. Of course, there are standards that apply here and you should certainly feel free to complain/ask questions about anything inappropriate, even if you aren't sure whether it is or not! All reputable academies and organisations will have a welfare officer, and you should be made aware of contact details when your daughter or son starts off. Such circumstances notwithstanding, you may find that the expectations or normal behaviours at the academy/organisation don't fit well with your own. Once again, discussion is the best first step. Coaches will sometimes not understand your concerns whilst, equally, you may feel a lot happier once you understand the logic of that particular practice. In closing, we should stress how important developing independence is for a young aspiring performer. S/he needs to be able to take control; so sensitivity and a willingness to let them handle things is a good thing, so long as basic safety concerns are addressed.

Staying with it without the dedicated support – is there a back door to elite sporting success?

In reviewing this situation and offering advice, we will stay as open and honest as we have throughout the book. After all, that is one big reason why you might be reading this – to get an alternative view.

So, right from the start we should stress that there is a lot of 'received wisdom' in sport. There are a lot of different ways to the top and there is certainly room for alternative pathways. Accordingly, you shouldn't feel that your son or daughter should necessarily conform to the stereotype as they try to enter or move up the pathway. The fact that the pattern of progression changes so much from country to country, sport to sport and even sometimes club to club shows that there should be a lot more tolerance and acceptance for different routes. What this means is that, so long as certain essentials are catered for, academy membership or the like is not essential in most situations. Furthermore, complete commitment and 'behavioural buy-in' to the whole academy package is also not an essential. Of course, appropriate behaviour is important but you may find that the expectations from the particular academy that you are joining just does not fit with your own, and/or your daughter's/son's, personal philosophy or standards. If this is the case, we would suggest that, as a first step, you 'audit' your stance, seeking advice from informed neutrals to see if you are, in fact, correct. Of course, you must try to ensure the 'neutral' bit. Especially when your son/daughter has potential, there will be loads of experts willing to tell you how green their grass is. Agents are another potential danger here, promising all sorts of things if only…. So, seeking a range of opinions (other parents, coaches, coaches in other sports, teachers, etc.) will help you to develop a more reasoned position. Having established that what you think has true merit, it is always worth seeking out the academy manager, programme director or whatever the head honcho is called to express your opinions and see how this is received and reacted to. We would suggest that, if your child is truly talented, there will always be some leeway and room for negotiation. The bottom line is not to feel that you have to accept *all* that you are told. Many of these essentials have already been covered in this book, so you can plan your alternative strategy with knowledge.

However…

There are a few caveats and notes of caution that need to be stated. For a start, it is very hard to get to the top in many sports without competing consistently against good opposition *and* with good teammates/squad members. Indeed, it might be that you should turn down a lower-level academy or training group *because* it might limit your chances for such experience. That said, it is rather hard to get any experience in a team sport if you aren't in a place with sufficient, like-minded others. Saying 'no' to a team sport academy is, therefore, a risky option, although late entry to such systems *has* worked in the past for some and will doubtless work for others in the future. If you chose to do so, or are forced into it, just keep playing and maintain a broad approach, with other games and the complimentary skills part of your programme. After all, a small but significant minority do make it to the top, without passing through the sausage factory. It just might be a bit harder but your call is whether it is worth it to ensure that your child is working in a system that is truly focused on her/him as an individual. These do exist, so playing a waiting game might work out for the best.

So in summary and for a variety of reasons, many pragmatically political in that it's just 'how the system works at present', academy setups seem to be almost essential at some stage in the pathway. As a result, the decision to join is more a case of when and where rather than if.

Expert perspective on Chapter 11

Dave Rotheram is an ex-professional rugby league player having made over 150 first-team appearances. He is now Head of Coach Development at the Rugby League. Prior to this appointment, Dave was Head of Talent and Player Development at the Rugby League. He has coached at all levels of rugby league from Junior

Elite through to Super League and Full International and worked as a Physical Education teacher for 12 years.

My working life has been spent around children and young people in sporting environments at all levels, from beginning as a teacher of physical education to working as a coach at all levels in the sport of Rugby League. Latterly, I have had the responsibility to lead the talent pathway in rugby league which has also coincided with my own children experiencing the talent pathway offers of two sports.

I once heard a conference speaker state that the best place to be a coach was in an orphanage. Reflecting on this comment, I find it to be wholly inappropriate and misguided. Parents are *the* biggest provider of finance, transport and social support to any aspiring athlete. What we as National Governing Bodies are acutely aware of, is that the provision of successful talent pathways will ensure the long-term success of the sport but also will sustain much craved public funding to allow that provision to continue. It therefore is in all NGB's/ professional sporting organisation's best interests that we keep parents not only fully informed as to what is going on, but provide advice on how to deal with the 'bumps in the road' along the way as a 'performance parent'.

This chapter provides guidance and support from every conceivable angle. It has considered everything from what to look for in a good programme to how to support inter- and intra-family relationships. One section of the chapter that is of particular interest is the one about reducing injury and optimising performance. This is most pertinent to team sports and one that is currently receiving close scrutiny in both codes of rugby. Dave and Áine provide good advice in not over-emphasising winning. In the real world, there will be times where winning will compromise the long-term development of athletes. This is particularly evident where athletes engaged in sports' talent pathways compete at multiple levels, for example at school and club. The competitive nature of our sporting landscape means that the best athletes are in demand so that competitions are won and reputations kept intact. This chapter provides parents with a knowledge and understanding 'tool kit' (e.g. what to look for in training plans and when rest periods should occur) to confidently challenge the system.

When parental support is most directly offered is often on the drive home from training or competition. The chapter provides some excellent 'top tips' as to the types of conversation that parents should instigate with their children. These simple messages are certainly good advice not only for parents but also for us as system builders to make sure that constant messages are being disseminated to those responsible for educating parents.

This chapter provides parents with a 'road map' with which to help navigate the well documented rocky road to success. This is truly compelling reading for any parent whose child is embarking on a sporting talent pathway.

In conclusion

The breadth of issues covered should demonstrate, in case you didn't know it already, that 'parenting your superstar' is a complex sport! Careful decision making and timing are crucial, with parents often having the capacity to make or break the outcome. Our biggest take-home advice, at the risk of using another aphorism, is that 'less is more'. Being a pushy parent, sweeping difficulties from your athlete's path whilst cornering her/his coach at every turn, is a recipe for disaster. It might make you feel like you are doing your best for your child but the evidence is pretty clear that this doesn't help anyone. In contrast, being listening and supportive, using subtle and honest questioning, developing an understanding of the process and building good open relationships with your son's/daughter's coach(es) are the key points for attention. Good luck with their journey!

PART VI

Transitions, roadblocks and other challenges

The majority of TD systems try to smooth the pathway for young performers and expend a great deal of effort and resource trying to counter the impact of naturally occurring life stressors. Providing an ultra-supportive environment by minimising challenges and allowing young performers focusing on their sporting commitments seems like a sensible or at least a face-valid approach. However, there seems to be growing recognition that facing and overcoming a *degree* of challenge is desirable for aspiring elites and, as such, should be recognised and employed, rather than avoided. The degree and nature of this challenge is important to consider; after all, the devil is always in the detail! In fact, the use of the term 'trauma' often seems to raise some concerns – due perhaps to the emotive nature of the word; there seems to have been some significant misinterpretations of the 'talent needs trauma' tagline we used in one of our papers! An Oxford English Dictionary definition of trauma would generate the following: 'from Greek, literally wound'; in short, anything from a small cut to losing a limb! We would contest that the use of trauma in the TD context is certainly more towards the band aid than the amputation end of the continuum, albeit that, at the time, the emotional upheaval from the trauma can be very real for individuals. For young performers, this structured trauma might include challenges such as playing up an age-group, out of position, deselection or selection for particular competitions, or increases in training load.

Of course, it isn't the trauma itself that is the causative factor for development. So how can you help the performer learn and benefit from the challenge? The difference between levels of adult achievement relate more to what performers *bring to* the challenges than *what* they experience. Therefore, it is essential that young athletes have the opportunity to develop PCDEs and coping skills, and have adequate social support, to ensure that adversity, trauma and challenge are interpreted as positive growth experiences. In this chapter we provide some guidelines about how a periodised and progressive set of challenges, preceded by specific skill development, would seem to offer the best pathway to success. The importance of preparing athletes for challenges, supporting them through the experience, and then encouraging positive evaluation and reflection should be a central focus to TD. Finally, we offer some suggestions, structures and systems which can be used to support the skill-based approach promoted. In short, some guidelines on how to facilitate this 'rocky road' are presented and discussed.

12
PREPARING FOR TRANSITIONS

Mind the gap! Supporting athletes through developmental transitions

Once a performer gets into the system, it isn't of course all plain sailing! As athletes progress they will encounter various transitions from both within and outside with their sporting context. Indeed, preparing athletes to negotiate these key transitions successfully might well be a key factor in helping them realise their potential. As you can probably recount from your own coaching or playing experiences, dropout is especially prevalent at key transitions, such as the move from underage to adult levels of sport, or out of secondary school into university, the workforce or full-time sport. Being able to find a balance between these different commitments as well as changes in environment, expectation and involvement is crucial. Therefore, in order to keep the talent pool as deep as possible, it is important that coaches, parents and other stakeholders proactively prepare young athletes for both the anticipated and unanticipated transitions that will be experienced as part of the developmental journey.

What is a transition? A transition can be defined as an event or non-event which results in a change in assumptions about oneself and the world, and in turn requires a corresponding change in behaviour and relationships; athletes must possess the skills, attitudes and competencies to adapt to these new situations. Of course, it is important that we remember that the young athletes do not experience 'sporting' transitions in isolation; remember the importance of understanding development from a biopsychosocial perspective that we discussed in Chapter 1? Transitions are a very useful way to understand how physical, psychological and social changes interact and impact on the developmental pathway of aspiring elites. Viewing any one perspective in isolation is likely to give a distorted picture and miss some key factors. Taking a holistic view therefore is critical, so it is important to understand how challenges in other spheres of the young athlete's life impact on their sporting trajectory (or indeed vice versa where sporting transitions impact on psychosocial development, for example). What could this look like? A high-performing young athlete may be physically ready to compete at senior levels of performance but might not have the social skills or confidence to benefit from such a transition. Instead, the young athlete may benefit from competing within his or her own age group as 'the star' and being allowed the opportunity to develop skills (e.g. leadership, self-regulation) that would benefit them in the longer term. The need to consider the orchestration of these transitions (as is the case with most TD issues) on a case-by-case basis according to the need of individual athletes is the key message here.

What happens during a transition?

Transitions are inherently stressful since athletes are uprooted from established behaviours and circumstances, and their usual patterns of action, and required to behave in new ways that fit the changed circumstances. We have already stressed through this book that TD is best thought of as dynamic and non-linear; therefore transitions within sport should be viewed as a series of events where athletes have to cope with new demands and find a balance between these demands and the resources available to them. A performer's ability to cope with these unstable periods of development is crucial, with research suggesting that psychological behaviours act as transitional mechanisms that guide performers into stable and more effective levels of performance (see discussion in Chapter 6 on the role of PCDEs). Again, this points to a skill-based approach to TD; the importance of proactively equipping young athletes with a toolbox of skills that they can draw on to cope with the challenges they face at various points in their development. Ensuring that athletes have the opportunities to develop and refine these skills in advance also helps build the confidence when they have to deal with 'real' transitional challenges. This supports the importance of the Teach–Test–Tweak–Repeat cycle of PCDE development we proposed in Chapter 6.

Characteristics of within-career transitions

When you look at the TD pathway, it is obvious that some within-career transitions are predictable and normative; all athletes will experience these as they progress. For example, the transition into senior levels of competition is predictable because of the structure and organisation of your sport. These transitions are easily signposted and effective TD pathways can implement a 'plan of attack' for supporting athletes into this higher level of competition and the challenges that ensue.

Other transitions are unpredictable and may occur unexpectedly or even not at all (e.g. injury, change of coach, selection or deselection). These transitions are generally unanticipated and involuntary, but occur in response to important events in the athlete's life. Non-normative and unpredictable transitions are obviously much harder to detect in advance, as they are not necessarily signposted in the same manner as predictable transitions. As a result, less attention is generally paid to preparing athletes for the non-normative and unpredictable transitions and performers are often in the midst of the 'crisis' before a plan is put in place. Given the idiosyncratic nature of these transitions (different athletes, even in the same team or sport, will experience different challenges or cope with the same challenge differently), support services aimed at supporting athletes through transitions should include frequent evaluation and adjustment at an individual level so that development plans can counter sudden and unpredictable events and transitions. Unfortunately, generic systems are the norm within sport, even though these may not meet the needs of all athletes. As emphasised throughout this book, an individualised approach supported by empirically grounded principles, should underpin work in this area.

A developmental model of transition

In addition to their degree of predictability, transitions can also be characterised by their origin (Wylleman, 2001); some transitions have an intra-individual, physical or psychological basis (for example, injury, growth spurt or decrease in motivation) while others occur within the performer's environment. The latter can be related to the individual's setting, psychosocial, educational or professional life. Wylleman and colleagues (Wylleman and Lavallee, 2004) proposed a model of transition that helps us understand what this might look like for a young performer. This model encompasses a holistic, life-span perspective spanning both the individual's athletic and non-athletic careers and describes the normative or predictable transitions that athletes are likely to face during their careers, as well as the origins of such transitions. The model consists of four interacting layers; (1) athletic; (2) psychological; (3) psychosocial; and (4) academic. The athletic layer reflects the macro stages of development (sampling, specialisation, investment, discontinuation; Côté, 1999). The psychological level outlines the stages and transitions that occur at a psychological level, namely childhood, adolescence and adulthood. At a psychosocial level, transitions that occur relative to the athlete's career include changing interpersonal relationships; your performers will experience changes in their family, friendship and even sporting relationships. The final level within this model describes the normative academic and vocational transitions that athletes encounter, such as moving from primary to secondary school, and from there into either higher education or employment. Figure 12.1 shows how this might play out for an 18-year-old rugby player who has just signed his first professional contract. The reciprocal and interactive nature of this model recognises that, for example, the athletic transition into the investment years coincides with academic transitions (e.g. transfer into third level), psychological transitions (e.g. transition from adolescence into adulthood) and psychosocial transitions (e.g. development of stable relationships, move away from parents). The young player is clearly faced with significant upheaval just as they are trying making a huge step up in their sporting career!

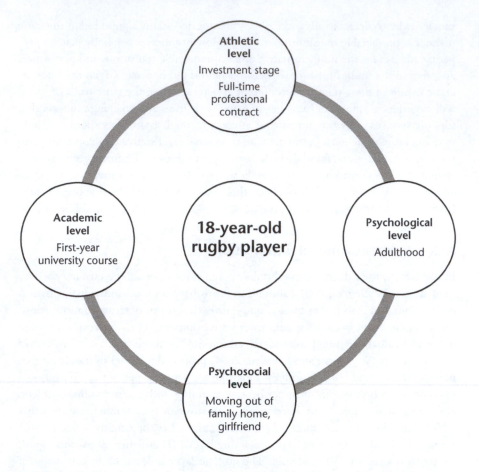

FIGURE 12.1 Developmental transitions experienced by 18-year-old rugby player

The swimmer represented in Figure 12.2 is faced with different developmental challenges as she tries to cope with selection to the National training squad. How does this information help us support young performers? Wylleman and colleagues (2004) suggest that this model should alert practitioners and researchers to the 'developmental, interactive, and interdependent nature of transitions and stages faced by individual athletes' (p. 517) and should highlight the need to take a holistic view when working with young athletes. Supporting performers through transitions seems to work best when all stakeholders work cooperatively with the best interests of the athlete and their long-term future in mind. The need for schools, sports and parents to understand what is happening in all areas of the young performer's life is crucial. Keeping lines of communication open and knowing when to pull back or forge forward (depending on what is happening) and doing this in a cooperative manner is a good starting point. Without this, something will have to give and the young performer (and his or her performance) will undoubtedly suffer.

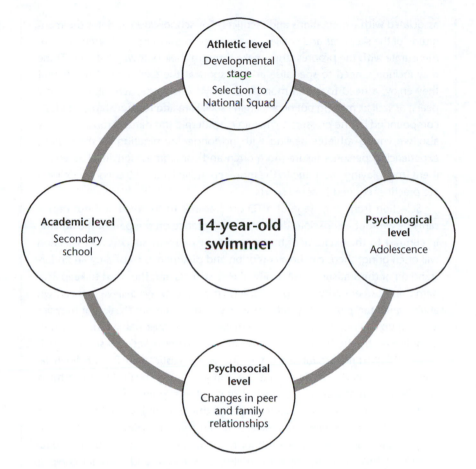

FIGURE 12.2   Developmental transitions experienced by 14-year-old swimmer

---

Expert perspective on Chapter 12

Iain Simpson is Director of Sport at Oakham School, an independent boarding and day school for girls and boys aged 10–18 years of age. The school enjoys an outstanding record of success at local, regional and international level and over 50 pupils regularly represent their county or country in their chosen sport.

This chapter reflects a lot of the issues that we see in a school context when we are working with young performers. At Oakham we support young athletes undertaking changes at various stages of their sporting careers whether that be moving onto pathways for the first time, moving through their stages successfully or falling off pathways when release and deselection takes place. In an upward trajectory, these transitions require athletes to adapt to changes in culture and required behaviour, and to deal with an escalated level of pressure associated with expectations and sacrifices. For school-aged athletes the magnitude of the sacrifices and challenges they face in transition will often be commensurate with the progress they make through their pathway's stages. These may include a need to specialise in their sport at the exclusion of sports that they enjoy; a need to spend more time away from home, school, family and peers; as well as missing out on a teenage social life and relationships. This is all compounded by the pressure to maintain academic standards. Transitions may also see young athletes dealing with no longer dominating in their sport, experiencing personal failure more often and sometimes deriving less enjoyment from playing sport due to the more repetitive focus of training or deliberate practice required in some sports.

Selection from one stage of a TD programme to the next will not necessarily be without a conscious decision or acceptance on the part of the athlete. In contrast to the excitement that academy or pathway success and selection will often bring, there can be a confusion and dissonance caused by an understanding of the statistical probability of elite success and the need to keep academic and career pathways open. Athletes may not always believe in their own ability, and fear, particularly in team sports, and sometimes think that they are 'making up the numbers' required to make programmes viable. This is further complicated by the hopes and expectations of parents keen to support their children's sporting aspirations yet maintain a realistic plan B. The financial rewards associated with 'making it' vary hugely between sports and so these can affect the motivation for academic or vocational provision.

Towards the end of secondary education the number involved in pathways reduces following progressive deselection, but those remaining all face transitions as they prepare to leave school and embark on future and often dual careers. At this stage, transitions can also involve club and contract choices, education choices and relocation, all as part of a move into senior sport and its own associated uncertainties. For those who are released, as is often the case at this stage, this transition involves decisions about whether or not to strive to pursue a future in elite sport, if indeed there is a route by which that can still be achieved.

In all cases of transition as part of a school programme we look to support young sportsmen and women in an athlete-centred and individual way. This support involves mentoring by adults who have experience of high performance and is extended to parents and family as well as those involved in an athlete's academic programme. The relationships that we create with pathway and academy coaches and directors are paramount to the assistance and information that we can provide and equally a breadth of associations allows alternatives where appropriate. We have to see ourselves as *part* of a pathway, not as a pathway.

How to support athletes through transitions?

It is all very well knowing what transitions and challenges athletes are likely to encounter, but how can we optimally support athletes at these critical junctures? First, it is important that we acknowledge links, overlaps and interactions between different levels of development as highlighted in Figures 12.1 and 12.2. If a coach is focused solely on an athlete's sporting trajectory then they are likely to minimise the potential impact of transitions in other realms of that individual's life. Finding a balance between the growing demands of the sports career and educational and psychosocial development seems the most sensible approach. The saying 'You are coaching the child, not the sport' is a sensible reminder of the importance of putting the needs of the individual to the forefront of your coaching practice.

The final section of this chapter deals with how to manage a dual career and provides some guidelines for key stakeholders about how to optimise that approach. All this evidence points to the need to consider the support and resources offered to young performers as they attempt to negotiate these transitions. Ideally these resources should be tailored to meet the demands posed by the multiple layers of Wylleman and Lavallee's model (2004). Without the skills to successfully cope with transitional challenges, even the most able performer is unlikely to realise their potential. Conversely, the young performer who is equipped with the skills to overcome these challenges, and offered the support systems to smooth their pathway (but not too much!), will maintain their involvement at their chosen level of engagement.

The timing of key transitions along any pathway to excellence is going to be influenced by the educational and sporting structures imposed on that sport; young gymnasts are likely to transition to the specialisation stage of development at a much younger age than a rugby player. UK and European athletes are likely to specialise later than their US counterparts because of different educational and sporting structures; Bridge and Toms (2008) noted that this pattern mirrored the educational changes and age groupings of sport within the UK, with athletes entering the investment phase at approximately 18 years of age (i.e. coinciding with educational (e.g. university) and competition structure changes). Of course, the timing of the transition into elite sport is also likely to be influenced by the demands of the sport itself. Again there isn't a 'one size fits all' blueprint for TD. For example, critical episodes, rather than age-defined events, appear to be more salient and notable transitions during development. Coaches, and others involved in the design and implementation of the pathway, should be cognisant of these timings as they prepare athletes to meet the demands they will inevitably face.

Managing the dual career

The adage 'give a busy man a job' seems to ring true when we begin to list the number of elite athletes who have also excelled in other areas of their life. There are many examples of athletes who have balanced academic and sporting careers and achieved at the highest level of both; Katherine Grainger, for example, won five Olympic rowing medals for GB while also completing her PhD in Law. These success stories can act as good leverage when you are negotiating with head-teachers and parents for access to young athletes. In the rest of this chapter, we describe how we can help athletes maintain a dual career, especially as the demands from both parts of their lives intensify. From both an individual and societal perspective, there seem to be multiple benefits for athletes who balance education and sporting commitments. Athletes who gain academic qualifications have been shown to be better able to manage (expected and unexpected) developmental transitions as well as being better placed to make a positive contribution to life after sport. Conversely, athletes whose sole focus was on their athletic career experience more negative consequences as they transition out of sport. Given that the pursuit of both academic and sporting excellence requires significant commitment and time, how can we support athletes as they pursue both goals simultaneously?

A dual career can be defined as

> the requirement for athletes to successfully initiate, develop and finalise an elite sporting career as part of a lifelong career, in combination with the pursuit of education and/or work as well as other domains which are of importance at different stages in life, such as taking up a role in society, ensuring a satisfactory income, developing an identity and a partner relationship.
>
> *(EU Expert Group 'Education and Training in Sport', 2012, p. 6)*

For young athletes, a dual career is usually a combination of academic and sporting pursuits while for older athletes a dual career might comprise a vocation or work combined with sport participation.

For most young athletes, their TD trajectory can be defined as either a *convergent path* where the athlete balances a sport career and academics but prioritises their sport career, or a *parallel path* where the athlete places equal importance on both their sport and academic careers. It is likely that the priorities for athletes will be highly individualised – some will prioritise sport over education and vice versa – and the extent to which they prioritise sport or academics is likely to be influenced by significant others (e.g. parents, friends) as well as social expectation and cultural norms. The key point here is that a dual career seems to be both appropriate and beneficial for the long-term development of young athletes. However, the realities of managing these competing demands have to be acknowledged. Education and sport both require significant investment of time and resources and these commitments increase in both domains simultaneously throughout adolescence. Therefore, maintaining these multiple demands can be extremely challenging for young athletes, especially considering adolescence is also a period of time where young people encounter a range of other stressors, including the challenge of growing up! The rest of this section will consider the benefits of balancing academics and sporting pursuits and how you might encourage athletes to maintain a dual career.

What are the benefits of a dual career?

Most young athletes that enter your pathway will not exit as World, Olympic or even elite athletes. For example, there are 12,500 players in the English Football Academy system and a rough estimation suggests that just 0.5 per cent of Under 9 players progress through to first-team football. If players have such a small chance of 'making it' (and similar progression rates are likely across sports), coaches and NGBs have an onus (and parents should also be keen) to ensure that young players are equipped for both progression in sport and a life after sport. There are, of course, some very pragmatic reasons for maintaining a dual career. Very few athletes, even those who compete on the international stage, earn enough money to live comfortably and certainly not for prolonged periods of time. Therefore, ensuring athletes have gained education qualifications that will allow them to transition out of the athletic world and into 'civilian' life should be an important part of the TD pathway.

Even for those players who maintain their involvement in sport, there appear to be several individual and societal benefits to having a 'dual career'. Maintaining a dual career helps young athletes cope with the transition from junior to senior sport as well as the transition to higher-levels training environments. Having a life 'outside sport' seems a very healthy thing. In fact, despite the extensive demands that academic and sporting pathways place on young athletes, successful TDEs recognise these benefits and are highly supportive of, and facilitate athletes' engagement in dual careers. Other benefits of maintaining a dual career include positive socialisation effects, higher employability (athletes can transfer the skills learned in elite sport to the workplace), reduced stress, a sense of balance and positive effects on an athlete's self-regulation. Athletes who maintain a dual career also seem to be able to maintain perspective and a realisation that there is more to life than sport.

At the individual level, having a dual career has been shown to promote greater balance; young athletes haven't placed all their eggs in one basket in terms of defining who they are and their self-worth. This is extremely important, as it limits the development of an exclusive athletic identity which we know has significant consequences for drop-out and life after sport. Athletes with an exclusive athletic identity – where their self-worth and identity is tied to their sport, 'John the Swimmer' – tend to experience difficulties when they transition out of sport, whether that is at the end of a long career or earlier along the pathway as a result of injury or deselection. In contrast, athletes who have engaged in a dual career tend not to have an exclusive athletic identity and are better prepared for transitions and retirement, have better and more established coping skills and are better able to access social support.

Although we all recognise the benefits of a dual career, it can be challenging, given that both sport and academics require significant amounts of effort and time. Maintaining both pathways simultaneously can be time consuming, and often results in fatigue, a loss of motivation for maintaining a dual career, and a lack of time and opportunities to participate in activities outside of sport or education.

Unless properly managed, maintaining a dual career can also lead to overload and associated increases in injuries, and may even result in the athlete failing to achieve their potential in either, or both, their sporting and academic endeavours. These factors might also lead young athletes to abandon academic commitments to solely focus on their sport. However, the positive consequences of a dual career, both in the short and long term, outweigh potential negatives, but the latter do point to the need to put structures in place to manage the pathway. What do these structures look like in the real world? Deirdre Lyons, Player Development Manager for the Irish Rugby Union Player Association (IRUPA), outlines how their Player Development Programme helps young rugby players undertake educational, vocational and personal development opportunities while pursuing and achieving excellence. In the final section of this chapter, we offer some guidelines that should underpin the support structures required to minimise disruptions to both elements of the dual career.

Expert perspective on Chapter 12

Deirdre Lyons manages the Player Development Programme at Rugby Players Ireland, and works on the ground as a Player Development Manager for Connacht Rugby. Deirdre has more than 18 years' experience working in high-performance sport, having previously worked at the Institute of Sport, Ireland and has a PhD in sports psychology.

This chapter reflects many of the issues that I deal with on a daily basis. Teenagers now view rugby as a professional career and Rugby Players Ireland realise the need to expand the duty of care to life off the pitch as well as on it. Each professional rugby team in Ireland has a dedicated Player Development Manager working with them to help players integrate personal development with rugby development. Our Player Development Programme is comprised of five pillars: career advice and guidance; education, training, and skills; social engagement; financial planning and management; and player wellbeing. All of these pillars support each other to foster personal growth and development. The PDP aims to maximise opportunities for our members while they are still playing, and ultimately support them for life after the game.

Over the course of a week, a PDM will proactively work with members of their provincial team, from sub-academy level (post-secondary school, but not yet on a provincial contract) through to senior professional players. We also work with players who have transitioned out of the game. This individualised support allows each player to place their own unique passions, values, skills and interests at the centre of their personal development plans. Our PDMs strategically focus on academy and sub-academy levels. Players at this level are encouraged to take part in academic education, or learn a trade or skills that they enjoy (e.g. welding, coding, blogging, barista skills). Engaging in non-rugby activities helps players to develop an identity outside of their game and provide them with outlets when rugby may not be going so well (e.g. injury, non-selection). Our role involves building relationships with academic institutions and various workplaces to offer choice and flexibility to players. We also work closely with the management at the clubs to ensure that we view the development of dual careers from a 'whole person, whole career, whole environment' perspective – as Áine and Dave say in the chapter, getting the culture right is key!

The transition out of secondary school can often be a huge change for young players – academically, socially and financially. Skills such as time management, communication, study skills are not just picked up as students enter third-level education. We run workshops and seminars with players on how to balance their time, identifying potential stressful periods around assignment deadlines and exams, tips for studying smarter (not necessarily harder) and understanding and developing their support network. We also work with other support staff in running cooking lessons, advice on sleep and recovery, even workshops on personal hygiene and health.

A huge focus recently has been on mental wellbeing. Through a public campaign, 'Tackle your Feelings', we have started the conversation with players that 'it is ok, not to be ok'. Issues, inside and outside of sport, can affect players in different ways. Injury, burnout, relationship problems, anxiety, bereavement, addiction, anger, money worries are just some of the problems that have come to our door. Rugby Players Ireland now have a network of qualified counsellors, psychotherapists, psychologists (sport, counselling, clinical, coaching) and chaplains to assist players. By helping players to cope with the challenges that they face we hope that talent loss could be minimised, and fundamentally that all-round development of young players is supported.

Maximising social support: guidelines for significant others

Of course, the responsibility for maintaining a dual career cannot rest solely with the athlete themselves. At the individual level, athletes need support from family, peers, coaches and teachers in order to manage the demands they encounter as they balance sport with other commitments. In fact, an athlete's ability to cope with developmental stressors and demands seems to be influenced by the support they receive from their immediate support network. This type of social support is likely to be particularly important at certain school and sport transitions phases. For example, it has been suggested that athletes might struggle to maintain their education when compulsory schooling ends, if they move away from home to train, or when they transition to university. Identifying these transition points, and putting the structures in place to support the athlete, is a vital step to maintain progress.

The challenges and benefits of a dual career will differ at different stages in athletes' lives. During the initiation stage of involvement, performers typically report a balanced life because neither sport nor education require too much time or commitment. During this stage, parents, siblings and friends all act as supporters and facilitators of sporting experiences and education commitments. As performers move into the development stage (generally during mid-adolescence), the commitment required from both education and sport increases but is usually manageable. Parents play a significant role during these years and are generally supportive and strong facilitators of the dual career. Of course, this isn't always the case and it may be that 'pushy mum or dad' might need some guidance from the sport about what is in the best (long-term) needs of the performer. To this end, the role of coaches and teachers is increasingly important in supporting the dual career and putting the appropriate structures in place. During the mastery stage, parents continue to play an important role but coaches now become both facilitative and restrictive of dual careers. The take-home message here is that a network of people help athletes manage the demands of a dual career and these multiple agents need to interact optimally, and coherently, to ensure the most effective TDE is created. In the next section we present some guidelines about how coaches, parents and educational and sporting organisations might work together to facilitate a dual career.

Implementing a supportive culture

It is important that the athletes' support network includes individuals who value education and the benefits of engaging in a dual career. Since the support network will include individuals from both sport and education it is vital that support is provided in an integrated manner. In a practical sense, this might mean that a point of contact is established in both domains, and regular and planned communication is maintained to monitor engagement in both sport and education. If all parties – the performer, coach, school and parents – know who the orchestrator is then the likelihood of managing the various demands is increased. Giving the young performer responsibility to manage this process is an important developmental task. This communication should be used to highlight specific times when sport and academic demands are likely to clash, thus allowing the athlete to plan in advance how to deal with this. This might be sounding a lot like the PCDEs we spoke about in Chapter 6, and it should! Ensuring your athletes have the skills to plan, reflect, communicate and seek social support when necessary were all highlighted as skills that allow athletes make the most of developmental opportunities. Simply, keeping a diary and up-to-date calendar is a simple tool for a young performer to help them manage the different demands they face from their various commitments.

You might be working or coaching in a sport that has not traditionally supported education as part of a dual career. Certainly, football is one sport where young players rarely maintained a dual career, with many players leaving school as soon as compulsory education finished. In this context, it is important to create a culture where education is supported and valued and key stakeholders are educated about the benefits of maintaining a dual career. If you find yourself in this type of environment, it might be that you need to think outside the box in terms of the educational structures that might suit your particular environment. This might mean that you need to find novel approaches to timetabling so athletes are not overloaded during busy or important times of the year and strategies are developed that allow athletes to manage the demands of a dual career. In order to change a dominant culture, it is also vital that all those involved with the athlete are informed about the benefits of a dual career and appreciate the benefits to an athlete's sport and academic performance that accrues from maintaining a dual career.

In conclusion

The benefits of proactively preparing young athletes for the (expected and unexpected) transitions they encounter along the TD pathway is hopefully the message that comes from this chapter. This approach is especially important for those of us working with young performers, who must balance a range of competing demands as they negotiate a challenging developmental trajectory. In addition to a skills-based approach, the importance of social support is a key factor in helping young performers cope with developmental transitions. If this is provided in a coherent and systematic manner then it is less likely that the athlete hears mixed messages. Although a dual career balancing education and sport can be a daunting prospect for athletes, schools and coaches, the benefits seem to outweigh the negatives, especially if we value the athlete's life after sport.

References

Bridge, M. and Toms, M. (2008). *Club sport and the developmental model of sports participation: a pilot study of the UK perspective*. European Association of Sport Sociology International Conference, Ljubljana, Slovenia.

Côté, J. (1999). The influence of the family in the development of talent in sport. *The Sport Psychologist*, 13, 395–417.

EU Expert Group 'Education and Training in Sport'. (2012). EU guidelines on dual career of athletes: recommended policy actions in support of dual careers in high-performance sport. Available: http://ec.europa.eu/sport/library/documents/dual-career-guidelines-final_en.pdf.

Wylleman, P. (2001). Understanding the role of parents and coaches in the development of athletes. Invited keynote address presented at the British Association of Sport and Exercise Sciences conference on dealing with parents, coaches and athletes: a European perspective, Glasgow, Scotland. In D. Lavallee, J. Kremer, A. P. Moran and M. Williams (2004). *Sport psychology contemporary themes* (pp. 209–233). London: Palgrave Macmillan.

Wylleman, P. and Lavallee, D. (2004). A developmental perspective on transitions faced by athletes. In M. Weiss (Ed.), *Developmental sport psychology* (pp. 503–524). Morgantown, WV: Fitness Information Technology.

13

THE TALENT TRANSFER PROCESS

How it works, how it *could* work better and how to make it work for you

Introduction

One thing that has hopefully become clear as you read through this book is that there isn't one route that typifies development. In fact, an overly linear and structured development pathway is likely to be a pretty ineffective way to translate potential into performance. As you know from your experience, an athlete's trajectory of development can take a number of different routes. Simply, there are multiple pathways that individuals may take as they progress in their activity. In your TD system, some athletes will be successful as juniors, some as seniors, and a very small percentage will achieve both junior and senior success. Other athletes will drop out of competitive sport at various points but will (hopefully) maintain their involvement for participatory and wellbeing motives. In some cases, individuals may initiate their involvement in sport at a recreational level before moving into more competitive settings. It is a complex picture! However, if we really are keen to keep as many people involved as possible, for as long as possible, it is essential that the TD pathway and sport system offer flexibility and 'return routes' as key features. In this chapter we discuss how we can help *all* young athletes maintain their involvement in sport, at whatever level they wish, whether that is in your sport, another, or even at recreational levels. We see this as a long-term approach to TD founded on the importance of equipping young people for challenge and choice throughout the lifespan.

Facilitating lifelong involvement: transfer along the Three Worlds Continuum

In Chapter 2 we proposed an approach to TD – the Three Worlds Continuum – that enables a flow between different, but interrelated, motives for involvement, namely *participation* (taking part to satisfy needs other than personal progression;

Participation for Personal Wellbeing – PPW), *personal excellence* (Personal Referenced Excellence – PRE) and *elite excellence* (high-level sporting achievement; Elite Referenced Excellence – ERE) (Collins *et al.*, 2012). Within the Three World's Continuum (see Figure 13.1), ERE and PRE are mainly concerned with competitive sport; the former defines excellence in terms of high-level performance where achievement is measured against others with the ultimate goal of winning at the highest level possible. Excellence in a PRE world is more personally referenced and as such accomplishments such as completing a marathon, improving a personal best, playing for a local club team, or hill-walking can be considered as the pursuit of 'excellence'. Typical motivations for the third category – Participation for Personal Wellbeing (PPW) – might include the improvement of one's social life (e.g. making and keeping friends), the enhancement of one's social identity (by being a member of a high-status group or club), personal renewal (through activity which is fulfilling), or the maintenance of aspects of self-concept (staying in good shape). The point here is that individuals will participate in sport and physical activity for different motives at different stages of their lifespan and therefore the TD pathway must facilitate effective and smooth transitions between these 'worlds'. When we present these ideas to coaches at conferences or training days, they are sometimes dismissed (we would say wrongly!) as 'not relevant' because 'I coach high-performance athletes'. Of course, you might only work within one of these worlds but the system and pathway (what happens before and after the stage you are working at) must consider how it supports the fluidity of movement that is a feature of development. In Chapter 15 we return to these management issues. For the time being, think of the Three Worlds Continuum as a framework that allows young performers stay involved throughout the lifespan.

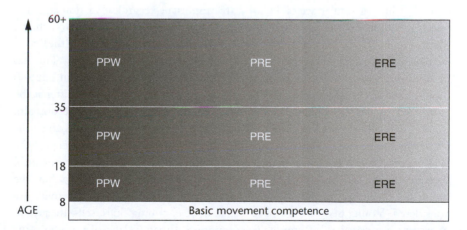

FIGURE 13.1 The Three Worlds Continuum

Note
PPW – Participation for Physical self-Worth; PRE – Personally Referenced Excellence; ERE – Elite Reference Excellence.

For those of us working with young athletes at the start of the pathway, it is important to note that the Three Worlds (PRE, ERE, PPW) are interrelated, at least in developmental terms. The proposition is that a common set of skills facilitates participation for these related but distinct motives. The message here is that the foundations of a good TD pathway will equip young people with the skills and competencies to maintain their involvement over the course of their lifespan. On this basis, young elite performers can drop out of a competitive pathway but still stay involved at a participation level, whilst late developers or returners can attempt to move into the ERE and PRE worlds at any age, practicalities notwithstanding. For example, a successful young athlete might choose to continue in their sport (or indeed in another sport) during adulthood at a recreational or participatory level while others may begin their involvement in sport at recreational level before moving into elite involvement at a later stage. Alternatively, an elite athlete should be able to maintain their post-retirement involvement in sport at more participatory levels if they so choose. As we will see later in the chapter, athletes may choose to change domain, termed Talent Transfer, in order to find a sport where they are more likely to achieve success. In short, at any age/stage and in progression from one to the next, easy movement between the Three Worlds is important; indeed under certain circumstances individuals may 'inhabit' more than one world concurrently. Preparing the young person for the road is as important as preparing the road for the young person!

PCDEs as achievement mechanisms for now and then, here and there!

What underpins the ability to transfer between different worlds? In Chapter 6, we described how a similar set of PCDEs are important regardless of domain. TD systems that promote PCDEs not only encourage and facilitate athletes to achieve their potential in their current performance domain but also allow for the 'cross fertilization' of talent into other domains at later stages of development. This has obvious implications for movement along the Three Worlds Continuum but also should increase the efficiency of the TD pathway by facilitating talent transfer at the elite level, as we will discuss later. Even if an athlete does not change domain, PCDEs will help them adapt their performance to the different situations and contexts inherent in their activity *and* the broad range of 'other stuff' challenges (the challenges of an adolescent lifestyle, for example) which can be equally powerful derailers on the TD pathway. As such, PCDEs are even more crucial when the significant challenges of prolonged engagement in sport and physical activity are considered. Young people must have the skills (e.g. coping skills, self-efficacy) to overcome associated risk factors (e.g. competing demands, lack of positive reinforcement) and steer a passage through the everyday stressors they encounter such as social and peer pressures. In essence, PCDEs act as a buffer against risk factors and contribute to a young person's ability to make appropriate choices about their physical activity involvement.

Recycling talent?

Reflecting on the multiple pathways that typify development, we now turn our attention to the ERE world and how sports might offer 'mature' athletes an alternative pathway to achieving success. One method that has received considerable attention is Talent Transfer (TT). TT initiatives have been adopted by various sporting organisations as a means of capitalising on the developmental investment made in previously identified athletes and fast-tracking athletes' progress in new sports where they may achieve success. Simply, the goal of TT is to 'recycle' an athlete's talent by seeking out already mature and experienced 'talented' performers to try a new sport, then develop skills to become equally, or more, successful in the new pursuit.

Structured TT initiatives

Across the last ten years, many sport organisations such as UK Sport and the Australian Institute of Sport (AIS) have invested large sums of money and significant political, intellectual and resource capital in structured and purportedly systematic approaches to TT (e.g. Tall and Talented, 2012, Girls 4 Gold, 2008, Sporting Giants, 2010, UK Sport) in an effort to capitalise on this approach. Specifically, during the London Olympiad UK Sport invested over £264 million in talent development alone (UK Sport, 2012). The English Institute of Sport (EIS) has even appointed 'Talent Scientists' to orchestrate the recruitment drive; notably, a discipline invented for this specific purpose. These specialists join a purpose-built 'Talent Team', individual discipline specialists who are responsible for providing the necessary investment to fast track an athlete to success. Similarly to the most common aspects of TT athlete recruitment, the sport science support primarily comes from motor control/skill acquisition and physiology specialists, with support from other disciplines (e.g. psychology, coaching) only coming in much later in the process, if at all. Hopefully, if you have got this far in the book, this approach should ring alarm bells!

In structured TT systems (Sporting Giants, and Tall and Talented are two examples from the UK), potential candidates are typically selected based on performance, anthropometric and physical profiles before talent confirmation and development phases at later stages of the process. Sporting Giants, for example, was the first TT initiative developed by UK Sport in 2007 and nearly 4,000 athletes were first selected based on meeting three criteria (between 16 and 25 years of age, over 6'3" for males and 5'11" for females, and with an athletic background) and then assessed using a battery of tests, including anthropometric (e.g. height, weight, arm span), power (e.g. vertical jump), speed (e.g. 5m, 10m and 20m sprints), endurance (e.g. multistage fitness test) and skill (e.g. sport-specific motor coordination tasks) assessments designed against profiles of elite athletes in the targeted sport. Following this assessment phase, a smaller cohort of athletes ($n = 58$) was selected to attend a 'talent confirmation phase' in sports thought to suit their physiological and anthropometric profile (i.e. handball, rowing, volleyball and canoeing). The importance placed on these test batteries as selection tools is exemplified by Gulbin's (Talent Scout Coordinator with the Australian Institute of Sport (AIS); Gulbin, 2001) suggestion that they 'have found what they are looking for' when an athlete met the world-class criteria on the Australian Institute of Sport cycling talent transfer tests. It would strike us as odd that potential could be confirmed through a single battery of tests! Indeed, the inefficiencies of these one-off and one-dimensional tests are encapsulated by this quotation from one of our research studies. In that study, we asked athletes to reflect on what helped them achieve world-class success. Reflecting on her physical profile, this Olympic medallist described how she would not have been selected into rowing based on the AIS TT criteria (a battery of physical, performance and anthropometric tests):

> Before Sydney, on the Gold Coast there was a project going on in Australia where they were going round the teams, measuring their physical attributes. They wanted to have your seated height and I wasn't even on the bottom of the scale so physically I wouldn't have made it [selection into rowing].
> *(GB Medallist at the Sydney Olympic Games, cited in MacNamara et al., 2010)*

It seems that TT might not be so efficient after all! Like other TI protocols, this approach to selection confuses determinants of performance (what the athlete can do, or how well they match a physical profile) with determinants of potential (what they are likely to do in response to an effective training environment). The key issue here is that a large number of potentially talented performers may be excluded from TT opportunities because of inappropriate identification measures that are based on set criteria designed to identify current performance rather than potential for development (Abbott and Collins, 2004).

Of course, there are strategic and resource implications to any talent identification model. Structured TT processes involve selecting those athletes who are most likely to be successful and from a pragmatic perspective this will involve some inclusion and exclusion error. There simply isn't enough resource to accommodate everyone so you have to make informed decisions about who will make the most of the TT opportunity. On this basis, picking tall individuals for basketball makes sense! However, what concerns us about the design of structured TT is the lack of an evidence base (or at least a peer-reviewed one). As a first step it would have seemed sensible to examine and understand the range of factors athletes perceive as facilitative of the TT process. Surely, asking successful TT athletes and coaches (and there are some very successful ones out there!) would have been a logical starting point to guide formal initiatives and maximise the investments made?

What are the benefits of TT for athletes and sports?

As standards in performance sport rise ever higher, coaches, sports and even athletes are searching for new avenues for recruitment and TT offers an alternate pathway for success. By transferring athletes from *donor* sports into *targeted* sports the probability of identifying athletes with the capabilities to compete at the highest level is thought to be increased by minimising adolescent maturational issues (issues concerning the RAE, for example) and maximising the developmental investment already made in these older athletes. In the UK, since 2007, over 7,000 individuals have applied to several targeted TT programmes offered by UK Sport with 100 athletes progressing into the World-Class system. These results suggest that there is considerable merit in TT initiatives that provide opportunities for athletes to maintain their involvement in elite sport as well as pragmatically targeting sports where success on the world-stage may be more attainable. TT may be particularly attractive in certain situations, especially in a high-performance, 'no compromise' culture that is evaluated and funded on the basis of medal success. In this case, sports are targeted that might be considered a 'better bet' because of a lack of depth worldwide, a high technical component (so money and investment is useful!), or a new status. Women's rugby sevens, for example, has certainly been a beneficiary of transfer athletes since becoming an Olympic sport. Being a relatively new sport, the playing populations in most countries are fairly small and therefore most nations have adopted a talent transfer strategy to identify the best athletes to compete for their country. For example, when Australia won the World Sevens series, the team consisted of players from diverse sporting backgrounds including rugby league, rugby union, basketball and athletics. If you coach in a sport with a small playing population, or in a sport breaking onto the competitive scene, TT seems to be a good strategy to fast track progress and accelerate the competitive edge of your team. No doubt the attractiveness of an Olympics is a useful carrot to attract promising players.

Reflecting this hunt for medals, TT initiatives will often target sports where there is an increased likelihood of success on the world stage. Bobsleigh and skeleton, for example, are frequently the destination for TT athletes because the return on investment in terms of medals would seem greater in minority sports than in global sports such as track and field; skeleton is not the usual choice of many aspiring athletes (at least in the UK!). Indeed, when it was introduced to the Winter Olympics there were only 100 registered female skeleton racers worldwide, and less than half of these had competitive experience on the world circuit (Bullock *et al.*, 2009). Given the low numbers, and the fact that the sprint start in bobsleigh counts for around 50 per cent of the variation in total race time, it seemed a logical destination for sprinters and gymnasts. The significant transfer between certain sports, summer and winter sports for example, is a phenomenon likely explained by cultural, topographical and pragmatic factors. What does this mean to you and your athletes? It might be that you need to think outside the box in terms of which sport your athletes are most likely to succeed in and facilitate that transfer for your athlete.

TT is also an attractive proposition for 'good, but not good enough' athletes who compete in very competitive events – they may have hit a performance ceiling, plateaued or aren't quite good enough to take the next step on the performance ladder. In fact, structured TT initiatives specifically target athletes who have competed at a high level in the donor sport as part of their selection criteria. The idea here is that these athletes understand the commitment required to train and compete at the highest level and presumably have the right psychological profile to be successful in the target sport. We have stressed the importance of psychological skills throughout this book and especially the need to consider how physical, physiological, environment and psychological factors all play a role in successful TT. Unfortunately, and as we have flagged elsewhere, this interdisciplinary perspective does not always inform TD decisions and certainly doesn't appear to be appropriately addressed during TT selections.

Optimising talent transfer for your athletes?

Be careful how you select!

There does appear to be strong evidence for *some* of the underpinning principles of TT. For example, Güllich (as described in Chapter 7) found a significant negative correlation between early specialisation and senior success, compared with a significant positive correlation between late specialisation and senior success. That research supports the basic tenet of TT: delaying selection until post-maturation so you can 'cash in' on the training history and experience of mature performers. However, the methodology of structured TT initiatives does not appear to have a strong empirical basis. As discussed, factors such as anthropometrics, physiology or required motor skills seem to be considered central to the selection process – pick the biggest, tallest or strongest and *then* train them. We have already made the case in this book that a range of factors, and their interaction, are key to success. Unfortunately, some of these, most notably psychology, seem to have been overlooked in structured TT programmes, at least during the initial selection process. A couple of years ago, we (MacNamara and Collins, 2015) wanted to discover athletes' opinion of what helps athletes transfer from one sport to another at the elite level. We interviewed seven successfully transferred, world-class level athletes and found that this genuinely elite sample (there aren't too many athletes who have achieved world-class success in two sports) attributed their success more to psycho-behavioural and environmental factors, as opposed to any anthropometric or skill factors upon which they may have been recruited by structured TT initiatives. The discrepancy between these findings and the processes that underpin structured TT initiatives certainly demonstrates the need for a stronger evidence base for TT initiatives and should alert practitioners to what they should (and shouldn't) be seeking during this process.

Expert perspective on Chapter 13

Toni Minichiello was Sportscoach UK Coach of the year 2012 and was British Athletics Elite Coach of the Year in 2009 and 2010. He coached Jessica Ennis-Hill from her start in athletics through to her recent retirement during which time she was Olympic Champion (2012) and four times World Champion.

I have had success helping athletes 'Talent Transfer' from athletics to bobsleigh and from athletics to cycling. The bobsleigh athlete went on to represent GB at three Winter Olympic Games (including a silver medal) as well as becoming World Champion. The athlete transferred to cycling gained a Bronze Medal at the Rio Olympics 2016. Based on this, and the fact that the World Championship Medals represent the only medals that bobsleigh have won at a Senior International global level since the 1998 Nagano Olympics, then I would say that Talent Transfer certainly can work!

These athletes had both been Junior International athletes within Combined events and represented Great Britain at World Junior Championships in Heptathlon. This multi-discipline background, I think, lends itself very readily to talent transfer as the athletes have had a multi-faceted skill and physical conditioning programme. Both athletes were in their early twenties before considering transfer and I believe that this well rounded background, not only in training but also having experienced the pressures and environment created by international competition, stood them in good stead to be able to cope with the high-performance rigours required for success at International level in other sports. These athletes were looking for opportunities to be successful in elite sport – the ERE world Áine refers to in this chapter – and saw Talent Transfer as their opportunity for this. The Talent Transfer experience for these athletes was informal and they did not go through an extensive testing nor a 'Talent Confirmation' process. There was no 'hot housing' of their abilities and no 'maybe' to their inclusion on a WCPP or Olympic team but a clear defined outcome goal; they were either in or out. This certainty, I think, enabled them to focus and commit over a very short time-span.

My experience of seeing other athletes attempt Talent Transfer is that the process can be too long, which creates doubt and uncertainty on the part of athletes and fed by any support systems (family and previous sport coaches). High-performing athletes want clear direction to an outcome and timeline because they want to commit to the goal of success, be that representation at the highest level or medals. The athletes I supported in Talent Transfer knew more or less straightaway that they were 'in' and didn't have to go through the rounds of selection and identification that were described in the chapter. This was a real advantage to their journey. The transfer sport plays an important role here; athletes want a sport that commits to them completely for a reasonable and specified period of time so that they in turn can commit to the sport in order to achieve the competitive outcome of medals. This is important because the transfer process will require life changes in terms of location and commitment.

High-performing athletes, to my mind, want to win medals and want to be on that journey as soon as possible. Talent Transfer offers that and gives them an opportunity, especially in the smaller participation sports that they have not experienced before. I am not convinced by the formal or structured TT systems described in this chapter. I feel that Talent Transfer systems are more concerned with collecting data, possibly too much data, which makes the analysis too drawn out; trying to fit within a particular number of brackets instead of realising that medal winning is more about finding an outlier not a norm. Working with Jessica Ennis-Hill, an athlete considered too small by her own sport governing body expert for her event yet winning two Olympic Medals and four World Titles, I feel adds weight to this reflection. I think that you need to look beyond the numbers to see who might really succeed. I think that a lot of what was said in the chapter is important: it is the size of the fight in the dog not necessarily the size of the dog that matters!

The TT coaching and environment

The extent to which the transfer environment differs from a typical high-performance coaching environment is also an under-researched, though potentially key, aspect of TT. It may well be that the 'transfer' coach has a significant role to play in facilitating TT, as s/he does at other stages of talent development and therefore attention to this facet of TT warrants attention. When we asked TT athletes 'what helped' they told us about how coaches provided them with an individualised learning environment and suggested that this 'fast tracked' their initial development in the transfer sport. The TT environment and coach maximised the athlete's previous experiences by encouraging athletes' input into training with coaches facilitating the transfer athletes to become 'agents of their own learning and transfer'. Given the experience that TT athletes bring, it seems sensible that coaches promote learning in the transfer sport by building on experience in the donor sport. Experiences at the top level of sport should be exploited by making links to prior learning and experiences. These results suggest that coaching style and agendas should usefully vary for TT athletes from that within the 'normal' pathway.

The need to be patient!

One of the attractive features of TT is the (purportedly) relatively short timeframe between entry into the sport and (hopefully) success. Sports can exploit the athlete's previous experience in the donor resulting in a shorter pathway than the traditional TD route. However, we suggest that alarm bells should ring when systems are so prescriptive and definite since development is anything but! For example, in our TT study, athletes described how a long-term approach characterised their TT environment. In contrast to the short selection and confirmation periods typically associated with structured TT, the athletes in our study felt that there was *no early pressure for results* when they transferred to the new sport. In fact, all the participants described relatively poor early performances before they adapted to the demands of the activity. Illustrating this, one athlete described how her initial performances were in no way indicative of her future success: 'I mean if you had seen my first couple of performances then you would have given me no chance! But the more I did it the better I got!' The lack of pressure to 'get it right straight away', and the suggestion that the athletes were given sufficient time, resources and attention to adjust to the transfer sport before they were expected to perform, was cited as key to their success. It is important to remember that these athletes were not part of a structured TT system but either self-initiated the process or were encouraged by coaches to change sport. It is likely that some of these athletes would have been dropped from TT programmes like Sporting Giants during the confirmation phase because they were slow to adapt to the new environment. This strikes us as rather careless given the success these athletes ultimately enjoyed in the transfer sport!

The age of selection to structured TT programmes is also worth examining. Initial applicants are usually screened based on demographics – typically athletes aged between 15 and 25 years are recruited. What is the basis of this and does this 'hard and fast' rule exclude potentially talented athletes based on a rather arbitrary criteria? Only two of the successful TT athletes in our study would have met the 15–25 years of age criterion associated with formal TT initiatives. The range of ages at which transfer occurred is perhaps indicative of the complexities of development in different sports and the idiosyncratic pathways that typify development in sport. Again, this is no one route to success or a single profile that typifies 'who makes it'. These findings suggest that an understanding and empirical evidence base of the time zones for effectively targeting and developing TT athletes is required as, without this understanding, potentially talented athletes may either be overlooked during the initial selection process or prematurely cut from talent confirmation phases. The health warning here? Be careful with prescription as having structures and processes that are too tight and rigid is likely to result in you missing out on exactly what you are looking for! Patience, a bespoke coaching approach and an athlete who has the psychological profile to maximise the experience seems to be key to TT.

Multiplicative approach to TT

So, what helps performers successfully transfer from one sport to another? It seems likely that it is facilitated by the identification, development and promotion of transferable, complementary and interactive elements (i.e. motor, physiological, perceptual, conceptual, physical, psycho-behavioural) in both donor and recipient sports. Unfortunately, psychosocial variables are either largely ignored or undervalued in structured TT, certainly during initial selection beyond a cursory inclusion in athlete specification: 'athletes must be mentally tough and competitive' is a typical, though rarely operationalised, requirement during initial recruitment. Once an athlete gets past this first step, a positive and empirically grounded feature of *some* TT programmes is the inclusion of a talent confirmation phase where selected athletes spend time in the sport system with a view to assessing how they cope with training and environmental requirements. The validity of this approach is well supported, stressing the importance of representative design during the selection process by employing tasks that are representative simulations of the performance environment; for example, tasks that represent variability, ensure decisions are context dependent, and consider individual differences. As such, transferees must have the skills and support (largely psychosocial) needed to successfully cope with these novel challenges.

Reflecting this, we would encourage thinking of TT as the broad, productive and supported use of acquired knowledge, skills and motivations as opposed to the direct and sequestered application of skills from one situation to another. Simply, the ability of a performer to take the 'whole package' of what they have learned from previous sport and apply that to expedite their development in the new sport. This suggests that those involved in TT should focus on assessing athletes' abilities to *learn* as the key factor. Simply, we should be placing more emphasis on an individual's capacity to learn rather than measuring what has already been learned. Indeed, our suggestion is that there is a need to consider and further explore the individual skills and characteristics required to meet the challenges faced in the transfer sport, along with an emphasis on appropriate coaching environments and timeframes associated with TT.

We would also urge people not to reinvent the wheel! It may make more sense to develop a comprehensive and well integrated TD system which would facilitate the transfer between sports of athletes who have already received investment from sport. These systems could then be supported by 'educated coaches' who have experience and understanding of the challenges faced by TT athletes. Such a system could then be supplemented by smarter recruitment. As an example, targeting transfer athletes by an appropriate age bracket, or use of skill transfer. Once these athletes have expressed interest, their previous experience of high-performance sport and the psychosocial assets it has left them with, can be analysed, to identify the athletes most worthy of investment.

In conclusion

In this chapter we have suggested that TT might be an innovative and productive means of maximising an individual's potential. Having said that, and echoing the warnings from Chapter 1 about scienciness and sticky ideas, we urge you to critically consider some of the structured and 'branded' TT initiatives against the evidence base that does exist. As always, we encourage the critical consumption of what is presented. The skills-based approach to TD that is stressed throughout this book, and in this chapter in particular, goes a way to meet the many agendas to which you probably work – elite sport, lifelong participation and physical activity. This may especially be the case for coaches working predominantly with young athletes. Ensuring that you equip young athletes with the skills necessary to make informed choices about their involvement seems to be a 'win-win' outcome that has positive repercussions for buy-in from schools, parents and, of course, the athletes themselves.

References

Abbott, A. and Collins, D. (2004). Eliminating the dichotomy between theory and practice in talent identification and development: considering the role of psychology. *Journal of Sports Sciences*, 22(5), 395–408.

Bullock, N., Gulbin, J. P., Martin, D. T., Ross, A., Holland, T. and Marino, F. (2009). Talent identification and deliberate programming in skeleton: ice novice to winter Olympian in 14 months. *Journal of Sports Sciences*, 27(4), 397–404.

Collins, D., Bailey, R., Ford, P., MacNamara, Á., Toms, M. and Pearce, G. (2012). Three worlds: new directions in participant development in sport and physical activity. *Sport, Education and Society*, 17(2), 225–243.

Gulbin, J. (2001). From novice to national champion. *Sports Coach*, 24, 24–26.

MacNamara, Á., Button, A. and Collins, D. (2010). The role of psychological characteristics in facilitating the pathway to elite performance. Part 1: Identifying mental skills and behaviours. *The Sport Psychologist*, 24, 52–73.

MacNamara, Á. and Collins, D. (2015). Second chances: investigating athletes' experiences of talent transfer. *PLoS ONE*, 10(11). Available: https://doi.org/10.1371/journal.pone.0143592.

UK Sport. (2012). 12 facts about 2012. Available: www.uksport.gov.uk/news/uk-sports-12-factsabout-2012-030512.

14

THE ROCKY ROAD TO SUCCESS

Introduction – the importance of a challenging developmental pathway

As highlighted elsewhere in this book, many of those involved in TD environments spend a lot of time, effort and other resource in trying to 'smooth the path' to excellence. We referred earlier to 'snowplough parents' who push all the difficulties from their child's way. Meanwhile, coaches make things as simple as possible for their athletes, avoiding challenges to keep the youngsters motivated and moving forwards.

As we said earlier, there appears to be a lot of sense in this, especially since eliminating outside pressures so you can fully focus on training and performance is the preferred system of choice for many elites, in sport and elsewhere. As we have stressed throughout, however, this is like many other uncritical downloads of the 'it works with elites, so of course it will work here' variety. Our point is hopefully made by the example in Figure 14.1.

As part of our ongoing research, we must have done well over 1,000 of these 'sketch your pathway' figures, examining performers, male and female, from a wide variety of domains. The idea is that the performer sketches his or her perceived performance level across the years of their progression to the top. For those who have made it, each one is very different; the only common feature is that it finishes at the top. The main point is that the pathway to the top is bumpy and idiosyncratic. Indeed, we would suggest that it has to be since, by contrast, those who promise much but don't make it (the 'Almosts' from our study reported in Chapter 7) do display a common path. Simply, these athletes are characterised by a fairly linear and smooth ride up to a certain level where, all of a sudden, the wheels come off and they either plateau or drop out of the sport altogether.

Progress to elite

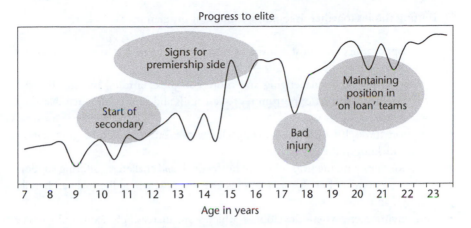

FIGURE 14.1 Athlete-drawn figure of his perceived pathway to the top

As this chapter will show, we believe that this sort of thing is causative. Excepting certain super-super champs, not *necessarily* the eventual absolute best but certainly high flyers from the moment they start, the challenges represented by the 'rocky road' are an essential part of the young athlete's development. Let's now consider how this might work.

Preparing performers to cope with, learn and benefit from the rocky road

As we said in Chapter 6, the Psychological Characteristics of Developing Excellence (PCDEs) are the curriculum we have designed for developing performers, providing them with a 'hand of cards' skill-wise, which they can deploy in different combinations to handle the different challenges they encounter on the pathway. Importantly, however, when used properly and integrated into the development path, the approach becomes a lot more than just a shopping list of mental skills.

For a start, we know that an individual's self-esteem is a big part of resilience – the essential bounce-back ability which is so important for rising in the 'School of Hard Knocks' which characterise most development pathways. We also know that having skills is only part of the puzzle; an individual must have the ability and willingness to deploy them, together with the confidence to keep trying if they don't work first time out. With regard to life experiences, we know that although some elites have experienced challenge and hardship when younger, there are even more who get knocked back by this sort of thing; perhaps even bearing the scars and working against the limitations for life. Finally, having mentors and a supportive environment seems to be key to generating the 'growth from adversity' which is currently being pushed as a big element in development programmes generally, and sport progression in particular.

Putting this lot together, it looks like the ideal programme will offer:

- the opportunity to boost confidence and self-esteem by successfully over-coming challenge;
- progressively more challenging and more complex 'hurdles' which offer the developing performer opportunities to test skills and gain confidence that they will work;
- support through naturally occurring challenges, but designed to grow rather than shield from the experience;
- relationships with mentors who will both check *and* challenge, offering support when appropriate but also standing back to see how the individual can handle things; and
- an environment where developing athletes are increasingly expected to take control of their future, seeking input from available and well informed sup-porters as needed.

So, reflecting this checklist we evolved the phased or 'periodised' approach which we summarise as:

Teach–Test–Tweak–Repeat

The general idea is as follows. First of all, young performers are taught the skills that they need. As described in Chapter 6, this is usually done in small bite-size chunks, with one or two aspects of the skill introduced, then supported as the performer tries it out in a simple context. For example, a nine-year-old might be shown how to use imagery to set themselves up to do a sporting challenge, then helped to work through using the skill over repeated trials. An 18-year-old might be encouraged to use self-talk as a help to keep going in a physical challenge.

Next, the skill is tested in a situation realistic to the sport. Nine-year-olds might do a cross-country run, whilst the 18-year-old is required to execute a technically complex task, interspersed with fatiguing physical work bouts. Ideally, these 'tests' are comparatively easy to measure, with clear and objective scores possible.

Following the test phase, which might be a single session or run over days or weeks (time periods generally increase with experience), individuals are debriefed on their experience, with feedback offered on what they did well but also how they could have improved their performance. Re-teaching or tweaking of the skillset can be used to build confidence and capacity. Finally, the process starts again.

As stated above, this cycle can increasingly be built into a periodised format. So young footballers will be warned of upcoming challenges (e.g. 'Your Tuesday night session is going to be challenging … make sure that you prepare well') whilst older martial arts students might go on a four-day training camp. In parallel, the chal-lenges become more multifaceted and complex; in other words, more realistic. This requires the performer to evaluate the challenge, think through it and make a plan, then execute using a range of skills in combination. As these more complex challenges come into play, feedback will also become more sophisticated. For example, the mentor could compliment the learner on his or her plan but question how well it was executed or how much the idea was committed to.

Recognise also that this approach embeds two other big features of effective performance under pressure. First of all, negative thoughts are almost automatically countered because you are looking at positive things to do. This, in turn, encourages the development of what psychologists call 'proactive coping'. That is you are thinking ahead of problems arising, thinking in advance what you can do to avoid them rather than only getting engaged when the fans are starting to get clogged! The other factor is, in our opinion, the most crucial one of all – preparation. All who operate in pressured situations acknowledge the importance of preparation, as enshrined in sayings such as 'Fail to prepare equals prepare to fail'! The approach suggested ensures preparation as a constant element in the performer's life, developing habits which will be effective both within and outside their sporting career.

We hope this doesn't sound too complicated ... we don't think it is at all. To be honest, this individualised approach is a feature of good coaching anywhere anytime, whether dealing with an individual sports performer, team athlete or even a squad or working group. The basis of the idea is the Do–Review–Learn–Apply idea which was enshrined by the educationalist Kurt Hahn within the Outward Bound Schools, which used adventure activities as the challenge for testing and stimulus for growth. Our main point here is that the quality of the debrief is key. Mentors, whether coaches, psychologists, parents or peers, must be committed to doing a good job, focused on challenging and supporting the learner. In short, the approach we suggest has underpinned good teaching for many years. All we are doing is offering some structure to the content (the PCDEs), the process (Teach–Test–Tweak–Repeat) and the progression which have always been a feature of growth.

In an ideal world, all performers will complete cycles of development throughout their time in an academy setting. In football setups, where players start as young as eight years, we have a 'curriculum' of teaching the skills, designed so that all have received, tried out and got feedback on them before the age of 16 (go back to Chapter 6 for an overview of this). Progressive support in the pro-like environment of youth football and beyond can then make use of the player's established armoury. Individual sports will set up challenge phases through tournaments, ideally preparing performers for the later selections which (whether they are right or not) are a common feature of current systems. Sensible design develops the curriculum to have linked elements of support (teaching the skills then supporting the learner as s/he tries them out) with challenge elements as tests. You will also see a sample of this presented in Chapter 6.

But what to do with those who coast through or are crushed by the test phases? And how do you help performers cope with the inevitable 'external trials' that are part of growing up?

How to generate *relevant* speedbumps along your developmental pathway

Well, the first thing to recognise is that learning to cope can start very young, with some quite simple domestic stuff. The approach, known as self-directed learning in educational circles, requires the child to solve problems for her or himself. After all, the logic goes, if you always solve someone's problems then they will probably let you keep doing it! You might consider this idea against the KR Crutch shown in Table 9.1, where the learner just absolves responsibility for feedback to the coach, with subsequent loss of quality learning.

Our point here is that encouraging the child to take charge and control stuff can start very early. For example, Dave is blessed with two *very* independent younger daughters who often insist on doing things themselves in their way. Rather than get irritated and brushing their hands away as he does the job, this is music to his ears! It might take a bit longer but now they can do it, it's one less thing to attend to and one more 'brownie point' to their confidence and self-esteem. Now if they can just learn to tidy their rooms.… OK, so miracles take slightly longer! But hopefully you see our point. The development of taking charge can start well before the child starts out on the academy trail.

So, assuming that all this has been started early, what you do as coach expect to happen as parent if your child is flying along? Well our point here is that, whilst it is very gratifying to see your son or daughter as the undisputed star of the show, this can be very bad for them in the long term. As we said earlier, losing out on the experience of coping with losing and disappointment, and having to handle pressure, means that you may arrive at the sharp end of the academy process with some skills missing. Parents and coaches may like to download the free version of our 'Superchamps' paper (Collins *et al.*, 2016; referred to in Chapter 7) and contrast the reported experiences of these achievers with the Almosts. In fact, for the academies and development programmes with which we work, the concept of 'speedbumps' has become an accepted feature of how to ensure potential high flyers get the necessary diet of challenge, together with the opportunity to develop their PCDE toolbox, that they will inevitably need. Collins *et al.*, 2016 examines this process.

As the paper suggests, there are several ways in which speed bumps can be built into the development process. In some sports, 'playing up' (working with older players, not mucking about!) is a good option. As other alternatives, getting youngsters to play in different positions, or in challenging circumstances (your left foot is weak, let's play you on the left) or against double marking, or with a points handicap will all work. Perhaps the best idea is the careful use of goal setting, which is covered in the next section.

For the moment, how about the other extreme, a young performer who is really struggling under the workload. Well, for a start the really switched on environment will generate a tolerance of this situation quite early. In other words, all members on the pathway will be told that they will face some strain at one time or another. Removing the stigma of being under pressure, of losing, or not being able to cope is really important. Good communication between coaches and parents, and then between parents and coaches and athlete (see Chapter 11 for some ideas here) will go a long way to helping the situation. More one-to-one coaching support will also help, whilst getting parents involved in both actual (e.g. practising challenging elements) and moral (e.g. role modelling how to handle things) support is another step. Finally, and given our emphasis on social support (the tenth PCDE mentioned in Chapter 6) we are all in favour of peer coaching and support. After all, almost all elite environments will involve some of the performers being under pressure some of the time. How great to generate an environment where this sort of thing is acknowledged, accepted and just dealt with!

We would like to stress that this isn't just 'cuddly fluffy bunny' thinking! *All* the elite environments we have worked in (and some were *very* elite and *highly* pressured) have peer support mechanisms built in; it would be a very strange pre-elite environment that didn't inculcate these same values and approaches as part of the norm. That isn't to say that all do, but we certainly suggest that all should, as a performance factor, not just because it is a humanitarian or kind thing to do. Surprisingly perhaps for some readers, martial arts gyms are one of the most collaborative and supportive places you will find. Perhaps it's something to do with beating the heck out of each other? Hopefully you hear our point, however. This is proper old school elite, not namby pamby stuff.

Goal setting

It is worth just repeating what is needed from the Teach–Test–Tweak–Repeat process. If done well, this will build confidence and self-esteem, focusing the learner on what s/he needs to do then introducing increasingly more complex challenges to provide practice (and more confidence) in playing the hand of PCDE cards optimally. As such, planning and review are integral parts of the process. So, goal setting is not only one of the PCDEs (see Chapter 6), it is also a key part of the rocky road process. Good use of goal setting will ease your path towards your targets, whether this is gaining a place in a particular team, winning a specific competition or recovering well from the injuries that are an inevitable part (unless you are made of steel/very lucky) of the performance pathway.

Now goal setting is a strange beast! Everyone talks about it, everyone uses it but slightly fewer use it well so that *all* the benefits are achieved. So herewith four important ideas to boost your goal setting skills, whether using as a coach or understanding and supporting as a parent … or maybe even using for your own domestic purposes!

1 SMARTER-R

There are almost as many versions of this mnemonic as there are articles on it, so don't be surprised if someone tells you a different version. No real worries here, though, as almost all match the same principles, with slightly different wrinkles and emphasis. For our purposes, the letters stand for and are defined and operate as follows:

- **S**pecific – The goal should be clearly defined and something that you can control or at least influence. So 'Stratford-upon-Avon FC to win the Premiership this year' is probably not a good goal!
- **M**easurable – It's good to have a goal which is measurable, either quantitatively against some performance or qualitatively against observation. So 'Lift 200 kg for one rep' or 'Look like you have better control of your pre-competition nerves' will work here.
- **A**chievable – Set a goal which you can see yourself achieving in the near future with resources and skills that you have or soon will. So 'Become a millionaire' or 'Be a senior international' are *dreams* for most 9-year-olds, but might be good *goals* for a 20-something just signing for a premiership team.
- **R**ewarding – Always useful if achieving the goal will give you something that you want (see the subsequent section on self-reward).
- **T**ime-locked – Pursuit of a goal shouldn't be a for-ever thing! Always try to set a target by which the goal will be achieved. For example, 'By December, I will be able to bench press 60 kg for one rep'.
- **E**volving – Clearly you want things to move on up, especially if you are on a development pathway. Consequently, you will revisit your goals at regular intervals, often in a formal set of regularly scheduled meets. But you should also feel free to tweak your goal in between as you reach the standard, if your circumstances change (e.g. more or less training time becomes available) or as it becomes clear that a different direction offers more potential.
- **R**egular **R**evision – So, like we just said, goal setting, evaluation and revision should be a regular thing, but not so often that you spend all your time in meetings. How often? Well how long do you expect this 'phase' to take? Use 3–4 months as a reasonable compromise. At a micro level, R-R will be an inevitable outcome of the Teach–Test–Tweak cycle.

The only other thing to mention here is that goals work better when they are recorded (some mnemonics say 'Ritten down' for the final R!), not just in the performer's head. Make sure that significant others (e.g. parents) know the goals, whilst coaches are living them with the athlete.

2 Process versus outcome

It is important to recognise that goals will have several dimensions, with process goals (what you have to do to achieve) feeding into outcome goals (what you want to achieve). There are a number of ways of doing this but one common and effective method is the Goal Ladder.

Figure 14.2 shows part of a Goal Ladder for a senior footballer on the way back from injury. All the goals are process ones, although they have an outcome 'feel' to

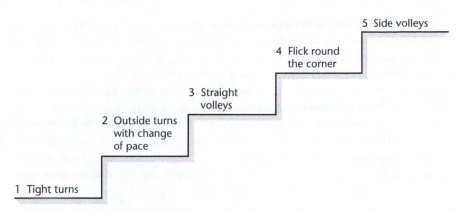

5 Side volleys

4 Flick round
the corner

3 Straight
volleys

2 Outside turns
with change
of pace

1 Tight turns

FIGURE 14.2 Goal Ladder for a premiership footballer in the later stages of recovery from knee surgery

them. Like many designed for this purpose, there are quantitative and qualitative elements to them, in that the 'side volley' stage, for example, will be evaluated by how good the shot is but also perhaps on how the injury feels afterwards, what the coach thinks of the shot, or even through some biomechanical/video-based analysis. The point is that designing the ladder helps to direct attention and also provides a way of measuring how the athlete is progressing. It also cements the planning process (the ladder in Figure 14.2 was developed by player, physio and coach for example) and helps the player to 'feel in control'. Using Goal Ladders, especially with combinations of process and outcome goals, is a very useful part of the Teach–Test–Tweak process. Coaches can usefully set this up at the Regular Revision sessions, just set simpler single goals for the test bits or, ideally, use all these in combination. The main thing is that achievement and progression up the ladder builds confidence.

3 Self-reward

Of course, goals are a lot easier to pursue, and processes a lot easier to stick to, when you can see that this will take you towards something that you really want. Especially for younger athletes, parents may feel like offering a gift for achieving certain successes, what psychologists call extrinsic (external because someone gives/does something to you) motivation. Many evangelise about extrinsic motivation being bad but we don't agree. So long as the performer is also developing intrinsic (inside – I do it to me) motivation as well, all works fine.

So, reflecting this idea, developing a young athlete's capacity and skills for self-reward is a worthwhile investment of time and effort for coaches and parents alike. As an example, let's return to the car journey home which was a focus in Chapter 11. We have already counselled against a sole focus on the result but outcome *and* process is another matter. So, win or lose, statements like 'I was really proud with your defending today' or 'Pleased with how you handled the pressure before the game ... you looked really in control' or 'Great encouragement for the rest of the squad ... looked like they really appreciated it' are good inputs. Using this type of approach, parents can 'model' self-reward behaviours: '*You* should be pleased with *this*'. As the social element gains importance into adolescence, stressing how well the behaviour was received by peers is another sneaky way of accentuating positive process.

Parents, coaches and teachers can start this as young as you like. Modelling the self-reward, telling the young performer what is good and encouraging or almost giving them permission to feel good about it is a good way to internalise behaviours. Rather like good manners – you do it because your parents and significant other adults praised you for it. As a result, the behaviour is internalised and you feel quite miffed when someone else doesn't do it. Like we said, a good investment of effort for the future.

4 Solution versus emotion

As the final strand of goal setting, it is worth looking at the types of challenges which young athletes will face and how they may best set goals and develop plans to deal with them. Psychologists talk about two types of coping, which are each suited to certain kinds of stressor.

Most sports challenges are best approached by use of solution-focused coping. In this style, the performer works out a plan of what to do, gets any additional skills that s/he is likely to need, sets some goals and then gets on with it. So, deal with anxiety on the start grid or in the changing room. The performer comes up with some more appropriate action-focused thoughts, might develop a few of the thought stopping/cognitive restructuring methods mentioned in Chapter 6, sets some process goals for how much better they want to feel and outcome goals around starting well, then gets going! Sounds easy doesn't it? Well there is a lot of challenge here, but the performer is in control of the challenge, so focusing on things to do and ways to control negatives (i.e. the *solution*) is entirely appropriate.

Now consider a challenge where the solution is *not* in the performer's control. Worrying about whether you will get selected is still partly controllable by you; you just switch off the 'but what if I don't ...' thoughts and focus your energy on what you need to do to perform better! No, we are thinking of a situation where you really don't have any control. Examples are serious illness in a family member, or how the team management are arranging things at a tournament. In this case, your focus is better on what you can control, the emotions you are experiencing, than fretting about the worries and what-ifs of the challenge itself. This *emotion*-focused coping is still about gaining control, but not trying to influence what you can't.

So athletes can make plans, set goals and employ the Teach–Test–Tweak approach to meet both kinds of challenge. Indeed, most elite sport (if not most life) challenge will require a bit of both. Imagine going to an Olympics. Broadly, there will be three phases, each with its own challenges and ways of coping.

1   Getting selected is a 'bit of both' challenge. Athletes focus their energies on performing well, getting into the right competitions to be noticed and arranging

their schedules so that they can hit the selection criteria. They avoid thinking about the what-if's, concentrating on what they can control.

2   Once selected and on the plane, in the holding camp or arriving in the village, they switch into emotion-focused mode. The Olympics, like many challenges, involve lots of waiting. Even worse, people try to organise your day for you, often with meetings, press conferences and the like, plus awkward, 'you must train at *this* time' style constraints. To counter, drop into sheep-mode, concentrating on doing things to distract from thoughts of the impending competition or the minor irritations of sharing with that large snoring shot putter. In short, emotion-focus.

3   Now it's the day of the event. You are maximally focused on *your* preparation, *your* warm up and *your* performance. It is now solution city!

Putting all this lot together should show you how goal setting and a set of related skills can be taught, deployed, tested and tweaked as an essential part of the pathway to the top. Lots of complexity here so, once again, breaking it down into stages, with regular evaluations to demonstrate progress and raise confidence, will keep you on the upwards path.

Expert perspective on Chapter 14

Robert Reid was the 2001 World Rally Champion. Since retiring from racing Robert has held several positions, including seven years as Performance Director for the Motor Sports Association and four years running development programs for Fédération Internationale de l'Automobile (FIA), including the FIA Institute Young Driver Excellence Academy.

This chapter deals with a concept that is often misunderstood amongst well-meaning parents; making an athlete's life as easy as possible in order to do well today certainly doesn't guarantee future greatness, and can often ensure future failure.

Many sports work by selling a dream to the parents and backers of young competitors; if only you can fund better equipment, have more practice, dedicate more time, then your son/daughter is destined for the top.

Whilst my domain, Motor Sport, is not unique there are certain commercial factors that exacerbate this phenomenon. Motor Sport is not cheap and is unlikely ever to be within the reach of many. This creates an opportunity and temptation to buy an advantage; go to a better team, use more new tyres, do more testing. Many win fairly easily at junior levels and then stumble when the competition gets stiffer as they progress through the ranks. The teams that run these drivers need to win today to attract the best/wealthiest drivers the next year, and many sponsors who are footing the bills want to be associated with winners today more than those with the potential for the future.

So whilst the costs of Motor Sport make this more obvious the end results are the same; athletes that fail to learn the resilience and adaptability needed not only to get to the top, but to stay there too. John Button, the late father of F1 star Jenson, often said that the reason Jenson was so great in the wet (he famously won the water-logged 2011 Canadian Grand Prix having been demoted to dead last after an incident half-way through) was that he couldn't afford wet weather tyres in junior karting and so when it rained Jenson had to make the best of dry weather 'slicks' in the wet.

There are no doubt elements of urban myth about this story, but the facts are that by creating a sub-optimal situation an athlete will learn skills that will come in very useful at tough times in the future. Rather aptly from a Motor Sport perspective this is often referred to as creating 'speedbumps'. It is important to point out that the key here is the way in which the athlete deals with the situation and gains from it, rather than the fact they had to endure hardship.

As Performance Director for UK Motor Sport I often saw examples of this: a driver who, whenever he dropped from the top of the timesheets whilst testing, fitted new tyres to propel him back to being fastest and then struggled towards the end of a race as the tyres wore down; drivers being dropped by sponsors or private development programmes after a couple of poor results who then came back stronger having had to fight to get a budget together and get back on the track.

In every sport there are opportunities to introduce and manage these speedbumps as a part of the athletes development program. In Motor Sport taking a mixed group of drivers into a low grip environment that would suit the rally drivers, and onto a race circuit that suits the race drivers, creates a situation where both are out of their comfort zones, learning from each other and building adaptability and resilience. This chapter gives an insight into managing the speedbumps to ensure the development of the skills needed both now and in the future.

In conclusion

As with many of the chapters in this book, there is a lot of inter-related stuff to take in. The Rocky Road has a number of side alleys, detours and ways to get lost, but also some shortcuts and motorways if you navigate well. Catering for all the elements described here will undoubtedly benefit your athlete/son/daughter, providing skills for the challenges encountered both now and in the future.

References

Collins, D., MacNamara, Á. and McCarthy, N. (2016). Putting the bumps in the rocky road: optimising the pathway to excellence. *Frontiers in Psychology*. Available as free download: http://journal.frontiersin.org/article/10.3389/fpsyg.2016.01482/full.

PART VII

Management considerations

15

DESIGNING AND OPERATING A PATHWAY

Introduction – management considerations for TDEs

Lord knows this is not a business management manual, neither are we management gurus! There are, however, several key factors which transfer well from the world of business to the management of performance environments. We start by listing and briefly considering them before we take a look at the area of specific interest; namely, the Talent Development Pathway. Unsurprisingly, perhaps, all these will be focused on aspects of leadership.

The first key factor is clarity. As a constant message through this book, there is a need for all TDEs to have clarity of purpose, with efforts hopefully focused on long-term development. As such, management should be very clear publicly, and consistent with this in private, in regard to the purpose of the academy or pathway structure and how it works. Of course, for various reasons long-termism may be moderated in certain sport-specific settings. In motorsport, for example, young drivers will have to demonstrate levels of good performance if they are to secure the funding and sponsorship which is so important for transition to the next level. Performance today may also be important in other settings, because of structural (e.g. selection to the next stage of the process) or local conditions. Whatever the reasoning, however, the leader should ensure that this is crystal clear.

The second factor is consistency. In other words, once the philosophy has been determined, how consistently is this pursued through the various levels of the pathway, and by the different individuals concerned? This is important in terms of sending clear and consistent messages to developing athletes, but also in keeping staff on track.

The final element is a core part of attaining clarity and consistency; namely, the extent to which all involved hold or at least subscribe to a Shared Mental Model or SMM. The concept of SMMs has come from what are termed high-stakes environments. Medical operating teams, firefighters, Special Forces and global sales teams all benefit from holding a similar set of weightings on what factors are important. This then extends to how these factors are interpreted and applied to designing and applying a solution. SMMs are also a primary method for attaining the aims of clarity and consistency.

Just to be clear, all these ideas are certainly not suggesting that management must impose a rigid system, or that coaches should be constrained to only work in a certain fashion. In our experience, TDEs work best when there is a clear structure and set of outcomes, then coaches are provided the freedom to work within these guidelines to achieve the set targets. This *might* mean that some individuals are more suited towards certain systems than others, or would be better in certain types of roles. In other words, 'picking and playing' your team to best effect. That is what the rest of the chapter is aiming to do.

Epistemological chaining, coherence and maximising return

Hopefully, one of the questions which might have occurred to you as you read through the Introduction is: where does the coach's individual philosophy fit into everything? One big factor is how the coach thinks people can best learn new skills and, in association with this, what 'knowledge' in the sport looks like and is best conveyed. The word used for this is 'epistemology', and it *should* play a big part in determining how the coach works.

We have done quite a bit of work on this construct with our colleagues and master coaches, David Grecic and Loel Collins. Specifically, we were interested in how it impacts on coach behaviour and athlete learning. Table 15.1 presents a simple way to think of epistemology and how it impacts behaviour: namely, by thinking of the two extremes.

Of course, even though these are extremes, and most coaches will fall some-where in between, you will still see examples of both ends of the spectrum. Hope-fully, you will also see that it is better to be sophisticated than naïve! Certainly, the levels of athlete involvement and the more comprehensive and personal nature of the goals for this approach should appeal to many coaches and parents. The way in which the coach's epistemology impacts on the whole coaching process is shown in Table 15.2, which provides an example of how the 'chain of reasoning and action' follows (at least sometimes) from his/her beliefs about the way people learn and the nature of knowledge.

Hopefully, you can see the logic in how the way in which I think knowledge is constructed flows through to impact every stage of the chain I use in planning and executing my coaching. There are a couple of things to note here, however. The first is that a coach's epistemological chain is not *necessarily* a direct or consistent link, either at the two extremes shown or anywhere in between. This is often due to a lack of thinking through the reasons for, and consequences of, a particular coaching style. Another common reason is down to coaches copying a method that they see, whilst not thinking through how it fits with their own beliefs and personal style. Whatever the reason, inconsistencies in the chain can be both confusing for

TABLE 15.1 The two extremes of epistemology

Naïve		Sophisticated
Knowledge is absolute and factual. It is possessed by experts, like the coach.	View of knowledge	Knowledge is relative and is constantly being discovered and refined. All can develop and possess it.
Learning is the acquisition of facts and experiences. A process of 'time served'.	View of learning	Learning is a never-ending process of seeing relative relationships in context. A process of constant reflection.
Authoritarian/benign dictatorship. I lead, you follow.	Relationship and environment	Mutual trust and respect. Athlete encouraged to experiment and try things out without fear of failure.
Success equals results, or at least tangible markers such as skills mastered, training performances achieved, etc.	Success	Success equals development of the athlete as an autonomous individual.

the athletes and decrease the impact of the coaching message, which needs to be clear and consistent to have maximum effect. In simple terms, coaches need to be coherent with their beliefs, providing their athletes with 'what they signed up for'. Furthermore, managers or senior coaches will generally prefer to work with coaches whose epistemology matches their own; another reason for being consistent in your belief to action chain. Pretending to be what you don't believe in is generally a recipe for disaster.

There is another factor at work here; and one which is, we would argue, the best way to enhance the impact of any coaching process. Simply, it relates to the why (or why not) something is done rather than just the what: you may recognise this idea from elsewhere in the book. We call the application of this 'Professional Judgement and Decision Making' or PJDM. Clearly, there is no one way to coach, and different methods will have different outcomes, as per the ideas we explored in Chapter 9. Crucially, however, the best coaches will be constantly going through a process of 'test and adjust', thereby making sure that they are using the absolute optimum blend of coaching tools for that particular athlete in this particular situation. In other words, maximising return is about knowing why you are doing things this way, and being prepared to change them to best suit the situation.

Now this isn't a book on coaching, so we won't go into the detail of this. In any case, the best thing about PJDM is the 'it depends' nature of what you get from using it, so this certainly isn't the sort of thing that you can be prescriptive about. Our point is that, under certain circumstances, even a naïve approach as described

TABLE 15.2 An exemplar 'epistemological chain'

Naïve		Sophisticated
Knowledge is absolute and factual. It is possessed by experts, like the coach.	View of knowledge	Knowledge is relative and is constantly being discovered and refined. All can develop and possess it.
Coach drives content and method. Athlete follows.	Coaching relationship	Content and method developed through negotiation. Both parties can suggest new ideas.
Coach sets targets and develops plan to achieve these.	Planning and goal setting	Developed in discussion. Increasingly athlete-led as autonomy and maturity develops.
Coach led. Changes of activity centrally driven; often working to a schedule.	Sessions	Work as agreed but either party can change direction based on agreed parameters.
Lots of 'drills' and part-skill practices. Coaching 'through the game' by stop, instruct and start.	Method	Challenges, problems and two-way questioning. Development through problem solving.
Coach is the leader. Stay here or move to another coach!	Outcome	Coach is increasingly the 'facilitator'. Relationship evolves towards mentorship or redundancy.

above may be the best option. So, as a parent, you want to see variations in coaching style employed – a sort of 'logical inconsistency' if you like, but within a consistent philosophy or set of goals. As a coach, and hoping that you are working towards the sophisticated end of the epistemology spectrum, you need to get used to thinking through the choices you have (lots of them, which is why coaching is so complex) and varying the blend for the best effect. Spending time auditing decisions (why I did this and whether it was the best option), not *too* much but certainly regularly, represents the best way to develop as a coach and the best way to maximise returns.

So, even though managers will usually prefer to use coaches whose epistemology matches their own, and consistency and coherence are valid aims for a coaching pathway, there will be times when alternative approaches are just what is needed. We now look at how this might work when designing a pathway, academy or organisational system.

Designing the pathway – what do you need, when and why?

Our ideas for designing the pathway are to apply the same sort of PJDM that the coach will use in her or his everyday work. This section is also worth a look for parents. It may be that you can gain some ideas about how the ideal environment for your daughter or son may vary through the development process. The key concept here is to think about the amount of variation in the training diet at each particular age and stage. Reflecting the ideas we discussed in Chapter 9, experiencing a variety of challenges is usually a positive feature, except when you are after rapid development. So, the question is how much variation is best and, furthermore, might this vary across the pathway?

We offer a perspective on this in Figure 15.1, based on work we have done with our colleague, Andrew Cruickshank, and Director of Coaching for British Cycling, Vinny Webb. As per our comments above, the 'direct and low variability' route generates a quick and consistent development. This would be characterised by almost identical messages, methods and objectives from all coaches in the pathway, or the same methods all the way through if you are working with a single coach. As ever, 'it depends'; so this approach is great if … In contrast, the very wide pathway (what we technically refer to as lots of ping-ponging!) offers *lots* of challenge and inconsistency to the developing athlete. This would be characterised by using a group of coaches with very different styles and objectives, or having one coach who was, to be generous, rather inconsistent in aims and method! Once again, it depends … This approach could work really well for a very driven, well motivated and intelligent performer, who can take in and process all the different things being thrown and take the most appropriate bits for him/herself. So, if dealing with an absolute prodigy, it is often good to let them work with a variety of different coaches and/or systems, providing a wide variety of challenge which will enable them to receive the fullest, most comprehensive education.

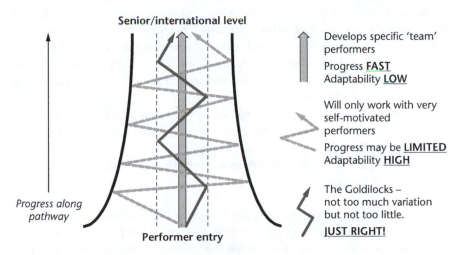

FIGURE 15.1   Routes to the top: effects of variation in the pathway

In the absence of such talent, however, our preferred solution is a compromise, the so called Goldilocks options (you know … just right, like the chair, the porridge and the bed!). Of course, this is a rather relative term – the 'just right' bit is a real example of PJDM in action. However, what is preferred are coaches and approaches that vary the stimulus for the developing performer around a core set of principles that ensure sufficient continuity. Accordingly, a manager or senior coach sets out these parameters, then coaches work within them, bringing their own styles and approaches to provide the important variability for the performer. If coaching a performer yourself, you need to make sure that s/he is getting a sufficiently varied diet, using the sophisticated end of the spectrum described earlier to talk things through and keep challenge levels optimum. Not too hard, not too soft … just right! Careful monitoring of progress, together with the Teach–Test–Tweak approach described in Chapter 14 should enable you to keep things on track. You might even use other coaches or training environments to 'spice things up' a little.

We hope that some clear messages come across from what is, inevitably given the topic, a complex area. Our key point is that variety is the spice of life, and a powerful factor in driving development. If producing an adaptable, multi-skilled senior performer is your aim, we would endorse the need for variability of challenge.

Culture change for TD directors

So, assuming that you have bought into the ideas presented in this book, you have responsibility for the pathway of an athlete or athletes *but* your colleagues aren't quite sure that this is the best way forward, then what you need is some culture change! We mentioned culture as an important if sometimes misunderstood or misused concept earlier in the book. Remember, 'what things are like around here'? Well, the Goldilocks culture, we suggest, will revolve around a number of providers (coaches, strength and conditioning specialists, psychologists, etc.) all buying into the principles set by the culture. It's incredibly powerful in determining behaviour. For example, the social setting or milieu around a coach plays a big part in how she or he coaches, how open to new ideas, etc. So working on the culture is a key management function for anyone with a responsibility for coaching systems and the outcomes they achieve.

Now there is a lot written about changing culture; some great, some nonsense but a lot that overcomplicates matters. So, staying with the KISS principle which has driven our approach in this book (we don't think it could be made much simpler!), we present the 'shepherd style' methodology of culture change. Three components as follows:

- provide a target or exemplar of good behaviour (the lead sheep);
- provide encouragement to move in that direction (good pasture); and
- challenge/sanction those not making the movement (sheepdogs snapping at their heels.

We hope the example isn't overdone and we won't get any rude letters about the animal welfare of farmers! Anyway, let's consider each of the stages, together with some real life examples (with no names and slight modifications to maintain confidentiality) that we have seen be effective and/or worked with.

Target of exemplar behaviour

The point here is that people are always happier to make a move when they can see an example of it working well. So, even if there isn't a perfect model of your eventual target, choose and use the 'closest fit' and use it to demonstrate the advantages of the changes you seek. Remember that what the model is achieving must be presentable as something desirable: more of this in the next section.

Although there are lots of good models, leaders can often seem reticent to endorse and praise selectively, to encourage this behaviour; something they seem far more comfortable doing with their own athletes than fellow coaches within a system. For example, given how many sports and sports administrators are publicly endorsing the 'long-term strategy', we are always surprised that so few follow through on this and name good TD coaches. As we said in earlier chapters, the skillset to coach elites is rare, not everyone can do it. Equally rare, however, but much less praised and perhaps less valued, are the equally complex skillsets that characterise excellent TD coaches. There have been some 'recent noises' in UK coaching circles that suggested a move to acknowledge this; for example, having the highest Level 4 award for both elites and, based on a different set of criteria, for TD coaches. As yet, however, not much has happened.

Senior coaches or managers might even 'shape' behaviour in their system. There are two ways to do this; first, focus on the positive features of a particular coach or environment, on the grounds that emphasising the 'right' bits will encourage them to be even more commonly used. Second, and in relation to this, leaders can publicise a 'made-up' model, stressing the good elements from several coaches or environments and showing how well they would work together. Whichever method is used, however, using every means to publicise and publicly 'reward' positive behaviour is a crucial part of any culture change process.

Encouragement for movement

Once you have identified and are pushing examples of what you want, the next step is to put in some form of reward to encourage more people to do this. As we highlighted earlier, humans are social creatures and coaches are no different. Many coach for very altruistic reasons, volunteering their time for the sport they love. Many will also appreciate public recognition, whether from external sources (hence our ideas on reward through publicity above) or internally, through recognition and praise from their fellow coaches, athletes and parents. Accordingly, and reflecting the SMMs we talked about at the start of the chapter, all elements of the coaching pathway leadership, from the Director of Coaching downwards, should be sending strong, loud, clear and consistent messages about what good practice looks like *and* who is doing it. This can be a challenge, especially in the current UK situation where glossy initiatives are often favoured over good solid 'bread and butter' coaching. We would encourage some open and critical debate so that the messages are clearer. After all, you often get what you wish for!

One idea that we have used is to attach a 'coaching ladder' to the profile of high flying elites: naming the coaches (starting perhaps with a school teacher who piqued their interest) that they have worked with on the way up. Offering some public recognition to those hard-working (usually always) volunteers would seem a low-cost way to kick-start the recognition process and encourage the principle of 'passing onwards and upwards' once your own skillset limit is reached.

Another is to offer incentives to environments (clubs, etc.) which generate the desired outcomes using the preferred process. So, for example, clubs can receive bursaries or 'kite marks' for retaining high numbers of young performers with demonstrably inclusive coaching focused at all levels of ability. It seems to us that this sends a far more workable and positive message than publicising the coaches of the local league winners.

Whichever methods are used remember that a reward must be rewarding for the person who receives it. Senior coaches, managers and leaders should meet and speak regularly with their coaches, so that they know what the workforce value and would like. After all, this works in coaching, so why not meta-coaching (coaching the coaches) as well?

Challenge those who do not move

Perhaps the most contested part of the strategy we have proposed, and used with success, is the idea that poor practice needs to be more publicly challenged. After all, even if a coach or coaches are giving their time for free, bad practice can quickly turn off large numbers of kids to the sport. In fact, it is interesting to see the dropout rates which occur later from coaches who emphasise early success, cutting those players who can't make a contribution. By comparison, environments that retain players, encouraging and catering for all levels of ability, are usually associated with healthy, thriving and upwardly mobile adult teams. The thing we can't work out is why those 'win early and at all costs' coaches are not questioned more publicly.

Of course, selection is a pragmatic feature of most high-level systems so, inevitably, some young performers are cut (we covered some of these issues in Chapter 8). Even here, however, there is surely a duty to do this with fairness and open-handedness. Furthermore, given the lack of accuracy in foretelling who will eventually make it, even high-level academies release at their peril; too many 'average age-group' players or athletes have come through to eventual success. You might take another look at the Superchamps versus Almosts idea we discussed in Chapter 7. Note that Almosts were very often thought of as the stars of the future, whilst Superchamps and champs sometimes laboured away in the middle tiers, only coming through later. In short, as a simple rule, almost all systems, at whatever level, will benefit from keeping more for longer!

There is also surely an important role for high-level academies and systems in providing role models of good and well grounded practice. We were amazed to see a manager of a high-status academy recently 'bragging' in the media when his junior age group team beat another by some 20-plus scores. We might be wrong but we assume that this isn't what the NGB wants as a general rule at junior level; after all that's what is said in their publicity material. So we were even more amazed that this comment, well reported and even endorsed by some, drew no negative comment from the sport's NGB reps. Being critical, in a fair, open and well reasoned way, is another essential component in selling the message and changing the culture!

Empowerment and derailment – keeping them with you

Applying all these ideas is likely to be a longer-term project. After all, what we are espousing is a TD process which is designed to bear fruit at senior level. That is a long time to wait and, human nature being what it is, some may lose patience and go for the quicker and more substantial rewards associated with a 'succeeding today' strategy! As such, the effective pathway leader will need to ensure that things stay on track. First, a focus on process will be more effective here. After all, the outcome is likely to take longer when you are aiming for senior success. Accordingly, developing and applying markers of good process, or as near as you can get to it, is likely to empower your coaches to stay with the programme. By far and away the best approach here is to focus on the coach's PJDM, using audits and peer reviews: other coaches looking at your process and the reasons underlying the methods you use. Unfortunately, many coaches only get looked at when they are taking an award or getting accredited for a new role. We would suggest that developing genuine 'communities of practice' is a good way to encourage this peer review. Such communities are an awful lot more than a set of breakfast meetings, ideally involving a group of practitioners who debate to gain agreement on objectives, share a common knowledge and vocabulary of coaching tools, and observe and critically discuss each other's practice. As mentioned above, such activities are best focused on bread-and-butter coaching, rather than on those who champion new but sometimes ill-founded and glossy initiatives.

The chances of derailment are also worth considering and countering. In the early stages of change, doing the new stuff is likely to be challenging and feel uncomfortable. Once again, this exactly parallels the athlete's experience in trying to make a change. Even later, when the new is not so original or discomforting, there may well be a 'social backlash', with some pushing for a return to the 'old and trusted' methods. We still suggest that honest and open debate is likely to be the best protection against the new processes getting derailed. Accordingly, keeping communication channels open and ongoing repetition and reinforcement of the new ideas is always a good idea.

Shaping your pathway – staff deployment and method issues

For this final section, we return to the ideas covered by Figure 15.1. You will have noticed (or if not have a look now) that the black outer lines of the pathway got gradually narrower, after starting from a broad base. Not only does this reflect the decrease in numbers as you move closer to the top, but also the idea that training will become more specific (but, reflecting comments in this book, not too much so) as things progress. As such, the senior first team or squad will be unlikely to use as broad a base of non-specific activity as the Under 11s! But might there be another reason to vary the degree of variability as the athlete progresses?

We suggest that which staff are deployed at which stage is another way in which variability levels can be, well, varied! For example, a more authoritarian coach, developing a more prescribed technical model may be appropriate at different stages, depending on the objectives of the programme against the progress of the performers. As such, the pathway might start narrower, using such a tight focus to build strong basics before freeing things up later. Or a tighter focus may be used just before the transition to the high challenges of senior level competition, to instil the personal standards, discipline and drive that will be needed. What's the answer? Well yet again, 'it depends' on what is needed when. What we are suggesting here is that, depending either on the personal style of the various coaches, or on the way in which the SMM of the pathway requires them to coach at each stage, a variety of shapes can be applied. This will be part of the PJDM deployed by the senior coach, manager or leader, who can deploy his or her coaching team for optimum effect, just as s/he might vary the positions allocated to performers.

In conclusion

The biggest take-home message from this chapter is an encouragement to think more carefully about the meta-coaching design of the pathway. The leader/manager has a number of ways to change the pathway experience; using different coaches with different epistemologies at different stages, team or co-coaching where one coach uses others to address specific aspects of development, or just changing the targets and methods through the application of culture change and SMMs. Many, if not all of the ideas presented in this book will apply at this higher (meta) level as well. Just make sure that you know why you are doing what you are doing, and critically reflect on whether a better blend or recipe could be applied, at sufficiently frequent intervals.

PART VIII

Conclusion

16

WHAT TO DO TO STAY AHEAD

Introduction

You have made it to the end, so what next? Throughout this book we have presented evidence-based guidelines about how to optimise the TD pathway. No doubt there were times when you thought 'Of course, I do that anyway', and if this is the case, well done! However, we would argue that a systematic approach to TD isn't always evident from NGB level right down to grassroots, and practices are adopted, maintained or discarded without the required criticality or investigation of their value. Unfortunately, in searching for the magic ingredient, coaches, sports and NGBs are often drawn to the uncritical adoption of practices (think of the widespread adoption of the 10,000-hour 'rule', LTAD or the need for early specialisation) without a consideration of the evidence base. In this final chapter we present some guidelines about how to be effective and critical consumers of research and applied practice in TD – the ability to differentiate, or at least question, the quality of the information offered and the importance of not getting caught up in the latest 'hot topic'. The importance of questioning the 'why' you should, or indeed why you shouldn't, is central to this criticality. We urge readers to maintain a healthy scepticism; question everything, ask for evidence and check things out for yourself!

Sorting the wheat from the chaff

It has never been easier to access information and the internet provides anyone who wants it with a mass of information at the touch of a button. Platforms such as Twitter and blogs are now at the forefront of knowledge dissemination and often the first port of call when we want to find something out – 'Let me just Google that!' A quick internet search will uncover thousands of blogs and tweets focused on talent development – everything from how to 'parent your superstar' to advice about early and late specialisation. These are undoubtedly powerful and impactful tools and, when used properly, can be an important method of information-sharing and collaboration. However, the extent to which the information is evidence-based rather than opinion-based is questionable. We are reminded here of Sturgeon's Law which suggests that 90 per cent of everything is crap! We can't stand by the percentage but we do urge you to exercise caution in what you believe and, in the absence of verifying evidence, the need to be careful about the veracity of the claims made. We are also not saying that academics should be the only gatekeepers of knowledge; they shouldn't. But the peer-review process does provide a level of rigour (though not always!) that is lacking in a 'free for all' online world.

There are two points to consider here. First, the quality of the information you consume and subsequently use is, of course, crucial. In an ideal world, information should be disseminated with quality assurance and, ideally, unsubstantiated opinion would not see the light of day. Online the quality of the information and, equally importantly, the balance of the information circulated, does not undergo any quality control. What are the consequences of this unfiltered data? First, you can choose what and who to listen to. The assumption is that people listen to people who hold similar views to themselves; we follow people on Twitter, for example, who share tweets about things that appeal to us. This self-selection builds up a shared community of individuals with similar opinions and, by virtue of preferential attachment, information gains credibility and traction in a 'rich get richer' fashion. Lots of people start tweeting and talking about something so it must be true! In much the same manner, people with opposing opinions can be unfollowed so those tweets do not appear on your Twitter feed. By doing this, the consumer does not have to contend with conflicting evidence or people questioning your stance. Social media is founded on connections and relationships that promote information sharing but has significant potential for negative impact when this is done in a self-selected manner. The ability to circulate ideas that are persistent and persuasive but potentially without evidence is a real danger. The bottom line is that such communication must come with, at the very least, a health warning or, preferably, a balancing argument. Those in positions of authority, whether that is academics, coaches, the NGB or other agency, have a responsibility to ensure there is an evidence basis to the information they share and agendas are not pushed! This is especially important when consumers of this knowledge – parents, or even the performers themselves – may be swayed by the authority (e.g. professional standing, accreditation or certification) of those sharing information, concentration of persuasive, (apparently) face-valid but evidence-lacking tweets, or the skills to filter the good from the bad. The take-home here? Listen to all sides of the argument and weigh up the evidence.

This brings us to the second point. With a sea of information coming at us from all directions, how do we sift out the misinformation and bogus claims, and get to the truth? The issue is not that everything available online, or indeed through other sources (coach education resources, for example), is inaccurate or not of value but that there is content that is both. How do we guard against hopping on every TD bandwagon while also demonstrating an openness to change and innovation? It is important to maintain enough scepticism so that you don't believe everything but at the same time are open enough to incorporate new ideas into your practice. Becoming a critical consumer and having a healthy scepticism is an important first step in how you consume information moving forward.

Becoming a critical consumer

As coaches or parents we rely on various sources of information – scientific studies, research reports, blogs and technical reports – to keep up-to-date with current practices in TD. However, most coaches and parents are not formally trained to evaluate this information which leads people to believe what they read, or what they are told, without questioning the evidence. This is especially true when that evidence comes from those in authority who 'should know better'. This kind of blind faith, an unquestioning belief in what is said, is anathema to critical thinkers. In science, for example, nothing is taken on belief or blind faith. Everything requires evidence, and every claim is (or at least should be) challenged.

So, should talent developers (be they parents, coaches or other key stakeholders) learn to think like a scientist? We think so! Unfortunately, critical thinking is not always a feature of interactions in sport (indeed it is more often than not discouraged!) and cheerleading rather than criticality is the prevalent behaviour. We would encourage stakeholders to behave more like scientists than cheerleaders. Could learning to think like a scientist, to question what is presented in a logical manner, help kill off misconceptions, bad practice and ill-informed decision making in TD? In turn, could this level of criticality provide confirmation for potentially good ideas? We think it can and should be a feature of practice. In the next section, we offer the reader some guidance about how they might do this.

How to think like a scientist

Carl Sagan, the noted philosopher, describes how easily we can all be fooled and then goes on to explain that scientists have been trained to cope with this reality. They have been equipped with what he terms a 'baloney detection kit' – essentially a toolkit for critical thinking. Sagan (1995) offers a set of cognitive tools and techniques that uncover errors, flawed thinking, false assertions, preposterous claims, frauds, pseudoscience and myths: simply, some very practical guidance on how to work out what is and is not 'baloney' (we are not as polite and might term this bulls★★t!).

The Baloney Detection Kit can be thought of as the tools of healthy scepticism that we can apply to everyday life. Sagan suggested that the kit should be brought out as a matter of course whenever new ideas are offered for consideration. Often these ideas are attractive because of who is proposing them (a figure of influence, authority, high stature, for example) or what they offer (identifying the next 'sure thing'). We can think of a number of TD initiatives that fit these descriptions! However tempting it is to adopt these ideas or practices on face-value, they should be (but haven't always been) examined for their truthfulness. If the new idea survives examination by the tools in the kit, it can be tentatively accepted.

Based on Sagan's work, we propose a checklist to help you assess the believability of a claim and sift through the noise of the TD landscape.

1 There must be independent confirmation of the 'facts'

Ask for the evidence and don't take things at face value. Thoughtful scepticism should be encouraged as it stops us adopting practices in good faith; you should ask, what is driving this decision, what is the evidence for it? Just because you read it on Twitter or in a blog doesn't mean it is true! Likewise, just because an approach is championed in your sport, doesn't mean it is the right thing to do.

2 Engage in debate

To detect falsehoods, Sagan 'encourages substantive debate on the evidence by knowledgeable proponents of all points of view'. Listening to both sides of the argument and weighing up the evidence allows you arrive at a reasoned position for accepting or rejecting a particular stance. This type of debate should be (but rarely is) a feature of policy development and practice in TD.

3 The authorities can be wrong!

'Blind belief in authority is the greatest enemy of truth.'

(Albert Einstein)

Sagan tells us that ' "authorities" have made mistakes in the past and they will do so again in the future. Perhaps a better way to say it is that in science there are no authorities; at most, there are experts'. I think that all of us who work in TD can agree with this statement! You shouldn't believe something just because your NGB, coach or someone in a position authority said it; God knows sports have made, and are continuing to make, a lot of mistakes! Again, look for the evidence and ask the question 'Why this way, and not another way?'

4 Spin more than one hypothesis

If there's something to be explained, think of all the different ways in which it could be explained. Then think of tests by which you might systematically disprove each of the alternatives. What survives, the hypothesis that resists disproof in this Darwinian selection among 'multiple working hypotheses', has a much better chance of being the right answer than if you had simply run with the first idea that caught your fancy. Unfortunately, as we have shown throughout the book, many

TD policies are too often driven by political 'neatness' (what makes for a glossy intervention) or by extremely secondary sources such as popular books (e.g. Syed, 2010) or social media. A much better approach would be to have a broader and more open debate, with the different perspectives presented equally to practitioners. How do you decide which idea to keep? Look for the evidence and let the data decide. If an initiative survives this level of scrutiny, it is worth running with.

5 Keep an open mind

Try not to get overly attached to an idea or way of doing something because it is your idea, or it is something that you have always done. Ask yourself why you like the idea and then compare it with the alternatives to find which is the best fit for your context.

6 Measure things

Quantifying things takes the ambiguity and guesswork out of decision making. Whenever possible gather data (or ask others for the data) to justify why you are doing what you are doing. This, rather than opinions and comments, offers a much better foundation for decision making.

7 Occam's razor

This convenient rule-of-thumb states that when you have two competing theories that make exactly the same predictions, the simpler one is the better. What does this mean? TD initiatives should be as simple as possible, but no simpler!

In conclusion

> 'If you always do, what you always did, you will always get, what you always got!'
>
> *(Henry Ford)*

We would suggest that talent developers spend a lot of time and effort designing the pathway and the resources required at different stages of development, but far less time and effort debating whether they are building the right product. It may be that sports and organisations have become so invested in some TID concepts (e.g. LTAD) that they have gone past the point of no return and it is difficult to change course or stop this momentum. In this chapter, and hopefully throughout the book, we have provided you with some of the tools to be an informed consumer and to navigate the information available. If you want to improve TD in your context, and give your athlete or child the best chance of success, it is important to put your sceptic's hat on; stick your head above the parapet (we think we do!), and question what is happening. Good luck!

References

Sagan, C. (1995). *Demon-haunted world: science as a candle in the dark*. New York: Random House.

Syed, M. (2010) *Bounce: how champions are made*. London: Fourth Estate.

INDEX